A NEW BRAND OF BUSINESS

A New Brand of Business

Charles Coolidge Parlin, Curtis Publishing Company, and the Origins of Market Research

Douglas B. Ward

TEMPLE UNIVERSITY PRESS
Philadelphia

TEMPLE UNIVERSITY PRESS
1601 North Broad Street
Philadelphia PA 19122
www.temple.edu /tempress

∞ The paper used in this publication meets the requirements of the American
National Standard for Information Sciences—Permanence of Paper for
Printed Library Materials, ANSI Z39.48-1992

Library of Congress Cataloging-in-Publication Data

Ward, Douglas B., 1961–
A new brand of business : Charles Coolidge Parlin, Curtis Publishing Company,
and the origins of market research / Douglas B. Ward.
    p. cm.
Includes bibliographical references and index.
ISBN 978-1-4399-0015-4 (cloth : alk. paper)
1. Marketing research—United States—History. 2. Parlin, Charles C.
(Charles Coolidge), 1872–1942. 3. Curtis Publishing Company. I. Title.

HF5415.2.W29 2009
658.8'3—dc22   2008047856

2 4 6 8 9 7 5 3 1

Contents

Acknowledgments   vii

Introduction   1
1   A New Era of Business   16
2   An Unlikely Leader   40
3   What Was Commercial Research?   58
4   Winning over the Skeptics   76
5   Barbarians, Farmers, and Consumers   91
6   Readers as Consumers   115
7   Chasing the Consumer, Protecting the Company   141
8   The Legacy of Commercial Research   168
    Epilogue   183

    Notes   185
    Index   221

Acknowledgments

I owe enormous thanks to many people who have helped make this book possible. First on the list is Maurine Beasley, who oversaw the dissertation from which this book emerged. She prodded, questioned, guided, and listened until I satisfied her skepticism. Her persistent but haunting "Why do we care?" burns in my ears every time I work through a research project. I am also grateful to Gene Roberts, Jim Gilbert, Doug Gomery, and the late Michael Gurevitch for their reading of an earlier version of this manuscript and for their encouragement in turning it into a book.

I extend many thanks to John Pollack, Nancy Shawcross, Lynne Farrington, and the numerous staff members and student assistants in the Rare Book and Manuscript Library of the University of Pennsylvania Library. Their gracious assistance and enthusiasm for their collections make the sixth floor of Van Pelt Library one of my favorite places to work. All of the photographs and illustrations in this book come from the Curtis Publishing Company Records housed in the Rare Book and Manuscript Library at Penn, and I offer my appreciation to the library for permission to publish them. Thank you, Nancy, for all your work in scanning the images. Special thanks also go to

Maggie Kruesi, now at the Library of Congress, who catalogued the Curtis Publishing Company Papers at Penn. Her early assistance was invaluable, and her careful work on the Curtis collection paved the way for my research. In addition, I am grateful to the staff of the Curtis Publishing archives in Indianapolis for access to the collection there, and to the staff of the John W. Hartman Center for Sales, Advertising and Marketing History at Duke University for their assistance in my visit there.

My wife, Juli Warren-Ward, has been supportive and patient throughout this project, as have my twin sons, Isaac and Ethan. Their curiosity about the project helped lighten the load, as did their perplexed queries of "Aren't you done with Curtis Publishing Company yet?" Well, I am, at least for now.

Lynne Frost provided an expert hand in shepherding this book through the production process, and Chel Avery polished the rough edges and asked just the right questions in her copy editing.

I appreciate the support of the Office of Research and Graduate Studies at the University of Kansas for providing a New Faculty General Research Fund grant, which helped me complete work on this book. And, finally, I thank the staff members of Interlibrary Loan at KU. Their expertise and persistence make them the unsung heroes of this and so many other research projects.

A NEW BRAND OF BUSINESS

Introduction

harles Coolidge Parlin gathered the notes for his speech, strode to the lectern, and looked out at the crowd of colleagues who had gathered in his honor. Three hundred fifty people from businesses and universities across the country had crowded into the Benjamin Franklin Hotel in Philadelphia that night—June 5, 1936—to pay tribute to the man they considered the founder of market research. Parlin, the manager of the Division of Commercial Research for Curtis Publishing Company since 1911, was hailed that evening as a visionary, a pioneer, an originator of the concepts and ideas of market research. Frank R. Coutant, president of the American Marketing Society, called Parlin "the daddy of all marketing research, whom we all recognize as the man who gave us most of the principles on which we work." Joseph H. Willits, dean of the Wharton School of Finance and Commerce at the University of Pennsylvania, led the group in toasting the man with the "penetrating mind" and the "prophetic insight." And Walter Fuller, president of Curtis Publishing Company, said that Parlin's work "has grown in reputation, it has grown in importance, and it has grown in the respect and appreciation of our company. That could not happen . . . if the results had not been very great."[1]

The accolades had not always flowed so freely. When Parlin began his work at Curtis Publishing, he was greeted with skepticism by many inside and outside the company. His mission was vague. Cyrus H. K. Curtis, the founder and longtime president of the company that bore his name, had given Parlin freedom to decide what needed to be studied and how he should go about his work, just as he had his fabled editors, Edward Bok of the *Ladies' Home Journal* and George Horace Lorimer of the *Saturday Evening Post*. That meant, though, that Parlin had little to guide him. He was new to the magazine industry and to the world of business. Partly because of that, the validity and integrity of his projects were difficult to prove, and the division he led provided no direct income or other tangible benefit to the company—not immediately anyway. "You have got a lot of figures," one man told him after completion of one of his early studies of department stores, "but how do I know they are good for anything?" Parlin had devoted many months to collecting and interpreting reams of information, but at one point he wondered whether he would have been better off "throwing pebbles into the sea."[2]

Those early, dreary days stuck with Parlin, and when it came his turn to speak at the banquet in 1936, he did so humbly. He reminded the group that he had been a high school principal in Wisconsin when he was hired by Curtis Publishing's Advertising Department to start the then-nebulous task of researching nationwide markets. He also reminded them that starting the Division of Commercial Research had been the idea of Stanley Latshaw, manager of Curtis's Boston advertising office. Parlin said he had simply taken Latshaw's idea and given it shape. He said his achievements had been possible only because Cyrus Curtis had been patient and had been willing to take a chance on something that someone else eventually would have tried and made successful. "If Columbus had not discovered America when he did," Parlin said, "someone else would, before long, because an age of adventure had already dawned.

And if the Curtis Publishing Company had not started Commercial Research when they did, sooner or later somebody else would have done so."[3]

It was Parlin, though, who was honored that night and who was lauded again and again for his pioneering work in market research. The Philadelphia chapter of the American Marketing Association established the Charles Coolidge Parlin Memorial Award in 1945, and Parlin was elected posthumously to the Advertising Hall of Fame in 1953. During his twenty-six years at Curtis Publishing, Parlin played a part in dozens of national and regional research projects, conducting much of the research himself by traveling the country and interviewing thousands of people as he shaped the early ideas of Curtis Publishing's market research. His second study, on department stores and the merchandising of textiles, was ranked by marketing scholars in the 1940s as among the most influential early works in the field. His later work was used by hundreds of companies in guiding sales of their consumer products. He forged friendships with early marketing instructors, exchanging ideas and even lecturing to classes himself. And many of the people who worked with him went on to lead market research departments of their own, further spreading the ideas and work that Parlin developed in the 1910s and 1920s.[4]

Despite such accolades and testimonials, we know relatively little about Parlin, the development of Commercial Research, or the thinking behind it.[5] His work has been widely noted by those in marketing,[6] but it has received only scant attention for its role in the development of advertising, media, or business, or in the rise of a consumer society. That is surprising because Parlin's employer, Curtis Publishing Company, has been widely noted for its importance in American journalism. The company's *Saturday Evening Post* and *Ladies' Home Journal* dominated the magazine market in both circulation and advertising revenue from the turn of the twentieth century until the 1930s. John Tebbel and Mary Ellen Zuckerman call the *Post* "the bible of middle-class America" in the early twentieth century. Frank Luther Mott calls Cyrus Curtis, the founder and business force behind the publishing company, a "bold and brilliant advertiser and promoter" and credits Curtis's willingness to advertise for much of the circulation success of his magazines.[7] Because Curtis magazines were so widely read, their content has also been the subject of numerous studies, often relating to portrayals of women,[8] and more recently their role in a consumer culture.[9] Likewise, Edward Bok, who edited the *Journal,* George Horace Lorimer, who edited the *Post,* and Cyrus Curtis have been the subject of several biographical studies.[10] Other researchers have looked at the financial problems Curtis Publishing faced in the television age.[11] We know far less, though, about Curtis Publishing as a company, about its corporate thinking or its business strategies during its heyday. And, despite its importance in the company's financial success, we know little about the workings of its Advertising Department. Curtis was among the first publishers to slash subscription rates below costs in the late 1800s and to rely on advertising revenues to make up the difference.[12] Because of that, the role of the Advertising Department grew increasingly important after the turn of the century, subsidizing the editorial work of such famed editors as Bok and Lorimer. The Advertising Department also played a large part in establishing Curtis's dominance in the publishing world, a dominance it used to influence the standards and practices of American advertising.[13]

Individual, But Also Societal Changes

Parlin's move from the nadir to the pinnacle of his field involved more than just one man carving out a distinguished career. (See Figure I.1.) It involved changes, both personal and societal, in the world of publishing and the world of business. In many ways, Parlin's employer, Curtis Publishing Company, was like the thousands of American businesses that slowly changed as a modern industrial society took shape during the first three decades of the twentieth century.[14] As Curtis grew larger and its bureaucratic structure became more complex, it sought ways to maintain contact with other businesses and with its customers—both advertisers and readers.

CHARLES COOLIDGE PARLIN

Manager of the Commercial Research Division,
and the bound volumes of reports, written by him,
dealing with market methods and conditions of
many industries

MANY years ago Curtis advertising representatives discovered that in order to sell advertising effectively they needed to be able to talk intelligently with a manufacturer about the manufacturer's business. Some of the questions asked them by the manufacturers were: What is the possible market for my merchandise? Through what sales channels can it be sold to the best advantage? Shall I use jobbers or shall I sell direct to the department stores? What margin of profit should the jobber and the retailer have? Shall I sell to the chain stores? How much sales resistance will I meet with dealers and with consumers? How can I get dealers to make window displays of my product? How can my own salesmen take advantage of the opportunities created by my advertising? How much advertising are other manufacturers applying to similar merchandise?

The answers to these questions were not to be found in books, for few books had been written on such merchandising problems. Then it was that the Curtis Company organized the Commercial Research Division to investigate these problems so that the Advertising Department might be able to answer accurately and helpfully the merchandising questions of Curtis advertisers.

The Division had a pioneer work ahead of it. Neither the United States Government nor any state

COMMERCIAL RESEARCH

By CHARLES COOLIDGE PARLIN

They went to the department stores. They interviewed the managers and their assistants. They discussed all manner of local and national merchandising problems with them. Then, when they returned to the East, they wrote the four volume report on Department Store Lines which became a work of basic importance.

They found that men and women bought in different ways. Men buy either at the nearest place, or as they are attracted by display, or by seeking out a desired brand, or at an accustomed store where they can say "Charge it" and escape red tape.

In women's buying they made a distinction between shopping lines and convenience goods that has been universally accepted as basic in merchandising. Women buy convenience goods in the same manner as men buy, but in shopping lines—that is, lines that involve styles that give a touch of originality to dress or home—women wish to see more than one stock before making a purchase.

It was found that department stores grew out of this desire to shop. No merchant can hold a monopoly of the department-store trade of a city; to sell shopping lines he must have competition. They found that

had ever taken a merchandising census. How much business was done by department stores nobody knew, and soon it became apparent that the only way to find out was to go and ask, store by store, city by city. In 1912, and again in 1920, Commercial Research representatives visited almost every city of over 50,000 population, and many smaller cities, from Maine to California, from Florida to Washington, and estimated the volume of business done by every department store in each of those cities and also the volume of business done by every wholesaler in general dry-goods lines.

three is the magic number in women's shopping—most cities up to 20,000 population having just three department stores—and that only three cities in the United States had more than seven full-line department stores.

In the same way, by actual field studies, reports were compiled and written on other basic industries. The report on Foods took up the problems of almost every foodstuff. Automobiles were investigated from practically every point of view including an estimate of just how much influence women have in the purchase of a Ford or a Rolls-Royce. Agricultural implements and The

Diamonds are chunks of coal that stuck to their jobs

Figure I.1   Charles Coolidge Parlin personally researched or oversaw dozens of market reports for Curtis Publishing Company. His work was promoted both externally and internally, as with this article in a Curtis employee magazine.

It promoted an attitude of service to both as it first carved a niche in the world of publishing, then tried to improve on its position in and increase the control it had over the marketplace.

One of the crucial means it used was marketplace information.[15] By using what it promoted as new scientific methods of knowing and understanding competitors, customers, and markets, the company saw itself as better able to chart a course in the modern business world. Through its magazines, Curtis helped disseminate information to millions of people. Through its market research department, it sought to gather information that it thought would help position itself against the competition and would better prepare itself for working with thousands of established and potential advertisers. Curtis also saw Commercial Research as a means of extending a hand of cooperation to American business in general. It rarely published its research reports in full, although it did make them freely available at its offices in such cities as Philadelphia, New York, Boston, Chicago, and San Francisco, and it encouraged advertisers and advertising agencies to make use of the information and insights. The idea was to improve clients' chances for success, with the hope that strong customers would become repeat customers in the highly competitive, yet lucrative, world of advertising.

Market research, however, did not appear with the waving of a magic wand. It had to be sold as a necessity for modern commerce. Even as businesses yearned for information, they often looked upon early research with suspicion. Could they trust the information? Could they afford to gather their own information? Did they really need information? Was it just a fad, something that would cost them time and money without ever paying off? Those were the types of doubts that Parlin and his colleagues at Curtis Publishing Company faced as they cobbled together their early market research. As the Division of Commercial Research evolved, it became more than just an instrument for gathering information. Parlin was forced to become a salesman, a public relations man, an advertising man, and an expert on circulation, sales, distribution, wholesaling, retailing, and dozens of other facets of publishing and business. Curtis Publishing looked to the division for economic forecasts and for help in planning strategy and direction of many different facets of the publishing business—all part of what one historian has called a move toward "bureaucratic rationality," administration based on logical and statistical rules rather than intuition.[16]

In the decades since Curtis established its research division in 1911, American business and industry have grown increasingly hungry for information about themselves, their competitors, their markets, and their audiences. By 1947, American business spent an estimated $50 million annually on market research, which it used to guide corporate decision making. Today, writes Eric Clark, research is a key part of all new products and advertisements, and "virtually nothing appears from a major advertiser or agency until it has been opinion-polled, test-marketed or copy-tested, submitted on the way to panels of consumers whose words have been turned into statistical tables or analyzed by psychologists." Billions of dollars are spent on researching products, markets, advertising, consumers, and public opinion, not only by companies, but by politicians, news organizations, advocacy groups, and just about anyone with the money and the desire to influence public opinion.[17] Businesses have come to rely on market research to gauge the "public mind" and to judge changes in consumer tastes, with the goal of turning consumer wants into corporate profits. For them, market research has become, in effect, the rudder on the ship of modern corporate capitalism. Applying what they call micromarketing, many businesses today use detailed information about consumers' preferences for such things as food, leisure, and an array of goods to target new products to people in specific regions, towns, neighborhoods, and even households. "The vision of the future is you can get whatever you want," said Robert Meyer, a professor of marketing at the Wharton School of the University of Pennsylvania. "Years ago, retailers and manufacturers would just be guessing where to introduce products."[18]

We often think of this availability and use of information as a late-twentieth-century phenomenon, a phenomenon built on technology, on electronics, on the ability to move information quickly. This "information age," though, is really just an expansion of needs, practices, and systems that developed decades, even centuries, earlier, as Steven Lubar has shown. The United States itself was formed with the notion that the wide distribution of information was essential to the well-being of a democratic society. That belief in information helped spur the development of such things as roads and transportation, a national postal service, and communications devices from the telegraph to the telephone to the computer modem. In the eighteenth and nineteenth centuries, savvy business owners found that information, when applied to trade, could position them to earn higher profits. Curtis Publishing took that idea to a new extreme at the turn of the twentieth century, emphasizing the role of information gathering in publishing, advertising, and other types of business.[19]

An Important Part of an Important Company

By focusing on Curtis Publishing, I attempt to show how that hunger for information about such things as product distribution, business competition, and magazine readership gave rise to market research during the 1910s and 1920s. Curtis Publishing, although certainly not the first company to conduct market research, was especially important in the development of research and business information because it showed that an individual company could compile information about national, regional, and city markets— information that many people of the time thought could be obtained only by the federal government.[20] As Curtis's research efforts grew, so did the company's promotion of that work. Curtis executives saw research as a means to distinguish the company from its competitors, in a sense to create a new brand of business—a business infused with Progressive notions of societal betterment. Again, Curtis was not the first or the only company to follow such thinking, but it was certainly one of the most important, largely because its sheer size and revenue dwarfed those of its competitors.

By 1890, the *Ladies' Home Journal* had pushed its circulation to more than 400,000, the highest of any magazine at the time. Thirteen years later, *Journal* circulation surpassed one million, and in 1924 surpassed two million. The rise of the *Saturday Evening Post* was even more spectacular. The *Post* had few subscribers and was losing money when Curtis bought it in 1897, and Curtis employees often referred to it as "the singed cat." The *Post's* circulation rose to more than 200,000 shortly after the turn of the century and soared to two million weekly in 1913, making it the widest-circulating magazine of the era.[21] Curtis's advertising revenues were even more impressive, growing from about $250,000 in 1892 to $850,000 at the turn of the twentieth century to nearly $10 million by 1912.[22] In 1923, Curtis estimated that its magazines accounted for 48 percent of the total advertising revenue of the thirty six leading national publications, and more than half of expenditures for color advertising in the same publications.[23] Between 1915 and 1922, the *Journal* carried about a third of the advertising in all women's magazines, and between 1918 and 1922, the Curtis farm magazine *Country Gentleman* carried about a third of the advertising in all farm publications, and for most of the 1920s outdistanced all other farm publications in advertising income.[24] By the end of the 1920s, the *Post* carried six times as much advertising as any other publication except the *Journal*, and the *Journal* carried nearly twice as much advertising as any other publication but the *Post*. Combined yearly advertising revenue for the three Curtis magazines exceeded $70 million in 1928—40 percent of the total advertising revenue of the sixty-four largest publications. In many ways, Curtis publications *were* the mass market of the early twentieth century.[25]

Previous histories acknowledge Curtis's importance as a business force but do little to explore the workings of the company. This book not only broadens the perspective on Curtis Publishing Company, but it revises several commonly held assumptions about Curtis mag azines and the mass media market of the early twentieth century. It makes no attempt to reduce the importance of editorial matter in the success of the *Post* or the *Journal*. (Without strong editorial appeal, any publication is doomed.) It shows, however, that Curtis Publishing's success was not built solely on the strength and planning of its magazines. Cyrus Curtis did not simply turn his editors loose and then wait for readers to snatch up copies of the magazines en masse. Curtis Publishing's success was much more complex than that.

That is, the magazines were simply the most visible component of a wide-reaching business operation.

The following chapters show, for instance, how Curtis used market research to provide feedback about the audience of the *Post* and *Journal,* to position itself among a growing number of publications that pursued advertising, to carefully chart the spread and growth of a consumer culture, and to reinforce its authority among businesses that advertised in Curtis magazines. They show how advertising and research established themselves as vital components of Curtis Publishing Company, and how those two components were used to improve the organization's trust and image. They also show how Curtis promoted a business ideology that stressed the value of science, research, and market information as important means of building credibility and increasing profit in corporate America; and how a symbiotic relationship between advertisers, publications, and advertising agencies strengthened as mass media emerged and developed. Similarly, without a highly structured circulation department that sold its publications aggressively, Curtis never could have achieved distribution that reached into the millions. And without a successful advertising department and business operation, the company never could have achieved the enormous profits that allowed it to expand, experiment, and reinforce its domination. In short, Curtis Publishing worked in many different ways to create the mass media marketplace in which it was so enormously successful. The market did not come to Curtis; Curtis aggressively pursued and shaped the market.

Challenging Assumptions

As this book explores the many facets of Curtis Publishing, it challenges several assumptions put forth by historians of advertising, consumer culture, and media. The early histories of American advertising were written by agency men, and modern researchers have taken for granted many of the assertions that the early writers put forth. Historians such as Jackson Lears, Roland Marchand, Daniel Pope, and Stuart Ewen have placed the locus of power in the emerging consumer culture in the hands of the advertising agencies and the manufacturers they worked for.[26] They began with the assumption that the agencies, because they so closely worked with businesses on the creation of advertisements, were the guiding forces of the advertising industry. They similarly regarded magazines such as the *Post* and *Journal* as little more than vessels for the distribution of messages created by the agencies and their customers. In doing so, they overlooked the influence that Curtis had—and used— in the development of modern advertising and market research. This book makes no attempt to cast aside the wide-reaching work or influence of the agencies. By showing the significance of the company's work, though, it argues that Curtis Publishing should be seen as at least an equal to the agencies in the development of American advertising and the creation and selling of a consumer society. Curtis, by its sheer size and domination of the mass media marketplace, was a power that the agencies were forced to deal with.

My intent in this book is to look at how and why Curtis developed its market research division and to follow the changes that took place during the tenure of Parlin, the division's first director. In that sense, this is a business history with Parlin and Curtis Publishing at its center. I have attempted to reach beyond that, though, and look for cultural and social reasons for the development and use of market research and the creation of market research departments. For the most part, though, I have chosen to concentrate on Curtis. Other scholars have done a good job of looking at the many players in early market research.[27] In doing so, though, those works often lose the nuance and intimacy that only a focused study like this can offer. Market research was not born in abstraction; rather, it involved real people who faced real obstacles as a profession formed. Only an in-depth study can tell that story. And though I tell a specific story, I also move between the specific and the general as I link Curtis Publishing to the broader currents of publishing, advertising, and business in the first four decades of the twentieth century.

This book also challenges another widely held assumption about Curtis magazines and other popular publications of the early twentieth century, as well. Although they are often grouped together as "mass" magazines that responded to middle-class wants and needs, Curtis publications and many of their competitors clearly coveted the readership of educated, upper-income elites. That was the audience that advertisers wanted to reach, and it was to those readers that the magazines tailored themselves and marketed themselves aggressively. The middle class was certainly important to Curtis and other publishers, but it was of secondary importance; the lower classes were, from a business perspective, superfluous. The *Post,* the *Journal,* and their competitors were indeed "mass" magazines in that they reached nationwide audiences in numbers never before achieved by American publications. Those "masses," however, were closer to a niche market in that they represented only a fraction of the population—a fraction targeted and defined by income. Curtis Publishing had neither the intent nor the desire to reach all of America; it wanted only that part of America that would and could purchase the goods of its advertisers.

In trying to understand the development of market research, I have drawn from many sources, disciplines, and philosophies, including cultural history, the history of marketing, the history of advertising, the history of business, the history of reading, and the history of journalism. Primarily, though, I have used a cultural approach applied to the world of business, creating biographical portraits of both a man and a business. In doing so, I have relied on several assumptions related to culture: that it is shared; that it changes; and that it can be understood by examining the public behavior and private thought of those who belong within a culture.[28] In this case, the public behavior consists of research reports, advertisements, published works, and speeches. The private thoughts consist of writings, confidential reports, or transcripts of private meetings. By examining both the public and the private, I have tried to create a fuller picture of how market research evolved.[29] In researching this book, I have drawn primarily from the Curtis Publishing Company papers at the University of Pennsylvania[30] and at the Curtis Archives in Indianapolis,[31] supplemented by the J. Walter Thompson advertising agency papers at Duke University. I have also drawn on many books, articles, advertisements, and trade journals of the era, using the Curtis research as a means of assessing assumptions that the company passed on to advertisers about audiences and the marketplace.

The research that Parlin did for Curtis certainly did not represent *all* the viewpoints or perceptions of the era's businesses, but it did represent the way Curtis Publishing Company viewed the marketplace and the consumer. The research represented, in effect, the reality of the marketplace as Curtis Publishing understood it.[32] Because of that, Curtis's marketing and research records are useful in helping to understand some of the positions the company took toward advertising and circulation. They are also useful in understanding how market research and other forms of information became incorporated into one of the most successful publishing companies of the early twentieth century. Through Curtis Publishing, I look at how the concept of market and consumer research was pitched to potential advertisers as a means of empowerment in the marketplace, but also how it was carefully presented to show that businesses needed to buy advertisements if they were to take full advantage of the research. That was the purpose in the end—to sell. In that sense, this is a study of strategy, not imagery, in an American business that gradually saw great opportunity and value in information that it could collect, analyze, and disseminate about the marketplace.

In writing this book, I have tried to concentrate on the narrative. I use theory again and again in my interpretations, but in writing, I have tried to weave the human experience into the broader fabric of social change.[33] So, in effect, this is a humanist history thoroughly grounded in the techniques and philosophies of social science history. No matter the approach, direct causal connections are difficult to establish in any study of historical thought or culture. Records that might point to valuable connections or developments are incomplete or even nonexistent. In many cases, people do not know themselves where they picked up an idea or how they developed a way of thinking. As Susan Strasser demonstrates, cultural shifts "happen piecemeal, with new developments interacting in complex ways and exhibiting contradictions and incongruities that frustrate the historian's effort to tell a clear story of cause and effect or even to provide accurate generalizations. People create those shifts by living their lives, making decisions that they may consider trivial or wholly personal but that have critical effects in the aggregate."[34] Those difficulties in causal links hold true with the development of Commercial Research at Curtis Publishing Company. In researching and writing this book, though, I have tried to trace some of the people, policies, thoughts, philosophies, and changes, not only in Curtis but in business, industry, and society, that were related to the origins of the research division. I have tried to weave the story of Curtis into the story of the changes that took place in American business and American advertising during the early twentieth century.

I have focused most of my work on the 1910s and 1920s, trying to explain and to understand the development of market research at Curtis Publishing Company. Chapter 1 looks at how doubts about advertising, combined with the company's belief in customer service, helped lead to the formation of Commercial Research. Chapter 2 looks at Parlin's early days at Curtis and at the problems he overcame. Chapter 3 looks at how the Curtis advertising staff gradually came to accept Parlin's work and eventually promoted it widely as a means of understanding the marketplace. Chapter 4 follows Parlin and his associates through some of their early studies and attempts to understand the guiding philosophies of their work. Chapter 5 looks at Curtis's move into the rural market, a market that the company saw as the real challenge if American publishing and American advertising were to create a true mass market. Chapter 6 examines the development of readership research as an extension of market research. It shows how Curtis Publishing Company increasingly viewed readers as consumers of advertised products and how its emphasis on a "class" readership translated into an elitist—even racist—view of the American public. Chapter 7 looks at the changes that took place in Commercial Research in the 1920s, especially in the way that Curtis Publishing became involved in the promotion of consumption through its work in sales quotas and in defending advertising. Chapter 8 follows Commercial Research into the 1930s and contains the conclusions of my research, followed by a brief epilogue.

This story begins, though, in 1910 as consumption was growing increasingly important to the United States economy and to the lives of Americans as the country underwent a series of revolutionary changes. Rural Americans migrated to cities, consumer tastes changed rapidly, and the number of consumer products available on store shelves grew enormously. Many manufacturers also sought to expand beyond regional markets, taking advantage of improved transportation and methods of production, and envisioning a truly national market for the first time. Similarly, they sought to create demand for national brands in areas like clothing and food that were dominated by store brands or by unbranded merchandise. This environment forced many marketers to shift their thinking toward masses of new, unknown buyers (consumers) rather than individuals they knew—or thought they knew—and catered to (customers).[35] That change occurred nationally, led by companies that produced branded products that were the same from Maine to California, and created a need for information about the newly forming mass market. Who were the buyers of nationally branded products? Where were these buyers? How could they be reached? Could a company afford to reach them?

Those were some of the questions that a young advertising executive in Curtis Publishing's Boston office was pondering in 1910, as he came to the conclusion that his profession, and indeed the world of business, was changing around him. The company had to change, as well, he concluded, if it was going to keep up in this new world. The question was, how?

1

A New Era of Business

Advertising had always seemed like a fairly straightforward job to Stanley Latshaw, head of Curtis Publishing's advertising office in Boston. Like a custom tailor, an adman tried to assess a customer, pay him due deference, and then create an advertisement that fit like a properly sewn garment, hiding the flaws while accentuating the positive. A good adman took what he could find about a client's product, wrote copy as speedily and as inexpensively as possible, and did his best to tell the advertiser's story. There was no use worrying about broader things like trade conditions or industry trends, or even the condition of the customer's company. A good product would sell itself. The advertiser rarely asked questions, and if there was ever a problem, a magazine could always fall back on "board of director copy"—an advertisement with a large picture of the business, a picture of the business's founder, and a few laudatory phrases. That always seemed to smooth things over.[1]

By 1910, though, those simple times that Latshaw remembered had all but disappeared, if they had ever really existed. As a consumer economy expanded in the United States, advertising turned into a lucrative business, and as it did, Latshaw and other executives sought new ways to cater to manufacturers so that Curtis Publishing could pull in as many advertising dollars as possible. Their thinking was infused with a morally grounded Progressivism and a Whiggish notion of unending progress, all wrapped in a cloak of upper middle-class managerial superiority that pushed them to act even as they denied its existence. Like so many others who helped create what Alfred Chandler calls the "visible hand of management," they saw themselves at the beginning of a new era—one in which they could guide capitalism along a path of their choosing—and they sought to make Curtis the emblem of that era.[2]

As Latshaw pursued that goal, he increasingly found himself on the defensive. Advertising was growing more expensive and more pervasive, and many businesses had begun to question not only its use, but its validity and expense. They no longer approached advertising with the blind faith of a wildcat copper miner. Rather, they looked at it as an investment, and they wanted to base that investment on sound advice. They wanted answers: How much did an advertiser need to spend to get results? How much were competitors spending on advertising? In what part of the country would an advertiser see the greatest results—and how long would he have to wait?[3] More stinging were the questions from advertising's critics, mostly jobbers (middlemen who sold their own unadvertised, branded goods), and store owners who did not like the smaller margins of profit created by the name brand goods that customers had begun to ask for. Wasn't advertising really just a tax paid by consumers and retailers? they asked. Didn't advertising greatly increase the cost of doing business and the cost of buying products? Didn't advertising waste everyone's money?[4]

Since the days of Hostetter's Bitters, Jayne's Expectorant, Mrs. Winslow's Soothing Syrup, and other patent medicines, advertising had been associated with the seedy and the disreputable, and into the twentieth century, the advertising world found itself running from the hucksterism of both past and present. "There is probably no subject on earth which is receiving so much concentration of mind force as advertising," the business manager of the *Philadelphia Press* told his city's Business Science Club in 1911. "Telescope and microscope are centered on it, and this, the commercial nation of the world, is giving it more attention than any other people."[5]

Latshaw was beginning to have questions of his own about advertising. He wondered just what his role—and those of other Curtis advertising representatives—was within the company. After all, Curtis's *Saturday Evening Post* and *Ladies' Home Journal* were the rising stars of the publishing world, each with a circulation of more than one million by 1908. Advertising for the publications virtually sold itself in many cases and would flow in whether Latshaw and his coworkers were there at all. So what was their mission? What could he and others do to earn their salaries? What could they do to make sure that Curtis Publishing, its customers, and—just as important—the advertising industry continued to thrive?[6] Between 1910 and 1915, Latshaw began to find answers to those questions within Curtis Publishing's long-established policies of service to its advertisers and readers. The company responded to the changes it faced with its own form of Progressivism: Company executives said they had a responsibility not only to set an example, but to see that others followed their lead. They saw themselves, in a sense, as guardians of advertising. By applying their influence, they contended, they could enhance the reputation of the company and of advertising in general. A movement was already afoot to try to make advertising more truthful and trustworthy. Curtis went even further, forcing advertisers to adhere to its own strict code of conduct—a code that had been in effect in some form since the 1890s.

To try to soften the criticism that the stricter rules would inevitably bring from clients, Latshaw and other Curtis managers worked to change advertising representatives from sellers to merchandisers.[7] Merchandisers planned the sale of products by considering buyers' wants and needs, promoted products in ways that would pique interest, and provided value-added services (such as warranties or other assurances of quality, and in Curtis's case, information about the marketplace and about consumers) to buyers. Curtis executives also prodded the Advertising Department as a whole to expand its "paternalism." That is, Curtis Publishing intended to watch over its advertisers and nurture them the best it could, reasoning that satisfied, successful clients would mean continued success for Curtis. One of the most important elements of this paternalism was the development of a market research division, which Curtis used to extend its influence in the marketplace by providing hard-to-find information that promised to help companies position themselves and their products for greater and more efficient sales.[8] None of the changes that Curtis sought came easily, though.

The Rise of a Powerhouse

Curtis Publishing Company was indeed one of the leaders in fostering the growth of mass market periodicals, mass advertising, and mass consumption at the turn of the twentieth century. American advertising was as old as American periodicals,[9] but the scale on which advertising developed around the turn of the century was unprecedented. The industrial revolution had given rise to more efficient methods of manufacturing, and improved transportation (from trains to automobiles) and communication (from the telegraph to the telephone to the typewriter) allowed products (including periodicals) to be produced and transported quickly, cheaply, and easily on a wide scale. By the late nineteenth century, these advances in technology had allowed corporate leaders to shift more of their attention from production to marketing and distribution. The United States, and especially its cities, had begun to expand rapidly, populated by tens of thousands of literate wage earners who, as purchasing power increased, became a ready market for the multitude of branded goods being created.[10]

The chief means of reaching this new consuming public was advertising. Advertising proliferated in magazines, newspapers, billboards, streetcar posters, store window displays, direct mailings, fliers, and just about anywhere else a trademark could be displayed. "Advertising, like everything else in this wonderful country, has developed too fast," the agent Earnest Elmo Calkins wrote in 1915. "This headlong rush has produced success rather than efficiency."[11] Between 1900 and 1914, the number of national advertisers rose from 6,000 to about 13,000, and as early as 1907, advertising accounted for half of the pages in most magazines. By one estimate, spending on advertising reached $600 million a year by 1911, and exceeded $1 billion a year by World War I.[12]

Cyrus H. K. Curtis was a strong believer in advertising, and he used it extensively as he formed his publishing company in the late 1800s. He began in 1879 with a farm paper, the *Tribune and Farmer,* and four years later, a section of that paper edited by his wife, Louisa Knapp, became the *Ladies' Home Journal.* Edward Bok took over the *Journal's* editorship from Knapp in 1889, guiding the magazine for thirty years and proving himself to be what Frank Luther Mott calls "one of America's foremost magazine editors."[13] The *Journal* was among what became known as the Big Six women's magazines, which had large circulations, a loyal base of readers, and large incomes from advertising.[14] Magazine readership rose dramatically in the early twentieth century as the country's literacy rate pushed past 90 percent by 1920.[15] By 1890, the *Journal* pushed its circulation to more than 400,000, the highest of any magazine at the time. In 1899, the *Journal,* with 820,000 subscribers, still led all magazines in circulation, outdistancing its nearest competitors—*Munsey's Magazine* (605,000) and *Delineator* (500,000)—by more than 200,000 subscribers.[16] Between 1900 and 1930 the *Journal's* circulation nearly tripled, while the U.S. population increased 62 percent. (See Table 1.1.)

The rise of the *Saturday Evening Post* was even more spectacular after Curtis bought it in 1897. It had only a handful of subscribers at the time, but circulation rose to more than 280,000 by 1901 and to two million a week in 1919, making it the widest circulating magazine of the era. (See Table 1.1.) A story that Bok recounted captured the flavor of the heady days of wild circulation growth: A friend once asked Cyrus Curtis at lunch what the circulation of the *Journal* was. "Now?" Curtis responded. "I really don't know. This morning it was two million."[17] Curtis often credited his successes to the power of advertising. In late 1889 and early 1890, when the *Journal* was only a few years old, he spent more than $300,000 of borrowed money to advertise the magazine. During the Panic of 1907, he spent $50,000 in one week advertising the *Post.* Throughout the 1910s, the company advertised nearly every week in *Printers'*

Table 1.1 Advertising Revenue and Average Circulation of Saturday Evening Post and Ladies' Home Journal

Year	Post Circulation	Post Ad Revenue ($)	Journal Circulation	Journal Ad Revenue ($)
1897	2,231	6,933	699,046	500,630
1898	33,069	8,659	740,933	536,795
1899	97,497	59,389	820,000	646,245
1900	182,515	159,573	879,048	692,102
1901	287,424	255,254	896,986	752,410
1902	314,671	360,125	1,000,000	956,698
1903	508,182	672,152	977,274	1,121,723
1904	638,969	838,765	1,060,881	1,201,022
1905	696,044	1,058,935	1,125,223	1,397,722
1906	681,095	1,123,359	1,179,001	1,566,419
1907	726,681	1,266,931	1,088,674	1,722,702
1908	897,835	1,617,434	1,106,745	1,622,784
1909	1,242,217	3,056,403	1,269,504	2,168,958
1910	1,567,601	5,008,948	1,306,123	2,515,837
1911	1,770,324	6,270,068	1,327,170	2,284,114
1912	1,920,550	7,114,581	1,757,677	2,457,006
1913	2,004,005	7,874,656	1,705,916	2,660,412
1914	1,983,142	8,213,242	1,566,957	2,544,417
1915	1,928,738	8,690,614	1,543,048	2,653,231
1916	1,849,667	12,089,727	1,606,030	3,361,865
1917	1,883,070	16,076,562	1,609,089	4,678,897
1918	1,934,361	16,935,236	1,626,518	5,709,105
1919	2,036,792	27,314,656	1,873,174	8,775,315
1920	2,061,058	36,228,092	1,910,586	11,148,360
1921	2,099,940	25,309,043	1,755,992	10,370,829
1922	2,187,024	28,278,755	1,895,239	11,414,144
1923	2,272,220	35,542,286	1,994,385	12,543,188
1924	2,324,487	39,935,825	2,376,072	13,657,392
1925	2,449,533	46,315,168	2,334,674	15,086,413
1926	2,724,876	49,158,904	2,336,532	16,172,535
1927	2,816,391	53,144,987	2,500,000	16,627,363
1928	2,929,343	48,661,580	2,531,287	16,617,968
1929	2,907,875	52,359,112	2,555,996	16,321,128
1930	2,924,363	27,551,104	2,581,942	15,590,980
1931	2,912,560	35,492,312	2,588,271	12,861,530

Sources: "Summary of Lines and Revenue from 1892 to Date," Curtis Bulletin 35 (Dec. 26, 1923); "Average Circulation," in Curtis "Dope Book," c. 1923, Curtis Publishing Company Papers, Rare Book and Manuscript Library, University of Pennsylvania, Box 130; Advertising in the Saturday Evening Post, 1926; Advertising in Ladies' Home Journal and Other Women's Publications, 1927; "Advertising in the Saturday Evening Post," Curtis Bulletin 101 (1928); Ladies' Home Journal Figures, 1927; Leading Advertisers for 1930, 1931, 1932; N. W. Ayer & Sons Directory of Newspapers and Periodicals.

Ink, the most widely circulating trade periodical for the advertising industry, and throughout the first three decades of the twentieth century, it was not unusual for the *Journal,* the *Post,* or Curtis's farm magazine *Country Gentleman*—and sometimes all three—to spend up to $35,000 a month on newspaper advertising.[18]

Financial Muscle

The large circulations that the Curtis magazines achieved worked in tandem with the amount of advertising that flowed in, putting the company in an enviable financial position. In 1905, Calkins and Holden estimated that the *Ladies' Home Journal* took in $135,000 in advertising a month—more than a third of the combined total generated by the ten highest-circulating monthlies, of which the *Journal* ranked first. During 1908, Curtis's advertising revenue exceeded $3 million, and during 1910 that figure more than doubled, to about $7.5 million. Between 1911 and 1916, the *Post* and the *Journal* accounted for about 45 percent of the advertising income among more than thirty leading publications that Curtis Publishing tracked.[19] (See Tables 1.1 and 1.2.) As the amount of money that American businesses spent on advertising rose, Curtis positioned itself to pull in an even larger share of that money by expanding and diversifying. In 1911, it bought *Country Gentleman,* a regional farm magazine that Curtis quickly transformed into a national publication. In 1912, the company bought controlling interest in the Home Pattern Company, which published *Ladies' Home Journal* patterns in a monthly known as *The Style Book,* and also published another magazine, *The Embroidery Book.* That year, Curtis also began offering *Journal* patterns and fashion articles to newspapers through the Ladies' Home Journal Fashion News Service. In 1913, it bought the *Public Ledger* of Philadelphia—a morning newspaper that added an evening edition the next year—and a New York fashion magazine, *Toilettes,* which it turned into a five-cent monthly called the *Criterion of Fashion.* That same year, it began publishing a house organ, *Obiter Dicta,* which it used to promote itself among advertisers, and it opened a Division of Publicity in New York City. The company opened an

Table 1.2   Curtis's Share of Advertising Expenditures, 1911–1922*

Year	Total for 36** Leading Magazines ($)	Curtis Share (%)	Post Share (%)	Journal Share (%)	Country Gentleman Share (%)
1911	18,354,130	42.0	31.0	11.0	—
1912	21,250,578	45.0	34.0	11.0	—
1913	22,367,195	46.0	36.0	10.0	—
1914	22,991,919	47.0	37.0	10.0	—
1915	22,665,280	47.8	36.9	10.9	—
1916	32,589,968	46.7	37.4	9.3	—
1917	42,005,367	50.9	39.9	11.0	—
1918	49,356,164	49.7	35.9	11.6	2.2
1919	79,767,785	49.4	35.7	10.7	3.0
1920	110,676,987	45.5	32.5	10.0	3.0
1921	77,479,732	48.4	32.4	13.3	2.7
1922	78,467,670	51.6	35.1	14.1	2.4

*Totals from advertisers spending more than $10,000.
**Total for 38 magazines in 1911 and 37 in 1912.

Sources: "Expenditures of Advertisers," Curtis Bulletin 25 (May 23, 1923); "Tables Showing Advertising Investments of Leading Advertisers Using $10,000 and Over in 30 Publications," 1916.

advertising office in San Francisco in 1913, adding to the offices it already maintained in Philadelphia, New York, Boston, and Chicago. Its advertising sales staff of twenty-seven in 1912 grew to forty-five by 1914, and expenses, including salaries, expanded so much that Curtis's board of directors summoned the advertising director to a meeting in early 1914 and told him to keep a tighter rein on finances.[20]

The expansion was spurred in part by the construction of a new plant across the street from Independence Hall in Philadelphia. (See Figure 1.1.) The nine-story building, which took up an entire city block, contained more room than Curtis needed at the time, and larger, more efficient printing presses allowed the company to print three magazines for not much more money than it had spent for two up to that time. With advertising revenues, especially at the *Post*, booming, Cyrus Curtis and his board of directors saw an opportunity to broaden the company's reach and widen its advertising base. Once it owned the *Country Gentleman* and the *Criterion of Fashion*, Curtis Publishing boasted that it had one of the most well-rounded groups of publications available to advertisers, "reaching

Figure 1.1   The Curtis Publishing Company building in Philadelphia.

with an almost unbelievable degree of efficiency every leading type of available consumer."[21]

One of Curtis's boldest moves during its flurry of expansion had nothing directly to do with the publishing of magazines. It had everything to do with understanding how those magazines worked in the commercial marketplace. Gaining that understanding became the primary goal of the new Division of Commercial Research the company opened in 1911. Edward Bok might have had the rare ability to read *Journal* subscribers' letters like tea leaves, *Post* editor George Horace Lorimer might have had a keen intuition in assembling editorial material, and Cyrus Curtis himself might have had the ability to spot both talent and commercial possibilities. The company's advertising representatives said they needed something more tangible to work with, though, especially if this ongoing expansion was to succeed. They needed more than just the Curtis name to back them up when they approached reluctant clients, more than just the trust of past performance. They needed something that would turn them into industrial experts and earn them better trust among clients. They needed facts.

Addressing the Critics

At Curtis Publishing's annual advertising conference in January 1913, Latshaw, who had been promoted the year before to assistant director of advertising, issued a stern admonishment to his colleagues. A few weeks before the meeting, he had asked each of Curtis's advertising representatives to compile lists of businesses that had quit advertising and to assess why they were no longer among Curtis's customers. The reports that staff members turned in made Latshaw fume. Most were incomplete. Many had been done haphazardly and showed little attempt at analysis. Either the men did not know the reasons for their clients' failures and had not taken the time to analyze them, or they did not understand the failures and did not know how to analyze them. Either way, the material they submitted was inexcusable, and Latshaw let them know it. He was not trying to blame anyone, he said. Rather, he saw the issue as too important to overlook. He reminded the members of the advertising staff that they were drawing salaries from Curtis Publishing; they were not working on commission, as many advertising salesmen in other companies were. There were no running tallies of the lines of advertising they brought in, no quotas, no attempt to measure individual productivity. Rather, Curtis judged its employees on the *quality* of their work. How then, he asked, should that quality be measured? What were they doing to earn their salaries? What role should they and Curtis Publishing be playing in the world of advertising?[22]

This type of soul searching showed an uncertainty at a time of change, not only in the advertising industry but also in the managerial ranks. Curtis's growth and bureaucratization—from a company with a handful of employees in the 1880s to one of more than 4,000 workers in dozens of departments in the 1920s—were typical of the changes that were taking place in American business at the turn of the twentieth century. (See Figure 1.2.) As operations grew, proprietors could no longer oversee or control all of their businesses' operations personally. They had to rely on a growing bureaucracy, a chain of command, and segmented groups of people whose jobs became increasingly specialized. Because of that specialization, their

Figure 1.2   The Curtis advertising staff in 1913. Charles Coolidge Parlin is the second from right in the second row. To his right is William Wellington Payne, one of his early assistants. Another assistant, Henry Youker, is at the far left in that row. Among other notable members of the staff are Edward W. Hazen, sitting at far left; Stanley Latshaw, sitting, fourth from left; and William Boyd, sitting, second from right.

view of the business was often narrow. This new class of white collar executives lacked the ability to see the complete picture of an expanding marketplace—or even an entire business—and lacked the authority to act unilaterally. They needed a way to broaden their view. This was an extension of what one historian calls a "crisis of control" that had plagued American business since the beginning of the Industrial Revolution, when the development and use of information processing and communication technology began to fall behind those of energy and its application to manufacturing and transportation. That is, businesses such as Curtis lacked the means for collecting information about their own operations, their competitors, their clients, and the marketplace, and needed a formal mechanism to help them make decisions and, ultimately, try to influence the marketplace.[23]

In a series of speeches during the first day of the advertising conference, Latshaw attempted to articulate his vision of Curtis Publishing's mission amid these types of changes. It all came down to a question of paternalism, he said. The company was the dominant provider of advertising in a business world that increasingly relied on advertising. That put Curtis in a position of influence, and the company needed to decide how to use that influence with clients. "Are we going to manage our affairs as though they were our own children, or as though we were participating in a foundling institution?" Latshaw asked. He stressed that helping current advertisers achieve success counted for more than signing up new accounts that were doomed to failure, saying that "it is better to raise the baby than it is to bring it into the world to die." Curtis Publishing, he said, needed to realize that it was *not* a "common carrier," open to all without scrutiny. It needed to delve further into the finances of its clients and turn away those that would not benefit from advertising. When an advertised product failed, Latshaw said, the publication that carried the advertising was always blamed. That hurt the reputation of the publication, regardless of any mistakes the advertiser might have made. "I think that the average man who fails is very much inclined to go on to the housetops and tell the neighborhood, the club, and every one else of the failure—not of *his* failure (few men are willing to admit that), but the failure of the *Journal* or the failure of the *Post,* going back of that, the failure of advertising."[24]

Edward Hazen, Curtis's advertising director, agreed that the company was going through a period of reconstruction and analysis, "a period of study of the why and the wherefore, and I believe that we have got to give greater thought, greater care and study to the why and wherefore in every case that comes before us." He, too, thought Curtis needed to exert more influence. Advertising representatives needed to be careful not to overstep, though, he said. "We cannot be so paternal as to assume that nobody else knows anything about advertising. We would make ourselves ridiculous. . . . We would be putting ourselves in a position to lessen our influence." Like Latshaw, he encouraged the advertising staff to raise the level of service it provided to customers. "It is not always the man that

receives the largest income that has the most money in the bank,"
he said. "It is the fellow that husbands what he gets and takes care
of it. . . . What we want to do is to keep these fellows that come in
and make them successes."[25]

Customer Service and Paternalism

This idea of paternalism that both Latshaw and Hazen expressed had
grown from a policy of customer service that Cyrus Curtis had
developed and promoted since he founded his publishing company
in Philadelphia in the 1880s. Between about 1890 and 1915, Curtis
Service (as the company called it) came to mean everything from
personally answering the thousands of letters that women wrote each
week to the *Ladies' Home Journal* to "censoring" advertisements in
the *Journal* and *Saturday Evening Post* so that readers could trust them
and so that reputable advertisers would not have to share pages with
hucksters. It meant investing in high-quality engraving and printing
equipment and buying high-grade paper for magazine stock. Above
all, it meant creating an atmosphere of trust, not only within the
pages of Curtis magazines, but in personal relations with readers,
advertisers, and even competing magazines.[26]

That idea of customer service had not always been well defined,
but the intent was usually clear. In 1889, in an effort to make the
Journal more attractive to reputable advertisers, Cyrus Curtis imple-
mented several bold changes—widely considered foolish at the
time—that would later form the backbone of his company's success.
Although the company's finances were shaky and its future tenu-
ous, Curtis doubled the subscription price of the *Journal* to $1 a year
and refused to allow any discounts. At the urging of Bok, the *Journal*'s editor, he did away with subscriber premiums—such things
as silverware and dress patterns offered as incentives to buy the
magazine—even though they were a widely accepted part of doing
business in the publishing and retail worlds. He also made a big bet
on advertising, pioneering the idea that advertising income could
largely finance a publisher's operations.[27]

Curtis lost thousands of subscribers after the new policies were put into place, but with those who remained he was able to claim a "quality," or affluent, readership that subscribed on the merits of the magazine, not as part of a promotional gimmick. He also lost thousands of dollars in advertising revenue after he banned patent medicine ads, then cosmetics ads, then financial ads, and eventually cigarette ads. After doing so, though, he told *Journal* readers that he would be personally responsible for any loss they incurred by responding to the magazine's advertisements. Writing in 1890, one observer noted that the contents of the *Journal* were "carefully guarded. . . . A doubtful advertisement would no more pass the eye of the publisher than would an article of immoral tendency receive the approval of the editor." As Bok later described it, Curtis "had cleaned house, wanted his readers to know it, and was prepared to back up his action and promised that he believed every advertisement in his magazine was reliable."[28] Curtis took his belief in customer service so seriously that he had a standing policy of never scrimping on anything that would improve the worth of the company's magazines to readers and advertisers. "To his editors he says· 'Give the public the best. It knows. The cost is secondary,'" Bok wrote of Curtis. "To his circulation managers he says: 'Keep the magazine before the public and make it easy for the public to get it.' To his advertising men he says: 'We know we give advertisers their money's worth, but it is up to you to prove it to them.'"[29]

The Broader Reach of Customer Service

Curtis was one of many businesses that began to focus more on customers and customer service at the turn of the twentieth century. The idea of customer service gained widespread popularity in American business between about 1880 and 1915, giving rise to such things as new kinds of consumer credit, a work force to cater to patrons, and spaces in stores for customer pleasure. Restaurants and theaters adhered to this idea of service, as did railroads and public utilities. "The chief profit a wise man makes on his sales is not in dollars and cents but in serving his customers," John Wanamaker, the Philadelphia department store owner, wrote in 1918. This attitude, notes historian William Leach, marked a turning point, of sorts, in industrial capitalism, and the philosophy of "the public be served" rose over that of "the public be damned." This concept arose partly from the tenets of Christianity and partly from the philosophies of liberal republicanism, but mainly in response to a need to improve the seamy image of business. At the turn of the century, industrial workers revolted against industry; farmers against railroads, banks, and land speculators; small merchants against large. Businesses tried to remake their public image by portraying themselves as working for the good of all.[30]

This devotion to customer service was especially important in the field of advertising and in the advertising agencies that handled the creation and placement of much of the printed publicity of the time. When the first agents appeared in the 1860s, they acted primarily as a clearinghouse, buying space in newspapers and magazines and reselling it to businesses at a profit. They provided a convenient way for advertisers to buy space in many publications through a single source. Service agents first appeared around the turn of the century, competing with the large space brokers by acting as advertising consultants, writing copy, helping with window displays, and generally doing whatever they could to assist the advertiser.[31] In the early 1900s, the agencies began to transform themselves into marketing advisers, helping businesses analyze their products and their customers, choose the best media, and create advertising and sales campaigns. One leading agent called agencies "the advertiser's partner . . . trained in technique and experienced in the fundamentals that underlie all the business."[32] Similarly, Curtis Publishing called agents "publicity specialists" and wrote in the early 1910s that the "better type of agency now offers brains, ideas, and service together with a real concern as to the customer's success."[33]

This emphasis on customer service had altered the relationship of an advertising agent and an advertiser until it became, wrote Earnest Elmo Calkins and Ralph Holden, two prominent agents of the era, like that of a lawyer and a client. It had to be built on trust and confidentiality. The agent needed to know as much as possible about the company he was working for: its margin of profit, its territory of operation, its possibilities for expansion, the arguments made by salesmen, and the extent and methods of competition. Just as important, the agent needed to have a clear view of the marketplace. Many agencies "push their service to a limit which a few years ago would have been regarded as quixotic," the advertising trade journal *Printers' Ink* wrote in 1911. Just how far an agency would go "depends upon the circumstances. The progressive agency is crossing a Rubicon or two every year." That same year, A. B. Freeman of the Nichols-Finn Advertising Company of Chicago said that the word *agency* had become outdated. Agents were really students of commerce, of economics, of distribution, and of trade conditions, and they knew the ins and outs of the business world, Freeman wrote.

> The time is at hand when the business man asks not "How much pretty copy have you written and how big is your institution?" or, "What do you charge for your service?" but "How can you help me to market my proposition to better advantage? What do you know about my market and the people I am trying to reach? Are you equipped to say how much money it would take to do a certain thing in an advertising direction? Are you in touch with concerns that have attempted or are doing the thing I want to do or something enough alike from which to draw a conclusion?"[34]

As part of this transformation, advertising agents and sales representatives began to form professional organizations around the turn of the century. Two national organizations, the Associated Advertising Clubs of America and the American Association of Advertising Agencies, extolled the benefits of advertising, claiming that it promoted virtue, improved product distribution, and continually raised the American standard of living.[35] Along with the trade journal *Printers' Ink,* the organizations widely promoted the creed of "truth in advertising," which was also one of Curtis's pet causes. "The advertisement which willfully or carelessly defrauds becomes worse than the thief," Curtis Publishing wrote in its *Advertising Code* in 1912. "It not only steals from its victims, but destroys the confidence which is fundamental to all business and essential to the success of advertising."[36]

Advertising *and* Selling

In at least one case in the early 1910s, Curtis advertising representatives took this idea of "What are you doing for me?" to the extreme to prove a point about the power of the Curtis organization. Responding in the name of Curtis service, they acted as salesmen for Warner Instrument Company, a maker of automobile speedometers. With Warner heading toward bankruptcy, members of the Curtis advertising staff in Chicago decided that it would be an excellent test case for what could be done with advertising in the *Saturday Evening Post* if that advertising was combined with skilled salesmanship. They persuaded Warner to run two-page spreads in the *Post,* and then they personally lobbied automobile makers to install Warner speedometers in their new cars. At the time, Curtis estimated, one of Warner's competitors, Stewart & Clark, had been furnishing 75 to 80 percent of speedometers for automobile manufacturers. Several months after the campaign began, the proprietor of Stewart & Clark summoned Curtis advertising representatives to his office, frantic about the gains that Warner had been making. He asked the Curtis representatives to work for his company, as they had for Warner. "Our reply," said Chauncey T. Lamb, an advertising representative in the Chicago office, "was, 'Nothing doing'; we did that to make Warner successful so that it should be an object lesson to the manufacturers of every kind of equipment for automobiles, that by advertising right in the *Saturday Evening Post* they could force the manufacturers of automobiles to use their product, providing it was high class; that we expected the success of the Warner Instrument Company to enable us to secure half a million dollars additional in advertising per year in the *Post* from other manufacturers of automobile equipments."

The ploy worked. Stewart & Clark signed a contract for two pages of advertising space in the *Post* each month and was eventually forced to buy Warner, once a weak and declining competitor, for $2 million. Advertising for automobiles and accessories in the *Post* continued to escalate, swelling the size of the magazine and making the Post *the* publication for marketing automobiles. By 1914, the *Post* carried 68 percent of all automobile advertising in the more than thirty competing magazines that Curtis tracked, and by 1923, it carried 83 percent of the more than $17 million that automakers spent on advertising in weekly magazines. The Curtis advertising staff, despite the strong-arm tactics it had used, assured itself and its clients that the only reason for Warner's success was the power of the *Post*.[31]

Creating a Conflict

Tactics like the those Curtis used with Warner came with consequences, though, and increasingly created tension between Curtis and advertising agencies as they all sought authoritative roles in a growing consumer economy. The problems and questions that the agencies faced were much the same as those that Curtis faced, and the work that advertising agents did, in many cases, was the same type of work that Curtis advertising representatives did: primarily selling advertising to manufacturers of consumer products, learning as much as possible about those manufacturers and products, and doing whatever possible to see that they succeeded.

On the surface, Curtis downplayed any conflict. To ensure that advertising was done right, the company said in 1912, a manufacturer needed the services of an agent. Curtis Publishing could not possibly look after each account, the company wrote. There were far too many advertisers to do that. Besides, many of those advertisers competed against one other, and Curtis could easily put itself in a precarious position if it favored one advertiser over another. The *Post,* for instance, carried advertising for twenty-two lines of men's clothing. "Could *we* give each of these twenty-two our 'clothing' best?" Curtis asked rhetorically. So, in theory, Curtis provided the medium; the advertising agent, who earned a commission from each advertisement placed, was to provide the service. "There is . . . no clashing of interests. Neither agent nor publisher can afford a failure," the company said.[38] Some agents did not buy that, and they worried that Curtis was trying to muscle in and save the money that went toward their commissions—usually 10 percent of the advertising bill. Those doubts grew during the summer of 1913, when Curtis broke from established standards and unilaterally changed its policy toward agencies. The company agreed to a long-sought-after increase in commissions—to 13 percent from 10 percent—but only if Curtis was "satisfied that the agent has earned it." That meant making sure that money was not wasted on poorly planned and poorly conceived advertising campaigns.[39]

Advertising had many critics, even as advertised products increasingly became associated with ideas like progress, freedom, liberty, and democracy, as Charles McGovern writes.[40] Advertising was blamed for, among other things, increasing the cost of living, discouraging competition, and forcing stores to carry brand-name goods that often had lower profit margins. Curtis could not answer all those criticisms with a single act, but by assuming greater control over agency commissions, it hoped to ensure that clients received an ample amount of attention and advice from agencies, thereby increasing the "efficiency" of advertising by giving campaigns a greater chance of success. If an advertiser succeeded, then so did the publisher. If clients were happy, they usually came back. And if publishers could point to repeat business, they could usually attract new clients. "Therefore, the most important work that the advertising agent is called upon to perform for the publisher is wide and conscientious service to his clients," Curtis Publishing wrote.[41]

In an obvious attempt to blunt criticism about the change in commission policy, Curtis said that it, too, was striving to provide greater service to advertisers, essentially stressing what Curtis had been doing for several years. Although Cyrus Curtis had screened ads for the *Ladies' Home Journal* early on, it was not until 1901 that it formalized a policy of "censorship." That policy not only reinforced a ban on advertising for patent medicines, investment schemes, and liquor, but set rigid boundaries for the content of all the ads it did accept, monitoring for such things as deception, extravagant wording, "undue boastfulness and exaggeration," and copy that "knocked" competitors.[42] As the company's advertising revenue grew, especially after 1910, it enforced the policy with increasing strictness, even though it cost Curtis $100,000 a year or more by 1913.[43] In its house organ, the company called censorship "costly and troublesome, but a distinctly necessary part" of the service the company offered. It admitted that censorship could seem "harsh and excessive," but that the driving force for the policy was the desire to make all advertising credible and respected. "We are striving to make our readers feel perfectly safe in dealing with advertisers by mail or in purchasing their goods in the stores, and perfectly confident that they will find such goods just as represented in print," the company wrote in 1912. "Apart from the consideration of honesty as a principle, it is self-evident that this unswerving standard benefits the public, the advertisers, and the publishers. If all advertising were strictly truthful, the purchasing public would soon recognize the fact and all advertising would be many times more profitable."[44] Curtis advertising representatives admitted that this type of outlook was idealistic, but they considered Curtis the flagship of the magazine industry, "the most powerful advertising organization in the world." If anyone was to uphold the standards of advertising, it was Curtis Publishing Company.[45] To reinforce that idea, the company began to broaden the argument for its publications, still pointing to their size and bulk, but also stressing the responsiveness and trust of their readers and advertisers.[46] It also sought to portray itself as the guardian of advertising, working to benefit the entire advertising industry, and in turn, all manufacturers and consumers.[47] And it began to emphasize and promote the work of various departments, especially a new Division of Commercial Research.

Envisioning a New Profession

The research department that Stanley Latshaw envisioned in the early 1910s was more of an evolution than a revolution for Curtis Publishing and for the world of business and industry (as I show in later chapters). Latshaw and other advertising representatives were already gathering information to help clients whenever they could. Cyrus Curtis himself took pride in investigating the marketplace before making decisions, and he admonished those who failed to do the same, especially when it came to promotion. Too many companies took no interest in their advertising, he told an interviewer in 1914. "They do not study it as they should and, what is just as bad, they do not permit any one else to study it for them. . . . It is rarely that an advertising campaign, started after a thorough study of all the conditions and all the factors and carried through with courage and patience, fails."[48]

Curtis's Circulation and Advertising Departments did just what Curtis described. In a book the company published in 1911, it sought to embolden its circulation agents by outlining the methods the company had used in achieving magazine circulations that were the envy of the publishing world. Those methods, which the company said had been perfected over the previous ten years, were really quite simple on the surface: Sign up as many salesmen as possible and offer them incentives to sell the magazines. Beneath this straightforward exterior, though, lay an intricate skeleton of work structures, incentives, expectations, and models for selling. The method, a variation of the idea of "scientific efficiency" that was spreading through the business world, involved 2,000 district agents who hired their own sub-agents to work directly with street salesmen, usually boys.[49] (See Figure 1.3.)

Curtis encouraged agents to break down their territory into city wards or voting districts. That way, they could compare population with the number of magazines they sold, spot weak areas, and know better where to concentrate their sales efforts. Nationwide, they were told, one copy of the *Journal* was sold for every sixty people. The ratio for the *Post* was one to every fifty, although district agents did better than that, selling one copy for every thirty-five residents. Using that model, agents were expected to adjust their sales methods and set goals for undersold areas. Planning was the key. "An attempt to cover your entire territory, by a general plan, without an analysis of the actual conditions by wards or precincts, is like shooting in the

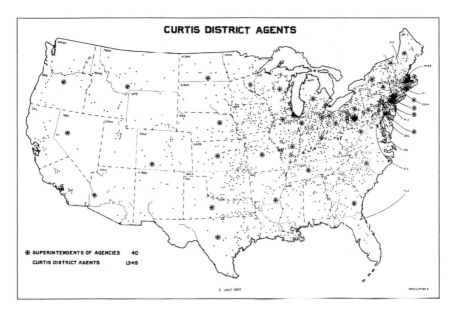

Figure 1.3   Curtis set up an elaborate network of superintendents and district agents to oversee sales of its magazines.

dark," Curtis Publishing told the agents. "You don't want to round up many more boys in wards where you already have as many boys as the population there will support."[50] The home office used a similar method to monitor sales in each state. Not only did it calculate a nationwide ratio of sales to population, but it calculated ratios for each state. When sales lagged in certain states, the company launched promotions to try to increase the circulation numbers. "Of course, the ratio of sales to population is not uniform in every state," the company boasted, "but it is more nearly so with our publications than with others."[51] That made a good marketing argument, but in reality Curtis's magazines had low levels of readership in the South, an area that it frequently marginalized in its promotional material.[52]

The Advertising Department had not analyzed its methods or goals nearly that precisely, but it, too, collected statistics to try to put its work into better context for staff members and advertisers. Beginning about 1905, members of the advertising staff met at least once each year at the home office in Philadelphia to discuss the state of the business, talk over any problems they were having, and refine any points of policy. At those annual advertising conferences, staff members shared information about businesses and industries they were familiar with. Individual representatives often specialized in areas like automobiles and textiles, familiarizing themselves with the workings of those industries and with the people and the issues involved, and in some cases keeping detailed statistics—mostly regional and connected to industries near the regional offices—to monitor industry trends and to identify areas that might be exploited for future advertising. Some of that information gathering became more formal in 1910, when the department formed a statistical division to tabulate the advertising and circulation figures of more than thirty competing publications. The new division began putting in spreadsheet form such things as total dollar volume of advertising and the amount spent by various industries and individual businesses. It also kept track of how the *Post,* the *Journal* and later, *Country Gentleman* compared with competitors in each category. Staff members were well versed on this accumulation of facts, but they sometimes found that bare facts alone were not enough to help them understand the industries they monitored.[53]

For instance, at a meeting of Curtis advertising employees in 1910, Melville H. Smith, a representative at Curtis's Boston office, reported that "the shoe industry offered a large and promising field for the development of national advertising in a big way." He presented national, as well as state-by-state, statistics on shoe sales since 1890, and noted the size of the industry, particularly in New England; the amount of shoe advertising in magazines, particularly in the *Journal* and the *Post*; the objections Curtis representatives encountered in discussing magazine advertising with shoe manufacturers; and how representatives could meet those objections. Smith noted that shoe advertising was "in an inceptive and experimental state but showing decided life."[54] And though Smith "aroused a consciousness" among advertising representatives that day, the reports that he and others presented alluded to some frustrations that the entire advertising staff was having in making sense not only of the shoe industry but of most other industries. Because the staff was so scattered, so was the information it assembled. The facts, statistics, and observations were too regional, too parochial to be analyzed on a national scale. Curtis's advertising offices might be in a better position to track the shoe industry if they would exchange information and observations about accounts, Smith told his colleagues. They would be better served, he said, if someone could tie everything together.[55]

Latshaw eventually convinced his superiors of the need for a full-time researcher in the Advertising Department, and in 1911, he set out to fill the job. He realized just how difficult that would be after he talked with E. Dana Durand, director of the Census Bureau, which had itself been made permanent only a decade before, but had become by the late nineteenth century the chief source of government data about business. Facts were easy to come by, Durand told Latshaw, but bald facts were of little use. What Latshaw needed was someone who could analyze those facts, put them into a context that advertisers could understand and appreciate.[56]

Latshaw spoke with several college and university professors about the research job at Curtis, but he rejected them all on grounds that they would be too likely to approach the work from behind a desk—"card shufflers," he called them. What he needed was someone who was willing to travel the country and search for ideas, someone who liked people and had a knack for conversation. He needed someone with knowledge of economics and statistics but also the skill to apply that knowledge to advertising, a quick learner who could become an expert in many different industrial fields. After a brief search, Latshaw decided he knew just such a person— a teacher he had in high school, a man with a quick mind and a penchant for public speaking. Latshaw took a train west from Boston to his home state, Wisconsin. That's where he found Charles Coolidge Parlin.

2

An Unlikely Leader

On the surface, Charles Coolidge Parlin was an unlikely candidate for a job in an advertising department. He was thirty-eight years old and had worked nearly his entire adult life as a high school principal and teacher. He had never worked in advertising or publishing, and he never had any such aspirations. During a job interview in 1911, Edward W. Hazen, Curtis's advertising director, asked Parlin what qualifications he thought he had for a position as a researcher on Curtis's advertising staff. Parlin was momentarily stumped. He eventually replied: "I think the most valuable one is that, not knowing anything about your business, I will not have to waste any of your time unlearning anything."[1] Twenty-five years later, that answer did not seem nearly as outrageous to Parlin as it did that night after speaking with Hazen. "I think . . . that the principal reason we do not learn more is that when we want to find out something we send out those who know the most about the matter and they come back with what they already knew," Parlin said in 1936.[2]

In 1911, though, after accepting the job as director of Curtis Publishing's new Division of Commercial Research, Parlin wished many times for more knowledge than he had. His job description was vague, and the executives at Curtis knew it was vague. They knew no better than Parlin what they wanted out of the new department. Hazen told the company's board of directors in 1911 that Parlin had been hired "to make investigations of trade conditions, with a view to use the information thereby secured in connection with the solicitation and development of new business."[3] The venture was as new to Hazen and other executives as it was to Parlin. Their general idea may have been to acquire information that would help them enhance their service to advertisers and to reinforce Curtis's position of dominance, but when it came time to articulate that idea, they could not. The idea to form the Division of Commercial Research had been Stanley Latshaw's, and the new department was located in Latshaw's office in Boston—significantly distancing it from both the home office in Philadelphia and the main advertising office in New York City. If the new project failed, Curtis could easily cut it loose without damaging the company's image.

During those first months at Curtis, Parlin found himself adrift many times. The expectations of him were low, and his future with Curtis was uncertain. Although Parlin was ignorant of the world of advertising, he shared a core belief not only with many in the advertising industry but with American business in general: a belief in the power of scientific knowledge. Parlin's background in education and debate had more than prepared him for his new role as a researcher. As an educator, he had spent many years learning how to gather information, how to analyze it, and how to present it so that others could understand it. His new career at Curtis was essentially an extension of those skills. Parlin had been persuaded to take the job in part because of Latshaw's insistence that "out in the minds of men there were ideas which would be of inestimable value if somebody would go out and catch them."[4] The world was changing rapidly, and Curtis Publishing needed someone willing to record those changes, someone who could gather information about the commercial marketplace and present it in a form—essentially a map of consumption—that would be useful to Curtis, its employees, and its clients. This would be a pioneering job, one without rules or guidelines, but also one with much potential. Parlin took Latshaw's message to heart. He was not the only one to do so, either. Throughout the country, business, industry, and government were beginning to discover the value of marketplace information.

A Reluctant Recruit

Parlin had not been easily swayed by Stanley Latshaw's offer of a job with Curtis Publishing. At the time of Latshaw's visit in early 1911, Parlin was the principal at Wausau High School in Wisconsin, and had been for nearly fifteen years. He was president of the state teachers association and was considering a job offer from the largest high school in the state. He felt, he later recalled, as though he were on the verge of making a real mark in state education. Although Parlin had dreamed of achieving greatness in other things—he had always wanted to become a lawyer—he had stuck with teaching and school administration. He enjoyed both, and that is how he had expected to spend the rest of his life.[5]

Still, Parlin had the qualities that Latshaw thought Curtis Publishing needed for its new research division. At the University of Wisconsin, he had been an important member of the debate team, and he had been a sought-after public speaker in both West De Pere (where he served briefly as a teacher and a principal) and Wausau, Wisconsin. Parlin, an elfish man with thin, dark hair and a relaxed smile, had the kind of affable personality that put people at ease, that made them comfortable talking about themselves and their livelihoods. Just as important, he was too restless to sit at a desk, and he seemed to have a mania for travel. During summer breaks from teaching, he occasionally worked as a guide, leading tour groups through Europe. Here was a man who would be willing to live forever out where the ideas were, Latshaw later recalled, "a man who could not only collect facts, but who would know one when he saw one." Parlin turned Latshaw's offer down three times. Latshaw persisted, and after Parlin received a fourth offer, he accepted. It was late June 1911. He taught his last class on a Thursday, boarded a weekend train, and reported for work at Barristers Hall in Boston on Monday morning.[6]

Making Sense of It All

The new job proved even more frustrating than Parlin had imagined. He knew his task would be challenging. This was, after all, a new concept: a department, within a major business, devoted exclusively to analytical research. But researching what? And where? And how? The material that Latshaw provided gave him little to go on. When Parlin asked for the company's sales materials, he later remembered, he was given a circulation statement about the *Ladies' Home Journal* and the *Saturday Evening Post* and a letter that "somebody had written in superlatives with no facts, asking a man to advertise codfish." He pushed it aside in exasperation. After spending three days going through other material that Latshaw had provided, Parlin was still no closer to deciding how to approach his new task. Where was the handle on this job? he asked himself. Had someone made him an offer, he later said, "I would have sold the job for two cents and gone back where somebody would tell me what to do."[7]

In early July, Hazen traveled to Boston from his Madison Avenue office to talk with Parlin about the work of the new Division of Commercial Research. Parlin hoped desperately that Hazen would give him direction. He showed the advertising director a long list of industries, arranged alphabetically, that he had compiled. "We cannot study industry, but we might study *an* industry," he told Hazen.

Agricultural implements came first on the list, and Hazen read no further. "We have just bought the *Country Gentleman*," he said. "Just the thing: Go out and study agricultural implements."

Parlin fished for more direction. "Where shall I begin?" he asked.

"Where you wish," was Hazen's matter-of-fact response. "I suppose they are manufactured around Chicago. That would be a good place to begin."

"How long do you want me to study agricultural implements?"

"Until you get ready to make a report. Then come back and make your report."

Parlin pushed Hazen for a more definite assignment. "How much money do you want me to spend studying agricultural implements?" he asked.

Hazen replied brusquely: "You do not understand us. Your job is to study agricultural implements. You go and get busy."[8]

The exchange between Parlin and Hazen contains important clues about the corporate culture in which Commercial Research developed. Parlin, at Latshaw's insistence, had been made a manager. As such, he was expected to function independently. Cyrus Curtis expected his executives to solve problems for themselves, and when any of them came to him for help, he was quick to say: "That's your job, not mine. . . . You have a mind of your own. Use it." Hazen, in essence, said the same to Parlin that day.[9]

The exchange also revealed Hazen's uncertainty about Parlin's role and about the whole idea of commercial research. Pointing Parlin toward agricultural implements made sense in that any information he came up with would help the advertising staff understand something they knew little or nothing about—agriculture and related industries. But in doing so, he was also pushing Parlin away from the company's star publications, the *Journal* and the *Post,* neither of which drew much, if any, agricultural advertising. Parlin's study of farm implements would have been of minimal use to the staffs of those two magazines. And because he would have no contact with the company' prime advertisers, he could do nothing to alienate them. Instead, he was sent off on a project related to *Country Gentleman,* which was then losing money and was widely expected to fail. It must have seemed a safe prospect to Hazen. As Parlin later described his early days at Curtis: "I had nobody to bother me, nobody wanted anything, nobody had any information. . . . More research operations have been brought to naught and more hearts of research men have been broken by being put on the outside fringe of a business than through any other means."[10]

That afternoon in July 1911, after Hazen's visit to Boston, Latshaw helped Parlin get started by arranging a lunch appointment with Grant Wright, editor of the *Eastern Dealer,* an agricultural trade publication in Philadelphia. Parlin left town that night. As he stared into the darkness through the window of the southbound train, he later recalled, he felt like Sammy Weller, a young lad in one of his favorite books, Charles Dickens's *Pickwick Papers.* Sammy's father had thrown his son into the streets of London so that he would learn to take care of himself. That, Mr. Weller thought, was the best training available. Parlin took comfort in that thought. He did not know how to approach the task before him, but then neither did anyone else. He would have to learn as he went along and adapt as best he could. If he was to succeed at this new job, he would have to rely on the skills that had brought him this far.[11]

"Talk Sense and You Will Have a Monopoly"

Growing up in Broadhead, Wisconsin, Parlin was a runt of a child who had a fondness for books and ginger snaps. He was a voracious reader of history and literature, especially the works of Washington Irving, James Fenimore Cooper, and Charles Dickens, and his keen memory earned him the nickname "walking encyclopedia." He struggled with spelling and penmanship, but he excelled in public speaking, which he first tried in grade school. He would later say that his ability in extemporaneous speech was his most valuable asset, and he carried with him a piece of advice that some sage had once offered him: "Don't tell stories. Everybody does that. Talk sense and you will have a monopoly on your field." Parlin completed seventh and eighth grades in one year and high school in three years. He was sixteen when he graduated, and he entered the University of Wisconsin in the fall of 1889.[12]

While at Wisconsin in the 1890s, Parlin was an important member of the debate team, which focused primarily on economic issues. When Wisconsin opened its Graduate School of Economics in the fall of 1892, Parlin and several other seniors petitioned the university president, seeking permission to take classes at the new school. When the president granted the request, Parlin booked himself almost entirely with courses in economics.[13] Despite Parlin's initial excitement about studying under Richard T. Ely—who was chairman of the Department of Social Sciences and who helped turn Wisconsin into a leading graduate program for social science and economics at the turn of the century—he gradually found the new graduate school less than attractive. Ely openly resented having seniors in his graduate classes, Parlin later recalled, and tried to drive them away by threatening to flunk them as a group. Parlin grew frustrated and left the university after the fall term, finishing his undergraduate degree by correspondence. He took a job as a high school teacher and a principal, an occupation in which he flourished until Stanley Latshaw convinced him that he was destined for something else.[14] Despite his frustrations at Wisconsin, though, the economic concepts he was exposed to there clearly showed through in his work at Commercial Research.

Overcoming Ambivalence

As Parlin researched his early reports for Curtis Publishing Company, he was not sure what he was looking for. His first study, written in late 1911, reflected both ambivalence and self-doubt. He admitted that a list he had compiled of the business done by manufacturers of agricultural implements was "based almost wholly upon general impressions rather than upon any definite data and is no doubt very inaccurate." In a section of the report that examined the advertising possibilities of implement manufacturers and retailers, he wrote: "I hesitate to express opinions on this subject to those more experienced in advertising."[15]

Between 1911 and about 1915, Parlin pushed aside that ambivalence about his new job and developed a general style of research, establishing a routine for his analyses that became the standard for all who worked with him.[16] He set out with the intent of making himself an expert on each of the general subjects he approached. Borrowing from economics and the social sciences, he started with what was known about the marketplace in trade journals, business catalogues, and government data, and then amassed facts and proceeded inductively with his analysis. He interviewed the prominent manufacturers, jobbers, and retailers—along with many consumers—in a given field, placing a high value on information he collected himself. He spent many months on the road researching each report, keeping detailed notes as he collected information, and forming theories about the workings of the marketplace and the interactions of businesses and consumers.[17]

For his study of agricultural implements in 1911, he conducted more than 175 interviews in sixteen states, Canada, and the District of Columbia with businesses that ranged from windmill makers to lightning rod makers, manufacturers of plows and planters to trade publication editors, engine manufacturers, and dealers in harvesting equipment. For a study of textiles and department stores in 1911 and 1912, he conducted 1,121 interviews in 165 cities, spending a year compiling information and writing the report. "The wider the scope of the inquiry and the more extensive the number of interviews the safer are likely to be the conclusions," Parlin wrote in 1914, again sounding much like a social scientist.[18]

In conducting his research, though, Parlin acted much like a reporter, seeking out experts in various aspects of industry and using their judgments to help form his own image of the marketplace. During the day, he conducted interviews. At night, he worked in his hotel room, often until well after midnight, poring over his notes and transcribing the interviews in longhand. Each transcript contained the date, time, and length of interview, along with Parlin's impressions of the people he spoke with. In at least one case, he even tabulated the responses into an opinion poll.[19] Each week he sent his notes to a secretary, who typed them and distributed them to Curtis's advertising staff. He hoped to keep the staff informed about his work, but he spent so much time away from the office, he could never be sure that anyone read the pages he had submitted.[20]

An Economist's Influence

Parlin never mentioned Ely's influence on his work at Curtis; in fact, he once wrote of his dislike for Ely. Ely's influence later became evident, though, not only in the theories that Parlin developed about the marketplace, but in the ways he went about his work and in the way he sought to reshape the outlook and strategy of businesses by endorsing the use of social science.[21] Ely was a German-trained economist who had been a professor at the newly formed

Johns Hopkins University for eleven years before moving to Wisconsin in 1892, and who trained many future leaders in the social sciences: Thorstein Veblen, Davis R. Dewey, John R. Commons, and Frederic Howe, among others. He believed in scientific investigation of practical business problems, and he favored descriptive writing that put problems into historical perspective. He also required students to think and write about the effects that their economic subjects had on the general welfare of society, assigning research papers on such topics as "The Economic Effects of Changes in Fashion" and "Advertising Considered From an Economic Standpoint."[22]

Ely saw society as an organism composed of interdependent parts whose functions were essential to the well-being of the whole. He also saw, early in his career at least, the acquisition of goods as tied directly to the "progress of civilization," though he later shifted toward a philosophy of "rational consumption."[23] He wrote in *An Introduction to Political Economy,* first published in 1889: "We have reached the highest stage of economic life that has ever been attained by man, and yet there were never so many economic questions pressing for solutions as at present." Ely and other antiformalist thinkers rejected notions of pre-ordained destiny and sought to explain social change by relating the past to the present, "to understand social evolution, not merely to proclaim it," as the historian William L. O'Neill writes. They also rejected the formalist idea that natural laws explained all human behavior. The antiformalists, O'Neill says, "preferred evidence to logic, experience to abstract principle." To Ely, economic knowledge was impossible without careful analysis, and he wrote that political economists needed to use induction, deduction, statistics, observation, and description in their studies.[24]

Parlin used all of those techniques in his market studies for Curtis Publishing. He made ample use of government statistics and compiled industry statistics of his own as he went about his work in the Division of Commercial Research. As a matter of routine, he turned the statistical data into charts and graphs, primarily as a means for identifying marketplace trends and for piecing together a rough overview of a market. In his report on farm implements, he relied on twenty-three pie charts to show how business was distributed (that six companies made 80 percent of plows, for instance), and seven line graphs that showed trends in the industry (as in the case of a shrinking number of manufacturers doing an increasing volume of business). In his study of textiles and department stores the next year, he used twelve maps and more than one hundred charts.[25] These charts became one of the signatures of his work, and he used them to emphasize things that others had overlooked. "Often," Parlin wrote, "we have found a manufacturer with the latest census reports at his elbow, but deeply interested in maps and graphs of the same census material as it applied to his own business, indicating that while he had perhaps read the figures, they came to him in a new light as he saw them graphed."[26]

Trading Information

Parlin found that his initial compilations of statistical data gave him credibility when he began to investigate areas he was unfamiliar with. "The man who is already informed and can talk the language of the trade soon inspires confidence and becomes a welcome visitor," Parlin wrote, "but on the uninformed the business world is too busy to waste time." Parlin became more and more sophisticated in his questioning as he immersed himself in his research, and he used the information he gleaned to "talk shop" with business owners. He often offered estimates of sales volume or turnover or the cost of doing business—prodding merchants either to confirm his figures or to offer other estimates.

Other times, though, especially in the early stages of a new report, Parlin asked general questions about a particular industry—how it worked, what the main companies were—and let the people he spoke with lead the conversations. What he found in many cases was that businesses would not provide information about themselves but that they were more than willing to provide substantial information about their competitors. At the John Wanamaker's department store in New York City, for instance, Ralph Helmer, the manager of the dress goods department, kept in his desk the estimated volumes of business for the city's fourteen largest department stores. He freely shared the information with Parlin, who obtained similar information about Wanamaker's from a Gimbel Brothers manager who used to work for Wanamaker's.[27]

Personality was also important in dealing with business people who were often suspicious of his motives, and Parlin used his skill as a speaker and a debater to gain the confidence of the people he interviewed. In many cases, he would have been turned away cold had he not been able to chip away at the suspicion, indifference, and occasionally even hostility of the people he encountered. One Wisconsin merchant burst into profanity when Parlin mentioned Curtis Publishing Company and the *Saturday Evening Post*.

> He would not give the ____ paper two cents of his money nor two minutes of his time—a paper that would favor LaFollette was no paper for him. I told him that since I was a Wisconsin man, his burst of feeling was intelligible; that under the circumstances I would not attempt to allay his wrath, but would bid him good morning. He said he did not wish to be discourteous to me, for he supposed I was not responsible for the editorial policy of the paper, and if I would sit down, he would be glad to be of service.[28]

In most cases, Parlin was able to use the Curtis magazines to his advantage. Nearly everyone he talked with read the magazines regularly and nearly all held them in high esteem. That seems to have helped break the ice in some cases, creating open-mindedness among some people who might otherwise have turned him away. That was the case with a Massachusetts merchant who was "at first rather inclined to be critical of magazine advertising and to argue that the magazine advertising increased the cost of goods to the retailer and hence the consumer. He became more affable later and said that he was accustomed to read the *Ladies' Home Journal* and especially the *Saturday Evening Post*." He then offered Parlin the information he had sought.[29]

Catching Ideas

Parlin based his approach to early trade investigations on Latshaw's premise that "out in the minds of men . . . were ideas which would be of inestimable value if somebody would go out and catch them." That is, Parlin proceeded under the assumption that Curtis Publishing needed to understand the workings of businesses besides its own, that the thinking behind those businesses could be synthesized and made to work to the company's benefit, but that business and society were in constant flux, in a perpetual state of change that required monitoring. His thinking reflected a combination of classical economics (that economic growth could better the human condition and that competition would keep individual self-interest in check) and Miltonian speech (a marketplace of ideas), but also of modern bureaucratic idealism (that the methods of science led to efficiency) and Progressive notions of specialization (that experts were needed to analyze complex problems and prescribe courses of action).[30]

The thread that held this patchwork of ideas together was advertising. Although Parlin discounted his role in advertising sales, he used his position as a researcher to scout for advertising prospects and, wherever possible, to promote Curtis publications as the most important media to use. In a final section of the 1911 agricultural implements report, Parlin wrote: "It was thought best to keep the advertising problem in the background and to seek only for industrial information." The bulk of the report—and later reports—funneled into the section on advertising, though, and Parlin pointed out the companies that seemed to be the best advertising prospects. He rated firms by the size of market and gave every agricultural manufacturer a "grade" based on the potential for advertising.[31] He also noted that the implement makers had generally used trade journals for advertising and that if Curtis were to gain their confidence, the manufacturers would "need to be educated as to the possibility of creating, through advertising, a pull from the farmers." The report itself was weighted toward manufacturers—the most likely prospects for advertising—and relied on them (nearly three-quarters of his interviews were with manufacturers) for most of the information.

At one point, Parlin even cautioned Curtis against accepting advertising from mail-order implement companies because doing so might upset the retail businesses tied to the manufacturers.[32]

This emphasis on advertising gave Parlin the direction he had so desperately sought when he started at Curtis, leading him during his studies of department stores and textiles (the stores themselves were not big advertisers in national magazines, but the manufacturers were); automobiles (which accounted for up to a third of *Post* advertising at the time); and food and household products (industries that collectively ranked second only to automobiles in their spending on national advertising during the 1910s and 1920s). Later studies focused on some of the other defining industries and issues of the era, such things as electricity, Prohibition, and radio—all important aspects of the emerging consumer economy. Consumption was transforming American life, and the Division of Commercial Research found its mission in analyzing the changes that transformation was making in manufacturing, distribution, retailing, and individual purchasing.

An Expanding View

The desire that businesses showed for economic information during Parlin's tenure at Curtis Publishing had emerged in the nineteenth century in what James Beninger calls a "crisis of control." Until the Industrial Revolution, economies ran at a "human pace." That is, products were made by hand, crops were harvested by hand, and trade was primarily conducted face to face. Industrialization sped up this process, and for several decades the means of processing and communicating information about business and industry lagged behind the ability to harness energy and apply it to manufacturing and transportation. Producers operated in a vacuum of sorts. They could keep track of their own businesses, which were expanding their ability to produce, but they had little knowledge of the overall marketplace, of supplies of raw materials, or of distribution and retail sales. Until the advent of such things as trademarks, consumer packaging, and mass advertising, manufacturers were essentially at the mercy of wholesalers and retailers, who continually haggled with them over such things as quantity discounts, profit margins, shelf display, and treatment of competitors' products. Increasingly, manufacturers sought out and used information about such things as business practices, competitors, and product distribution as a means of better influencing the marketplace and their own destinies.[33]

Large-scale mass production had also created a need for managers to oversee the many facets of business and industry. These new professional executives were expected to take a long-range, broad view of the marketplace—a much different perspective than the proprietor of a small, local business had in the nineteenth century. They sought the advice of specialists on the potential effects of decisions, and they attempted to use information to help control some of the uncertainties of the marketplace.[34] "The manager who *knows* his market conditions and can accurately forecast the needs of his trade, can seize opportunities for immediate profit which his less market-wise competitor must forgo," the trade journal *Printers' Ink* said in 1915. "That is one of the reasons why selling knowledge is so indispensable a part of the equipment of a competent executive."[35]

One of the early manifestations of this desire to control the uncertainties of business was scientific management. First put to use in the 1890s, scientific management sought to eliminate waste and reduce production costs while prodding factory workers to increase their productivity.[36] This thinking spread into the advertising industry at the turn of the century as industry leaders called for making advertising more efficient and more predictable by focusing on the right people with the right publications and the right products. As early as 1879, the N. W. Ayer advertising agency conducted what is often credited as being the first market study, wiring state officials and publishers across the country, requesting information about grain production for a client, and using that information to create an advertising plan.[37] "The present-day tendency on the part of the experienced advertisers," wrote the advertising agents Earnest Elmo Calkins and Ralph Holden in 1905, "is to get at the facts—to reduce the art of advertising to a science—to develop what may be called the mathematics of advertising."[38]

Applying Psychology

This "mathematics of advertising" was primarily an attempt to use the new social science of psychology to develop theories about how advertising worked and how it might work better, including such techniques as "keying," or coding, coupon ads so that advertisers could determine which publications drew the most responses, and the use of experiments in which people were asked to view a variety of trademarks and to tell which left the greatest impression and what product was associated with each trademark.[39] At the Lord & Thomas advertising agency in Chicago, Albert Lasker, a young salesman, nurtured a "record of results" department and made it a prime selling point of the agency. The agency's clients submitted weekly reports about such things as responses to advertisements and sales that could be attributed to retail campaigns.[40] In Philadelphia, the advertising agent N. W. Ayer & Sons used its information bureau to collect clippings and statistical information and to conduct research into product use.[41] And in New York, the J. Walter Thompson advertising agency said in 1904:

> When a manufacturer or merchant comes to us for advice about putting his goods more prominently before the public, we investigate his possible market. We look around to see whether the field is entirely covered by his rivals, whether he could obtain at least a local foothold, even if a national trade was denied him. We study with painstaking fidelity the exact status of his branch of industry and its susceptibility to development.[42]

One of the most prominent proponents of applying psychology to advertising was Walter Dill Scott, a professor at Northwestern University, who focused on using advertising to influence minds through such means as perception, suggestion, and the association of ideas.[43]

The agencies were among many other businesses that had delved into research. In 1911, the *Chicago Tribune* claimed to have "accurate knowledge of Chicago as a market," information that it said it would provide "to manufacturers who want to know the best and quickest way to secure distribution." It later backed up those claims with publications like its *Book of Facts,* which stressed the importance of the Upper Midwest and promoted the *Tribune*'s reach in that area.[44] In mid-1911, the two-year-old Business Bourse of New York, under the direction of J. George Frederick, former editor of *Printers' Ink,* announced that it planned to provide research in selling and advertising, including "tests upon consumers for labels, trademarks, color schemes, and even for advertisements along psychological, optical science and other lines."[45] That same year, the Harvard Business School created its Bureau of Business Research "for the purpose of investigation of business problems, primarily for the problem of distribution of products." It began publishing a journal two years later with a "distinctly tentative" report on the shoe industry, with a promise that its future work would provide "valid conclusions of great practical and theoretical importance."[46]

By the early 1910s, according to the marketing historian Lawrence C. Lockley, "there was a considerable amount of market research going on—enough to allow conclusions on techniques gradually to crystallize, and to broaden the interest of the business public."[47] *Printers' Ink* carried many articles that referred to market research either directly or tangentially as advertising practitioners discussed the logistics and results of research.[48] By 1914, there was no lack of self-proclaimed "experts" willing to conduct market analyses, *Printers' Ink* said, but it warned businesses to be wary, saying: "An engineer who offered complete specifications for a million-dollar viaduct for $50 would get scanty consideration, and the same reasoning applies to the 'expert' who promises a complete market analysis for the price of a round-trip ticket to Omaha."[49]

Showing How It Could Be Done

The reference to cost was telling because the collection of national data about business and industry was time consuming and expensive. As Parlin traveled the country conducting research for Curtis, he found that many people—including W. A. Scott, one of his economics professors at Wisconsin—were surprised that an individual company was taking on such ambitious nationwide research projects. In many cases, the people Parlin spoke to thought that only the growing authority of Washington could force businesses to divulge financial information that was usually considered sensitive and confidential—a claim that the government itself made.[50] Government agencies were indeed the most prolific sources of data on industry and society, especially during the Progressive Era. The census office, the primary compiler of national statistics, achieved permanent status in 1902.[51] In the early 1800s, the statistics it gathered were used mostly by congressmen, local politicians, and almanac publishers, but those statistics grew more elaborate and sophisticated in the late nineteenth century as the census charted the growth, industrialization, and urbanization of American society.[52] By the end of the century, business associations, reformers, and university professors lobbied for the census to include more and more information that they could use, helping change the census from strictly a tool for the apportionment of Congress to an instrument to monitor the state of American society.[53]

By the turn of the century, several other governmental agencies had begun compiling nationwide statistics as well, mostly through such administrative work as collecting taxes and logging the arrival of immigrants. The federal Bureau of Education produced annual or biennial statistics on public school systems, the Interstate Commerce Commission published extensive information about railroads, and the Geological Survey published statistics on mineral production. Agencies such as the Bureau of Corporations and the Bureau of Statistics followed everything from production to transportation to marketing, as well as imports and exports.[54] George Cortelyou, secretary of commerce and labor, said in 1904:

One of the most important methods of aiding commerce is to give to those engaged in it such definite information regarding existing conditions as will enable them intelligently to determine the classes of articles which can be most profitably produced, the sections to which they should be produced, and the agencies through which they can best be placed before prospective customers.

His department, which was created the year before, was doing just that with monthly and yearly statements on exports and semiweekly statements on commercial conditions.[55]

Local governments also sought guidance through research, especially as they tried to rid themselves of long-entrenched corruption. New York City's Bureau of Municipal Research was formed in 1906, and it became a model for similar agencies in Philadelphia, Chicago, Cincinnati, Milwaukee, and other cities. A university bureau movement soon followed as academia sought, as a public service, to collect and furnish information on all phases of city government, from administrative problems to control of public utilities. The first university bureau was created at Wisconsin in 1909 as an arm of its extension service. The University of Kansas established a similar bureau about the same time, and others were created at Illinois (1911), Washington (1912), California (1913), and Minnesota (1913).[56]

Despite this wealth of information that emerged from various government agencies in the early 1900s, businesses began to find that many important statistics were still missing, especially those related to retailing and distribution. In 1905 there were no accurate lists of such things as drugstores, grocery stores, or hardware stores, the type of goods they carried, or the volume of goods they sold each year—lists that would help map patterns of consumption. At the time Parlin undertook his study of textiles and department stores in 1911 and 1912, no consumer-product distribution census had ever been taken. He noted in 1914 that the federal government had compiled "numberless volumes of statistics on manufactures, but it throws almost no light at all upon the statistics of jobbing and retailing." Until the late 1920s, the government focused primarily on production. Detailed information about an emerging consumer society had yet to be gathered. That is where Parlin and his colleagues found their niche.[57]

3

What Was Commercial Research?

I n his reports for Curtis Publishing Company, Charles Coolidge
Parlin seized upon both the emerging agenda and the trusted
ideals of American business to provide himself a foundation of
credibility. The thinking behind his early research reports represented many of the principal concerns of contemporary business and
industry: the potential of national advertising, the importance of the
consumer, the potential of national and regional markets, the value
of expert opinion, the future of the jobber and the retailer, the
potential and also the weaknesses of government data. He also followed a line of thinking that had long been espoused in American
society but that was taking on new importance in an emerging
information age: that knowledge was power. "Knowledge is the
foundation of modern merchandising," Parlin wrote in 1914, "and
as competition grows more intense, it becomes more apparent that
the manufacturer must know in order to succeed."[1]

That belief in the power of information guided Parlin and his
colleagues as they began to form a core philosophy for the Division
of Commercial Research. With little guidance from within the
organization, and with little practical knowledge of the world of

advertising, Parlin drew from his background in education, debate, and social science, and from the statistical research that was emerging in government and business at the time, as he sought to explain the marketplace in systematic ways. In the end, his reports were almost anthropological, describing the culture of department stores or farm implement dealerships, taking into account the thinking of the manufacturer, the distributor, the retailer, and the customer and how they all interacted to create consumer sales. Sales—as well as the actions of industrial concerns in the marketplace—were not random, not caused by chance. They could be codified and explained if the right factors were investigated.

The work that Parlin and his Division of Commercial Research did was hardly as neutral as "explaining," though. Each research project was guided by the biases and aspirations of the company, its employees, clients, and competitors. In most cases, Parlin did not ask new questions as much as he asked questions that people thought they had answers for but had never investigated for themselves: How did individual businesses fit into the broader scope of an industry locally and nationally? How was the chain of distribution between producer and consumer set up, and did it operate efficiently? What areas of cities, states, and the country offered the most potential for sales of new products and increased consumption of existing products? What cultural influences affected the operations of business and the choices that people were offered and made in purchases?

As Parlin and his staff began to establish a routine for their work and began to give shape to the idea of Commercial Research, four core ideas guided their thinking and their approaches: that the market for consumer goods was a national market, not just a regional market; that rural areas and farms offered the greatest potential for sales growth and represented, in many respects, the true national market; that advertising, especially Curtis advertising, was essential for extending the reach of a product; and that information about consumers and the marketplace was essential for creating company strategy and for expanding the base of consumer products. Those guiding forces were not immediately apparent to Parlin, though. They began to take shape as he proceeded with his work, as he interviewed people in business and industry, as he spoke with his colleagues, and as he was forced to answer a crucial question about his work: What was commercial research?

Facing the Skeptics

As he moved from city to city, interview to interview, in 1911 and 1912, Parlin began to clarify the purpose of his work. At the Studebaker Corporation in South Bend, Indiana, he was forced to explain his intentions to several people before he spoke with one of the company superintendents. "What is there in it for us?" the superintendent asked. Parlin replied: "Directly nothing, sir. The Curtis Publishing Company desire this information that they may better use their advertising pages to develop industry."[2] In 1913, when Parlin and Henry Sherwood Youker, his first assistant, compiled an *Encyclopedia of Cities,* they described their work as a search for "accurate, first-hand information on industrial conditions throughout the country."[3] And when a skeptical manufacturer questioned the worth of Parlin's textile study, Parlin explained that the intent was "to find those tendencies which are fundamental and were therefore probably enduring, and separate them from the tendencies which were ephemeral and would be changed in a year or two, perhaps in a day."[4]

The idea of "fundamental tendencies" or "fundamental economic laws"—such things as consumer tastes and the general conditions of the national or regional economy or of a specific industry—became central to Parlin's thinking during his career. Through observation and qualitative analysis, he tried to identify important components of American culture and determine how manufacturers and retailers could turn those cultural ideals into increased consumption of consumer products and, ultimately, into increased profit. These "laws" or "tendencies," Parlin said, differed from "fads" or other short-term economic or social tendencies. For example, in his report on the automobile industry in 1913 and 1914, Parlin said that motor cars had tapped into long-held desires for improved "individual rapid transportation." The desire for automobiles went deeper, though, and was based on utility ("it facilitated business and broadened one's horizons"); a desire for distinction ("a longing for the possession of a rare thing that would separate the owner from the common herd"); a fad ("a craze in which the psychology of the masses impelled individuals to make purchases not warranted by their needs or buying power"); and a shortage of supply (which heightened the desire of the other three aspects).[5]

As automobiles became more common—between 1904 and 1914, production grew from about 20,000 to about 400,000 cars annually—the dynamics of desire for them changed, Parlin said. People found that the automobile shortened distances, made new places available for easy travel, and provided stimulation through outdoor riding. What once was a fad, Parlin said, had become a "permanent desire." He predicted that automobiles would continue to become more common and would be a vital part of American life for many years to come.[6] Relatedly, as the supply of automobiles caught up with demand, the dynamics of buying changed. People no longer rushed to purchase whatever automobile was offered, but instead scrutinized the choices more closely. Men, especially, had learned about automobile mechanics and quizzed dealers about such things as carburetors, radiators, motors, and ignition systems. Owners also found that automobiles could be quite expensive to operate and maintain, and so before they bought a new car, they began to compare models for costs of such things as tires and fuel. They had also seen many manufacturers go out of business. That made getting parts and accessories difficult and therefore made the cars of defunct companies worth less than others. So before buying, many people began looking into the financial soundness of a company and the kind of service it and the dealer would offer, gathering information themselves in much the same way the business world was gathering information about consumers and the marketplace. The "purchaser of today is very different from the purchaser of yesterday," Parlin wrote, "and retailers have been compelled to revolutionize their methods in order to meet the changed demands of their patrons."[7]

Like the textile market (which he had studied the previous year), Parlin said, the automobile market was being shaped by several

additional underlying factors: the larger the city, the higher the
expenses for a merchant; the farther west a company was located in
the United States, the higher its costs, mainly for shipping; and the
higher the grade of merchandise offered, the higher the cost of doing
business. Other changes had begun to take place in automobile
retailing by 1914 as well, Parlin said: Cars had begun to be sold on
credit; merchants needed more start-up capital than they had in the
past, and they needed salesmanship and "mechanical ingenuity" to
see to repairs; heightened competition had forced price cutting,
which reduced retailers' margins of profit; trading in secondhand
cars had created a competing market of sorts for the new car dealer;
and manufacturers had begun to produce annual models, which
reduced the selling season and required that old models be sold off
each year, often at a heavy discount.[8]

These types of tendencies governed all business, Parlin said, not
just the automobile business. They could be understood, but like
the laws of nature, they could not be changed. Businesses that "go
with the economic currents ride to prosperity, while those who try
to stem the tide are doomed sooner or later to failure," Parlin said.[9]
Understanding these "economic currents" required research. "Every
manufacturer," Parlin wrote in article for *Printers' Ink* in 1914,
"should know where his goods are sold, who buys them and why
they are bought, what type of men are selling his goods to consumers, what influences are affecting them, what their sales methods and
sales costs are, to what extent they are real factors in making sales
and to what extent they are only order-takers." He said manufacturers also needed to understand the geographic distribution of a product: regional differences, rural versus urban, even variances within
a city. That was especially important when dealing with a jobber, a
middleman who often knew little about retailers' problems or about
the geographic breakdown of sales. The manufacturer also needed
to study potential markets and how they could be developed, he
said, what new uses could be found for a product, what obstacles
might exist to new sales and how they could be removed, how
retailers could be recruited, and how consumers could best be
reached. (These questions are similar to those that later arose when

the J. Walter Thompson advertising agency began setting up its market research operation.)[10] In other words, Parlin sought information that would break down barriers to consumption.[11]

Scientific Influence

The scores of interviews that Parlin conducted provided the basis of his reports, and he made generous use of the material he gathered in his qualitative analyses of industries and the marketplace, melding the philosophies of social science with the profit-driven motives of industrial capitalism. Parlin's notions of science were really those of applied science. That is, he sought not to understand business, society, or the human condition as a means of intellectual exercise and a higher order of learning, but rather to help businesses improve their profit margins. He did not offer the technical expertise that engineers used in applying new technology to industry, but rather he offered the methods of a social scientist and an economist in helping businesses understand the dynamics of marketplace capitalism and how businesses could position themselves in new markets and against competitors.[12]

At the heart of this philosophy, as Susan Strasser writes, was the idea that markets were malleable and constantly changing as new products entered into the mix. Through research, businesses came to see an opportunity not only for understanding markets, but for creating them. Demand, they thought, could be manufactured just as products could be manufactured. Under the old producer system of supply and demand, the exhaustion of a supply told manufacturers it was time to produce more goods. The new mass market, which used enormous amounts of raw material and required a large labor supply, needed more extensive information if it was to operate smoothly. This mass market sought predictability, and market research gradually came to be seen as an important tool for understanding the market and predicting how it would respond to a product.[13]

Parlin engaged in considerable prediction of the consumer market, but he saw his job not primarily as a means to predict but as a means to interpret. His market studies often amounted to portraits of various industries within the overall marketplace. Because the figures he received from merchants and manufacturers often amounted to estimates or even wild guesses, he developed formulas and theories, based on his observations and on information he trusted, that could be applied to areas that were in doubt. For instance, he estimated the volume of business of department stores by taking into consideration the amount of floor space in the store; how closely the merchandise was packed; the class of merchandise; the number and appearance of the clerks; the number and appearance of the customers (important because people with more money spent more, he said); the location of the store; and the "mercantile possibilities of the city," which, along with the store's location, determined the class of patrons. He combined his estimates with the estimates he obtained in interviews, and he revisited a store if the estimates varied greatly.[14]

A Philosophy of Buying

Parlin also identified the consumer as the key to all merchandising and was one of many in the business world who helped create a vision of the consumer. Businesses had always thought of the consumer in some sense. Production was useless without someone to consume the end product. And yet, in most minds, production was clearly king. In the late eighteenth century, in his classic *Wealth of Nations,* Adam Smith wrote that "in the mercantile system the interest of the consumer is almost constantly sacrificed to that of the producer." The importance of the consumer grew in the century that followed, but so did an ambivalence about that increasing importance. In 1882, the political economist Robert Ellis Thompson argued that "mere consumers" who failed to recognize the importance of production—and to participate in such a system—were self-defeating. Ten years later, economists who studied consumption struggled to be seen on an equal plane as those who studied production, and "economic man"—the term economists often used to explain self-interested consumer behavior—was seen as someone more interested in acquiring wealth than in acquiring goods.[15]

As Charles McGovern writes, though, in the 1890s use of the term *consumers* replaced *the public* and took on a meaning separate from the long-used *customers*. That change took place, he says, because producers of goods became increasingly separated from those who bought and used their goods. Those producers never met face to face with buyers; that was a function of retailers. After 1910, advertisers and marketers like Parlin began to shape the idea of the consumer, melding it with the idea of citizen and infusing it with notions of progress. They saw these new citizen-consumers as wielding great power in the marketplace, yet they also saw them as malleable children who needed to be "educated" with advertising.[16]

Parlin acknowledged both of these issues in his early studies. In his analysis of the farm implement market in 1911, he said that farmers held the real power because they bought the equipment that manufacturers made and that dealers sold. He pursued that idea further in his study of department stores in 1912. Manufacturers, jobbers, and retailers had been fighting among each other for control of and prestige in the textile market. Amid this competition, the voice of consumers, especially that of women,[17] became more powerful than any of those that controlled the merchandise. Both manufacturers and retailers sought to expand their trade and their profits, but they could not do so without catering to the wants of the consumer in a mass market. Researchers might gather data about such things as production, distribution, sales, and profits, but the underlying purpose of any such work was understanding the psychology of the consumer, or as Parlin said, the "philosophy of buying."[18]

For instance, he explained the structure of department stores with a theory of how people—especially women—shopped. Women were crucial to department stores, Parlin said, because women scrutinized major purchases much more than men did and insisted on comparing values—but only in certain types of goods. Parlin divided purchases into three categories: convenience goods, emergency goods, and shopping goods—categories that quickly became touchstones of marketing. Convenience goods were small, insignificant items that people needed in everyday life, things like groceries or apron gingham or stockings. These types of goods were bought at the most convenient locations, as were emergency goods—things like medicines or other necessities that people needed in a hurry. Shopping goods—things like dresses and suits and high-grade underwear—required deliberation before purchase. Women investigated purchases of these goods thoroughly, comparing styles and prices to make sure they got the best value.[19]

This comparison shopping, Parlin said, had in large part shaped the structure of the modern department store. The largest and the smallest cities each had no fewer than three stores in which women could compare values, and in all the cities he investigated, he found a uniformity in per capita spending on these types of merchandise. He said the stores themselves had done much to shape the psychology of buying by stocking a variety of goods that made comparison possible, and by buying advertisements that promoted bargain hunting.[20] "But viewed as a movement, the department stores have succeeded because they have filled an economic need. They furnished shopping facilities, and women's trade quickly followed a natural course toward concentration."[21]

On the production end of consumer products, he divided industries into two broad categories: those that made "utilities" and those that made "style goods." The consumer bought utilities, he said, "solely on the basis of quality or efficiency for the price and without thought of their pleasing his taste or fancy." He gave the example of agricultural implements, which were strictly utilitarian and had no hint of cachet. Style goods, on the other hand, appealed "to individual tastes and fancies. In general they are the lines that involve the element of adornment and display," such things as clothing, jewelry, and household furnishings and decorations. Many items, like clothing and furniture, fell into both categories. The distinction was important, though, Parlin said, because companies that manufactured utilities "tend toward concentration, while those dealing in style items move toward dispersion of the market," essentially seeking out narrower niche markets.[22]

Illumination in Selection

Besides the theories that Parlin used, his selection of research topics illuminates the thinking behind Commercial Research. For the first study of agricultural implements, the selection of a research area was happenstance. The next three studies (of department stores and general textiles, automobiles, and food products and household supplies), which consumed Parlin and an assistant for nearly five years, were clearly not. Department stores, the subject of Parlin's second study, were not big advertisers in Curtis's national magazines. Rather, they spent large sums in local newspapers. The makers of textiles (such as women's and men's clothing and other goods sold in the department stores) were big advertisers, though.

Similarly, Parlin's *Encyclopedia of Cities* (1913), based in part on department store sales, gave Curtis advertisers a sense of how cities and regions compared in terms of wealth and sales of consumer goods, and how exploitable those areas might be for new products. His studies of the automobile industry (1914) and the food and household products industries (1914–1917) were of major importance to the *Saturday Evening Post* and the *Ladies' Home Journal* (See Table 3.1.) The *Post*'s explosive growth in the 1910s and 1920s was fueled in large part by the automobile industry, which accounted for about a third of its advertising revenues,[23] and by advertising from manufacturers of food and household products. The *Journal* likewise carried a large amount of advertising from makers and distributors of food and household products, such companies as Procter & Gamble, Palmolive, Pepsodent, Postum Cereal, and Quaker Oats.[24] Curtis had a clear interest in better understanding the workings—and the potential—of both markets. A continuing boom in the sales of automobiles could have meant (and did mean) an ongoing boom for the *Post*. If the automobile were only a temporary phenomenon, as some people thought, then *Post* ad salesmen would need to look to new areas for advertisers.[25]

That sort of reliance on national industries forced Curtis to take a broad view of the marketplace. For example, the textile study and

Table 3.1   *Post*'s and *Journal*'s Shares of Total Spending* in the
Largest Categories of Magazine Advertising, 1911–1915

Category	Year	Total Spending ($)	*Post* Share (%)	*Journal* Share (%)
Food	1911	3,009,318	18	18
	1912	3,472,007	19	18
	1913	3,274,764	22	18
	1914	3,457,358	21	18
	1915	3,366,210	19	18
Automobiles	1911	1,863,088	54	0.7
	1912	2,213,231	55	0.6
	1913	1,918,491	62	0.5
	1914	2,115,286	68	—
	1915	2,663,643	52	6.0
Soap, cleansers	1911	872,585	13	20
	1912	1,052,194	13	22
	1913	1,169,453	16	22
	1914	1,225,318	18	21
	1915	1,223,540	16	20
Toilet goods	1911	999,593	19	10
	1912	1,245,287	19	15
	1913	1,226,708	19	14
	1914	1,398,742	22	17
	1915	1,300,137	20	16
Miscellaneous household	1911	953,903	15	17
	1912	978,195	17	19
	1913	909,781	20	19
	1914	973,816	21	17
	1915	877,644	22	19

(continued)

the *Encyclopedia of Cities* that Parlin and Youker produced in 1913 (and that two other staff members updated in 1921) were relatively simple in their design, but they acted as a census of retail distribution nearly twenty years before the government conducted a similar, more extensive study. For each city in the United States with a population of more than 5,000, the Curtis studies provided such information as how many people from a region regularly shopped in each city, what nationality or race those people were, whether the city was primarily residential or industrial, what the primary

Table 3.1 *Continued*

Category	Year	Total Spending ($)	Post Share (%)	Journal Share (%)
Women's ready-to-wear clothing	1911	944,812	5	32
	1912	962,603	4	31
	1913	845,301	6	31
	1914	746,194	6	33
	1915	565,288	2	34
Musical instruments	1911	752,827	25	7
	1912	922,024	35	12
	1913	841,680	42	11
	1914	709,550	35	13
	1915	791,469	36	8
Office supplies	1911	710,936	44	6
	1912	817,320	52	3
	1913	706,306	55	4
	1914	743,990	49	4
	1915	548,357	58	2
Tobacco	1911	299,569	64	0
	1912	587,897	67	0
	1913	717,824	58	0
	1914	953,640	43	0
	1915	1,313,369	59	0
Men's ready-to-wear clothing	1911	516,023	73	0
	1912	532,930	77	0
	1913	584,277	82	0
	1914	576,498	85	0
	1915	543,726	82	0

*Among 38 magazines in 1911; 37 in 1912; 36 in 1913–1915; 40 in 1916.

Source: "Leading Advertisers, 1911–1916," Curtis Publishing Company papers, Rare Book and Manuscript Library, University of Pennsylvania, Box 121.

industries were, and what the leading department stores, general stores, or dry-goods stores were. The information was based on Parlin's observations and travels, and on letters that he and Youker had sent to city clerks in the areas they could not visit. Samuel Kinney and Milford Baker used much the same format when they updated the volume eight years later, adding estimates of the wholesale grocery business for the 108 largest U.S. cities, providing comparative data not only on the grocery business but on department stores and wholesale dry goods for 1912 and 1921.[26]

In the original *Encyclopedia of Cities,* Parlin admitted that many of the figures were little more than estimates, but he thought that even such estimates should be "suggestive to a sales organization." That is, they mapped the general amounts of consumption in each city, based on department store sales, and provided one of the first means of comparison for the volume of retail business by city. "The volume of department store business in any city is the result not of chance but of economic conditions," Parlin wrote, "and if these conditions are understood, the amount of department store business may be computed with considerable accuracy."[27]

Other Commercial Research studies through the mid-1920s were often more narrowly focused, but all analyzed industries and issues that the Curtis Advertising Department considered important. Such studies as "Farm Tractors" (1916), "Canned Soup" (1917), "Electrical Industry" (1917), "Oleomargarine" (1919), "Canned Beans" (1919), "Coal-Tar Dyes" (1919), "National Prohibition" (1920), "Automobile Tires" (1920), "Motor Trucks" (1920), "Automobile Markets" (1920), "Retail Hardware Stores" (1920), "Machine Tools" (1920), "Department Store Lines" (1920–1921), "The Gas Industry" (1921), "Radio" (1925), and "Automobiles" (1926) carried matter-of-fact, mundane titles, but their contents contained analyses that interpreted contemporary issues for Curtis employees and reinforced the use of advertising, especially Curtis advertising, as crucial to success.[28]

For instance, "Coal-Tar Dyes" used a combination of interviews and questionnaires to compile information about one of the main concerns in American fashion in the 1910s: color of clothing. Before World War I, Germany had supplied three-quarters of the dyes used in American-made clothing. That supply was cut off during the war. Afterward many companies and consumers refused to use German-made dyes because doing so would be seen as anti-American. The substitute dyes created in the United States were widely considered inferior, though, and clothing manufacturers refused to guarantee the color retention of their products.[29] As in nearly every Curtis study, the dye report insisted that advertising could be used to overcome "unreasonable prejudices, and to create a favorable attitude" toward new products, in this case, American-made dyes. Within these justifications for advertising also lay Curtis's justifications for a consumer society—primarily that advertising and the ensuing consumption it encouraged helped manufacturers (by enabling them to sell more and to retain the best employees), employees (by pushing them to work harder and produce more and better products), and consumers (by urging them to buy more) to achieve higher and higher standards of greatness. That is, advertising and consumption all meant "progress" of the nation. "Advertising will help every factor in your business as it has in that of many great American manufacturers," the dye report said.[30]

Despite claims by company executives that Curtis wanted only the best advertisers, the question put forth in Commercial Research reports was rarely *whether* to promote a product, but rather *how best* to promote that product. Commercial Research promised that through the wise application of market information it could point the way to efficient distribution and, in turn, greater profitability. In doing so, it not only justified the use of advertising but argued for the necessity of continuing market research. That is, information (research) explained the importance of providing more information (advertising), which in turn spurred product sales and created a need for even more research so that businesses could keep up with a dynamic marketplace. Consumerism was changing not only the culture of American society, but the culture of American business.

Purpose in Form

The presentation of the Commercial Research reports, although not crucial to their contents, nonetheless was an added means of enhancing their credibility. Bound in black or red leather and embossed with gold lettering, the volumes contained from a few dozen to a few hundred pages of typescript text. They had a serious, authoritative look, much like an academic thesis or dissertation. The text of the reports was double-spaced on one side, with hand-drawn charts, maps, or graphs, and occasionally photographs inserted on left-hand pages within or at the beginnings of chapters. Various sections of the reports were divided by cover pages, to which were attached embossed leather tabs with descriptions of the sectional contents or letters for an alphabetized index. The early volumes often contained foldout U.S. maps that showed the routes Parlin and his colleagues had taken and the cities they had visited on their research trips. Each report also contained single-spaced transcripts of each interview conducted. The interviews were dated and placed chronologically either at the back of various volumes or in a volume of their own.

Although the general physical characteristics of each report were similar, the size and organization of individual reports varied. Parlin's first report, the study of agricultural implements, was a single volume of 460 typescript pages, of which more than 150 pages were taken up by single-spaced transcripts of interviews. Parlin's analysis required about 100 double-spaced pages and took the form of an extended outline. It had four appendices, including an overview of agricultural implement manufacturers, and a ranking of those manufacturers based on Parlin's assessment of their advertising potential.[31] The textile study, Parlin's second report, consisted of three volumes and 2,805 pages of double-spaced analysis, single-spaced interviews (1,121 of them), indices, appendices, charts, and maps. A fourth volume consisted of more than 200 pages of textile samples.[32] Parlin and Youker's study of automobiles consisted of five volumes,[33] and their study of food products and household supplies consisted of six volumes.[34] Later reports were generally less voluminous—sometimes amounting to only a single thin volume—although through the 1930s, the Commercial Research reports often consisted of at least two volumes and hundreds of typescript pages.[35]

The reports were prepared by an office staff that ranged from about ten to thirty people through the 1910s, with a substantially larger staff in the 1920s and 1930s. One copy of each report went to the advertising director, one to Parlin, and at least one to each of Curtis's advertising offices in New York, Boston, Chicago, San Francisco, and Philadelphia.[36] The sheer bulk of the full reports prevented Curtis from mass producing them, although company executives' initial skepticism of Parlin's work gave them little incentive to distribute the reports widely.

The exhaustive nature of the reports served two purposes, though: First, in many cases no one had ever assembled such information about distribution, selling, and consumption on such a wide scale, and Parlin and his colleagues saw a need to examine nearly every scrap of information they could find. Everything was new and everything was potentially useful. At the same time, their credibility was on the line, and they used their voluminous findings as a shield against criticism. If people had doubts about the validity of the reports, they could read the interviews, check the sources, and see for themselves where the information had come from.

Parlin was also concerned about the confidentiality of his sources.[37] Many manufacturers, retailers, and jobbers spoke candidly with him, and he seemed compelled not to violate their confidence by circulating proprietary information or comments. Also, by keeping the reports in its offices, Curtis could easily control who saw Parlin's research and could prevent competing magazines from copying the material and passing it off as their own.

No log of who looked at the Commercial Research volumes has survived, if one was ever kept. The main points that Parlin made, though, were widely disseminated. Curtis advertising representatives frequently took Parlin's reports with them when they made calls on customers, showing them the work that Commercial Research was doing.[38] The company also encouraged advertising agents, manufacturers, wholesalers, and retailers to stop by one of Curtis's advertising offices to look over the books in detail "under proper conditions," presumably with a Curtis employee present.[39] The company seems to have tried to increase a desire for Parlin's full reports by limiting access to them, especially in view of a widespread promotional campaign that Curtis undertook for Commercial Research in 1913 and 1914.

Condensed versions of the reports—frequently based on speeches that Parlin made—were often printed and widely distributed by Curtis and by the organizations to which Parlin spoke. Others appeared in trade journals, such as *Printers' Ink,* and in various house organs and specialty publications. In the early 1920s, the company kept "a selected list" of 700 advertising agents and a mailing list of

8,000 names of advertisers and potential advertisers to which it sent promotional material.[40] During the 1910s and 1920s, Parlin was sought after as a speaker at meetings and conferences around the country. He spoke to such groups as the National Dairy Council, the National Coffee Roasters Association, the Davenport Bed Makers of America, the Machinery Builders Society, the National Hardware Association, the Associated Advertising Clubs of the World, the Kansas City Tractor Show, and the National Association of Credit Men. Although no record of the exact number of speeches and presentations he gave survives, by his own estimate he spoke at more than one hundred meetings with automobile manufacturers after his report on automobiles was completed in 1914; and he had more than two hundred meetings with equipment manufacturers and advertising agencies after he and an assistant completed their report on the farm market in 1917. He continued on a similar pace into the 1920s.[41]

Reaching a National Market

Although Parlin and his staff espoused the virtues of Curtis advertising, they were careful to temper their observations about the effectiveness of that advertising, emphasizing that manufacturers needed to tie advertising to an overall marketing strategy. They did not tell businesses how effective their advertising would be, but they did offer a plan for putting advertising campaigns into motion. With his textile study, for instance, Parlin took merchants into the aisles of department stores and offered them a glimpse of how their products were perceived and of the problems they would have to overcome if they were to succeed.[42] In doing so, he tried to bring the fuzzy notion of national markets into sharper focus by mapping trade areas, providing statistics and opinions, and showing connections between the local, the regional, and the national. He pointed out regional quirks that helped account for trade variances in each area, and he used maps to plot marketing strategies for national advertisers. The advertising that many businesses used might have been national, but the merchandising of the products was regional, subject to the quirks and attitudes of regional culture. Distribution was often scattered. Costs varied greatly depending upon the point of distribution. And regional or local tastes and prejudices meant that the same product would not always sell the same in every market. If a product was to succeed, the regional variances had to be studied carefully.[43]

It was the national market, though, that Parlin held out as a sort of holy grail for manufacturers. He tried to paint with a broad brush and make his studies relevant to entire industries, and sometimes to several industries. His marketplace evaluations provided a standard that businesses could use to compare themselves and their competition nationally. They helped Curtis clients see beyond their own products and regions and to think about the national marketplace as a whole, helping to open the path to the vibrant mass market of the 1920s and beyond.[44] "Do not make the mistake of seeking localized markets—aim for the vast national markets which will benefit every one of your thousands of producers," Parlin told the National Coffee Roasters Association in 1915.[45]

In the end, Parlin's reports were textbooks for advertising sales men, primers on the workings of business, industry, and distribution. They were a map of the marketplace, in the form not only of trends and sales figures, but in a listing of businesses and their key executives, what he called a "Who's Who among Manufacturers." As Parlin put it: "In general, retail and jobbing figures are merely the measure of human wants and economic possibilities, and when once the fundamental principles have been ascertained and the extent to which sectional, racial, industrial, and climatic conditions modify these fundamental tendencies is understood, one may estimate with a fair degree of accuracy the probable market for a given section."[46] Within the pages of Parlin's reports were the ground rules and the guideposts for the emerging consumer culture. The immediate challenge, Parlin discovered quickly, was finding converts to this new brand of business.

4

Winning over the Skeptics

The potential of Parlin's first report, not to mention the Division of Commercial Research as a whole, was difficult for many in the Curtis organization to see in the beginning. Parlin's early research was taken lightly by many company executives and staff members who were no doubt uneasy about basing their livelihood on someone else's untested observations.[1] In its book *Selling Forces* in 1912, the company emphasized that advertising agencies were expected to investigate the marketplace to better serve customers—something Curtis had been doing since mid-1911. During the Division of Commercial Research's first two years, however, the company made no printed announcements of its existence,[2] even though Curtis advertised nearly every week in the trade journal *Printers' Ink,* ads in which it instead emphasized the size and growth of its magazine circulation, the influence of the *Journal* and the *Post,* and the affluence of their readers.[3]

By late 1913, after Parlin had completed in-depth studies of the agricultural implements and textile industries and had compiled a city-by-city census of consumer product distribution based on department store sales, the skepticism of Curtis employees gradually began to wane. Edward W. Hazen, Curtis's advertising director, was still concerned that many members of the advertising staff had not grasped the importance of the work, though. Curtis Publishing was spending a considerable amount of money on research, Hazen told staff members, because the future of the company could hinge on it. Hazen called Parlin's work "so broad, and so fundamental," and he allotted several hours of a three-day advertising conference in January 1913 to a discussion of Commercial Research and the value of information "to drive home into the mind of every one of you that here is something that we have got to take seriously." Parlin's work "will broaden your horizon," Hazen told staff members. "You cannot do very much in the advertising business or in any other business without brains, trained brains, and a good stock of information." Parlin's work "will give you a conception of the fact that there are a lot of things to be known, things pertinent to your work, pertinent to the success of the advertisers with whom you come in contact. The purpose of this work is to give you vision, enable you to see, so that you can help others to see."[4]

The increased emphasis that Curtis executives began to place on Commercial Research seemed to be spurred in part by the interest that Parlin's work began to generate when it was shown to manufacturers. As he was completing a four-volume, 2,805-page work on department stores and textiles, Parlin went on the road, speaking to organization after organization about his findings. He did not always turn skeptics into followers, but he usually piqued interest in his work and helped to weaken barriers that many manufacturers had used to shield themselves from advertising or from Curtis Publishing. In late 1912, he spoke to the board of directors of the Hamilton-Brown Shoe Company about the textile report, and as Floyd T. Short, a Curtis advertising representative who accompanied Parlin, said: "They listened to it with respect; they got something that they did not have before, and yet it had nothing to do with shoes."[5]

In Minneapolis, Short took Parlin's report to Northwest Knitting Company, whose proprietor was notorious in his distrust of anyone peddling advertising. When Short showed up for an appointment, the proprietor kept him at the office for more than four hours, insisting on more time to read Parlin's textile report. Parlin had a similar experience when he interviewed John Willys of Toledo, one of the leading names in automobile manufacturing. Willys had reluctantly granted Parlin a short interview but ended up speaking with him for nearly three hours, saying that Parlin knew more about automobiles and their marketing than anyone he had ever known. Cyrus Curtis likewise noted that when Parlin spoke to a group of skeptical textile manufacturers in 1913, they "were much astonished and said so." The stir that Parlin's work had caused, Short told his colleagues, "merely shows you how a good man, a live man, takes to it, and how valuable we can all make it to ourselves, and to the company if we will study it, learn it, and talk it." William Boyd, manager of Curtis's advertising office in Chicago and later the company's advertising director, was so impressed with Parlin that he asked him to speak to as many people as he could gather from the city's advertising agencies. At two luncheon meetings, Boyd said, Parlin "held the attention of those men as I have very rarely seen a group of men listen. There was hardly the quiver of an eye-lash and not a man left the room; and when he stopped there was a tenseness in the atmosphere that you feel when a man has made an extraordinarily brilliant impression."[6]

Parlin's remarks at the meetings were not recorded, but throughout his career, he based his speeches on the conclusions he drew in his research reports, providing advice about such things as merchandising, selling conditions, advertising, and distribution. He quoted liberally from the reports, and he used them to ground his arguments in the facts he had gathered and in the categorizations and generalizations he had made. His sweeping study of department stores in 1912, for instance, not only provided an overview of store-by-store sales and operations in the 165 cities he had visited, but offered theories and advice on how these stores interacted and competed, how customers responded, and how textile manufacturers needed to understand these responses and interactions when they introduced new styles and new merchandise, especially nationally advertised lines.[7]

In his report the next year on automobiles, Parlin used a nearly identical approach, but he also emphasized that the influences that guided people's purchasing decisions of most products, including textiles and automobiles, were national. If auto dealers in a hundred cities across the country were to compile a list of their six or eight best-selling cars, Parlin said, the lists would be nearly identical. The reason, he said, was that supply had caught demand. No longer could a producer make any type of car and expect it to sell. The problem had shifted from one of producing to one of selling, and the most powerful influences in selling were national: the merit of the product, the strength of the national advertising, and the efficiency of a national sales organization.[8]

Parlin said that the way to achieve successful national sales was to pull the market, not push it. The pushers, such as plow makers, had produced their products first, and then tried to force them upon consumers. They had to adapt their products to local tastes, and the many variations had increased production costs. The pullers created a public desire for their products first through national advertising, and then let consumers come to them. By creating a national demand for a product, Parlin said, the producers could standardize the merchandise and sell the same product in all regions, rather than try to adapt a multitude of products to the many and varied regional cultures. In the end, he said, that would mean larger profits for aggressive businesses.[9] And in the end, that confident promise of steady profits through understanding of national and regional markets, merchandising, and consumer thinking was what allowed Parlin to create a stir among the people he spoke with. By the turn of the twentieth century, the business world was caught up in consolidation of many industries (including the auto industry) and in expansion of products nationally. Its trend was toward basing business decisions on solid planning and toward guiding day-to-day operations with well-substantiated facts. Parlin drew from that interest and showed how knowledge of the marketplace could be used in the drive for profit. He advocated a new means of doing business based on study and interpretation rather than on faith and gut instinct. As he did, he quickly earned a reputation as "the man with the facts," a reputation that was, in large part, fashioned by his superiors.

High Expectations, and Caution

Despite the increased faith that Curtis staff members showed in him and his work, and the increased notoriety he began to receive, Parlin tried to keep his work in perspective. He did not try to diminish what he had done, but he did try to make the advertising staff realize that the market information he had accumulated was still very narrow in scope and prone to revision and correction. With a plea heavy on metaphors, he tried to temper some of the enthusiasm that was building among his colleagues in 1913:

> We do not want to go out with the idea that we made an investigation into this big field or that big field and that we learned all about it. The sea of human knowledge is limitless, and is a high and moving sea. You can dip out but a single cupful, and yet it is full. So we have only a small portion of human knowledge, and let us be conservative in what we say about it.[10]

Parlin's plea for caution went unheeded, for the most part. Company executives seemed to sense the potential that Parlin's work held for improving company credibility and for attracting the attention of advertisers. Increasingly, they drew from and promoted his work, and they also put him in a position of authority. During the spring of 1913, for instance, Parlin instructed nine new members of the advertising staff in how to conduct small trade investigations in the New York City area, as part of a six-week training program known as the Curtis School.[11] The classes were aimed at broadening their understanding of advertising and, in a sense, indoctrinating them in the Curtis culture. The representatives were tutored by the more experienced members of the advertising staff, as well as by manufacturers and members of the trade press. Each afternoon, they either worked with Parlin or on their own, researching and writing reports on such topics as cement, roofing, and paints and varnishes. "These men were thus taught the importance of a knowledge not only of general advertising conditions, but also of specific conditions in the trade and markets of each advertiser," the company wrote. Just as important, Parlin was placed in a role of authority, legitimizing him and his work not only for the new staff members but for experienced representatives, as well.

By late 1913, Commercial Research emerged as a crucial component of Curtis's business strategy, and the company began to place Parlin's work at the center of a campaign for service, quality, and responsibility in advertising. It used Commercial Research to try to push advertising agencies toward greater service for clients and to promote Curtis publications as *the* source for advertising. Curtis's advertising staff began to promote the value of knowledge about markets and consumers, holding up Commercial Research as an important source for hard-to-get information about merchandising.[12] The company also promoted Parlin and his division within the pages of *Printers' Ink* and other trade publications, as well as in the *Saturday Evening Post* and in Curtis's *Public Ledger* newspaper in Philadelphia. It later reprinted some of those advertisements in book form, and it made its case over and over in its house organ, *Obiter Dicta*.[13]

Instructing Advertisers

In that house organ in September 1913, the company called Commercial Research its chief means of rendering service to advertisers. In the book *Selling Forces,* which Curtis issued that year, the company also said that "no publication should inaugurate the advertising of a manufacturer without first investigating." No longer could advertising representatives accept only the manufacturer's word about trade conditions and business conditions. Members of the advertising staff had to find out for themselves, the company said. "The Curtis Publishing Company today investigates the problems of its advertising clients long before it knows who its particular clients are to be." More specifically, it said the duty of the Division of Commercial Research was "to search out the exact facts about various industries and trades, manufacturing and selling conditions, trade tendencies and future possibilities." Commercial Research informed advertising representatives about national markets and how those markets could be entered; equipped representatives with the information they needed to advise manufacturers about broader approaches to advertising and merchandising; and allowed them on occasion to provide specialized service to clients, *Selling Forces* said. The book emphasized that the division was staffed not by advertising men but by "experts in research." Its work was described as original but not partisan, and the information it compiled was available only because of Curtis Publishing Company's unique position in the business world. The book said it was doubtful that the research reports "could be duplicated by any other private business institution in the United States. Manufacturers would be unable to obtain the large amount of information" needed to gain the confidence of retailers. "Retailers would be similarly handicapped in dealing with manufacturers. The prestige of The Curtis Publishing Company, and its reputation for impartiality, make it possible to gain entree to the hundreds of sources which are being drawn upon."[14]

To a large extent that was true. Curtis's size, wealth, and prestige allowed it to undertake projects that few other organizations were willing to try. National research was expensive, and Curtis was willing to spend the money to pursue an untested proposition: that exclusive information about markets would enhance its standing in the business world and ultimately lead to greater profits for itself and its clients. In its advertisements promoting the role of Commercial Research, though, Curtis used many of the same tactics that it advised manufacturers to use with consumer products: It emphasized trust and exclusivity; it questioned the adequacy of companies that failed to embrace its advice and products; it sowed doubts about manufacturers' ability to move into the future alone; and it set itself up as a catalyst for transformation in a time of great change.

In a series of *Printers' Ink* advertisements that began in October 1913, Curtis seized on cultural uncertainties about change, raising questions about managers' ability to trust their own instincts as they moved companies into a national market. It coupled that uncertainty with a Progressive belief in expert opinion and science, promoting the idea that science and knowledge would allow businesses to succeed. For instance, Curtis linked information to increased wealth by describing how Curtis's researcher could sort through statistics and understand the *reality* of the marketplace. In one ad, it pursued this idea by giving the example of how census statistics could mislead the uninitiated. According to the census, Curtis said, the dollar amount of carpeting sales was three times greater than that of rug sales. Among consumers, though, rugs outsold carpeting 10 to 1. The reason, Curtis said, was that carpeting was used in public buildings, apartment houses, steamships, and trains, all in high-dollar contract work. Consumers, who made their purchases in retail stores, preferred rugs—a fact, the company said, that a novice would most likely overlook. "Reliance upon untranslated statistics to point out the way is apt to result in misdirection," Curtis wrote. "There are conditions—and perhaps a compromising past— behind the statistical statement which you are disposed to accept without modification. . . . Advertising campaigns based on a careful study of the sources of statistics, rather than upon bare statistics themselves, have the advantage of insuring the plans as founded on real conditions."[15]

In that and other advertisements, Curtis promoted itself as the company with the answers, although it did not promise grand success as much as it promised the knowledge necessary to avoid disaster. It portrayed manufacturers as eager to plunge into the marketplace, but uneasy about strategy. "There are many manufacturers who have little information of this type regarding their own markets," a Curtis advertisement said in November 1913. "There are many who are not ready for big advertising but who must first go through a period of commercial introspection, that they may know where and to whom they should advertise. It is to this class that the agent and publisher may bring aid in research."[16] That is, all industries had hidden pieces of information that if not exposed could mean the difference between success and failure. Companies new to the national marketplace and to national advertising should ally themselves with Curtis if they wanted to succeed, the company argued. Curtis played off companies' financial fears and portrayed itself as a kindly, knowledgeable, paternal figure that would take a new company under its wing and graciously teach it to maneuver through the maze of modern business. "If . . . the advertiser is not wise to this degree," the company wrote in another ad in November 1913, "if he has not all the reins collected before the start, he may pay a heavy penalty and learn by dear experience. For the loose rein might perhaps have been the guiding one."[17]

More Familiar Links

Other advertisements tied Commercial Research to science (the "Alpha and Omega of successful selling," and "The Weight of Evidence"), but appealed to widespread belief in pragmatism by stressing that the marketplace information that Curtis gathered was practical, not theoretical.[18] "This analysis of field conditions is as thorough as painstaking and intelligent effort can produce. Theorizing was eliminated," the company said in an ad in January 1914. Curtis researchers "communicated direct with the men who own and operate automobiles, who buy and use tires and lubricants, and great care was observed to avoid error in the assembling of computations, tabulations and totals."[19]

Curtis also put Commercial Research on the same plane as technology (which was generally seen in positive terms), linking it to the automobile (an advertiser who proceeded without research was running on one cylinder) and to electricity (a business that proceeded without research could not complete a circuit). "Lighting the way" was a favorite metaphor, with Curtis ensuring advertisers that it could provide "illuminating facts" that would light up the path of successful merchandising.[20] Those early advertisements for Commercial Research often took the form of parables, and they sent the message that the ignorant and the unknowing manufacturer would not last long in a market of predators. The first few ads did not refer to Parlin by name, but rather made the case that Curtis

Publishing Company, and only Curtis Publishing Company, could obtain the information that advertisers, and even nonadvertisers, needed to know if they were to spend their money wisely in the marketplace. Beginning in early 1914, though, the ads began to take a more straightforward approach, indicating that Parlin and his Division of Commercial Research were becoming recognized, as in this ad from March 1914:

> Mr. Charles Coolidge Parlin, manager of our Division of Commercial Research, has completed the first volume of a report on Food-stuffs. This volume has special reference to Pacific Coast industries. The contents of the volume and the conditions under which it is available for use by advertisers and agents are described in the forthcoming issue of *Obiter Dicta*.[21]

Curtis also began to print snippets of Parlin's analyses of the textile and department store markets in its advertisements. After his report on automobiles was completed, the company placed an ad in *Printers' Ink* listing some of the questions and topics the 3,000-page report addressed:

- What is the future of the automobile industry?
- Why have some manufacturers failed?
- What types of cars are going to persist?
- Is monopoly possible?
- Will there be a $750 class?[22]

By piquing readers' curiosity about some of the key issues of the automotive world, the company hoped to draw industry officials to Curtis's advertising offices to learn more.[23]

Setting the Agenda

The extent to which Curtis actually prodded advertising agencies and competitors into providing market research—as it claimed in the early 1910s and later—is difficult to determine. Parlin was among a group of scholars, advertising executives, and business executives who began promoting the idea of marketplace studies before World War I. Although for several years he led the only such department among American businesses, several university professors began speaking and writing about the importance of market research.[24] Clearly, though, the evidence suggests that Parlin had considerable influence in shaping the early field of market research. The company he worked for, Curtis Publishing, was an aggressive advertiser and publisher of two of the widest-circulating magazines in the United States. As such, it was in a position to help set the agenda for advertising agencies and other publishers. Those other businesses may not have reacted immediately to what Curtis was doing, but they certainly could not ignore it.[25]

When Fred E. Clark, a marketing professor at Northwestern University's School of Commerce, compiled a bibliography of the "most helpful" books and articles in the study of marketing in the early 1920s, his list of 108 works included four by Parlin, along with the Curtis book *Selling Forces,* to which Parlin most likely contributed.[26] Only one other author, L.D.H. Weld, had more works than Parlin on Clark's list.[27] Weld, a former Yale University professor who went to work at Swift & Company in 1917, said that he had been inspired by Parlin's work and persuaded Swift to let him start a market research department.[28] Paul W. Nystrom, who turned down a job at Curtis Publishing in the 1910s, also credited Parlin with inspiring him to set up a research department at U.S. Rubber in 1916.[29]

In 1916, the J. Walter Thompson Company, one of the most prominent advertising agencies of the time, considered material it received from Curtis an important source of information about trade and industry.[30] It thought highly enough of Parlin's research on automobiles and foodstuffs to recommend that his work be distributed among all company employees. Stanley Resor, then a Thompson vice president, wrote that the company's Cincinnati office thought that Parlin's food report "contains not only a good deal of valuable information, but has a direct bearing on the advertising of food products. . . . Any one with a food product problem who does not consult this report is, in Cincinnati's opinion, passing by a very valuable tool." A few years later, in compiling a list of books for new staff members, Thompson made Parlin's collected research studies part of the required readings.[31]

Parlin's ideas flowed to some of the other pioneers in market research, as well. He regularly traded information with Ralph Starr Butler and Paul Nystrom, two early marketing scholars at Wisconsin, as well as Paul T. Cherington at Harvard. (Cherington later worked for J. Walter Thompson and became one of the prominent figures of early market research.) He also lectured at the Harvard Business School in 1913 and 1914 and at other universities, telling about his work, his methods, and his ideas about the workings of the marketplace. When Joseph H. Willits, a professor and later dean of the Wharton School of Finance and Commerce at the University of Pennsylvania, created a class in merchandising in the 1910s, he pored over Parlin's reports and translated them into class material.[32] In 1919, one of the early scholars of marketing, C. S. Duncan, called Parlin a "shrewd and careful investigator" and said that Curtis had done more work in market research than any other publisher. Several companies, including Swift, tried to hire Parlin to create market research departments for them. He turned them all down, although those companies eventually hired some of his assistants.[33]

Into at least the early 1920s, the analysis of retail goods and shopping philosophy that Parlin had made in his department store study in 1912 was regarded by businessmen and scholars as the basis for understanding consumer buying habits.[34] Marketing scholars later ranked it as among the most influential early works in the field, and terms from that study, like "shopping goods" and "convenience goods," are still part of the lexicon today.[35] Parlin's speeches were also widely reprinted by organizations to which he spoke. In 1923, in the foreword to a pamphlet based on a Parlin speech, the American Face Brick Association summed up an enthusiasm that many others expressed about Parlin's work, telling members: "There's food for thought in Mr. Parlin's remarks. Read them MORE than once."[36]

By the late 1920s and early 1930s, Parlin was so widely known that he and his work were parodied by the humorist Robert Benchley at a national meeting of the Association of National Advertisers, and the essay was later published in one of Benchley's books. In the parody, "The Woolen Mitten Situation," Benchley followed Parlin's staccato style of emphasizing major points and important questions, and even constructed a chart that looked as if it had come from a real Commercial Research report. He told those gathered at the conference: "Most of you have been shown some of Mr. Parlin's reports—in strict confidence—giving you the inside dope on the distribution of your own product and proving that, by using exclusively the Curtis publications—their names escape me at the moment—you will not only reach all the public that you want to reach but will have enough people left over to give an amateur performance of 'Pinafore.'"[37]

Benchley's humor underscored the position of Curtis in the world of publishing. As one of the largest and most influential companies regularly and systematically gathering market information in the 1910s, Curtis Publishing helped set the standard for the type of research that would later be done and for the approaches used in acquiring that information. In 1936, Parlin said that during his first five years at Curtis, the company had no competition in gathering national market data, "and during the next five years, I think most if not all of the operations which were started were a direct result of the Curtis operation."[38] Those remarks were certainly exaggerated, although they held some truth. During his twenty-six years at Curtis Publishing, Parlin was credited with developing or refining such market research techniques as a buying-power index, city maps that show purchasing power by neighborhood, and the study of consumer attitudes and buying habits through door-to-door surveys. He also helped develop an innovative means of applying readership statistics to sales quotas—statistics that not only assisted advertisers but that reinforced advertisers' belief in Curtis publications as the most important media for promoting consumer products.[39]

To say, though, that Curtis Publishing had a definite aim in establishing its Division of Commercial Research would give Parlin and the managers in the company too much credit for definitive planning. When the division was started, they had no definite goal, no idea of what the mission should be. Two years after Commercial Research was formed, the company feigned foresight, writing that it "investigates the problems of its advertising clients long before it knows who its particular clients are to be."[40] Such a definition of mission was as fuzzy as the early ideas behind the division. As hazy as those ideas were, though, they were not shapeless. Nor were they as completely innovative as they were later portrayed by Parlin's peers. The origins of Commercial Research lay in a broad movement that sought to make advertising a much more predictable factor in modern publishing—in essence, to turn advertising and market research into science. In 1950, the marketing scholar Lawrence Lockley wrote that Parlin's work "dramatized this fledgling science" of market research and "afforded the precedent many other firms were to follow. . . . These were studies of marketing structures of the industries—broad in sweep, yet affording guidance where none had previously been available."[41]

Parlin's influence aside, the most important legacy of Commercial Research may have been Curtis's promotion of it. The company made the types of arguments that businesses still use today: that a company is foolish if it does not know as much as possible about the marketplace it is getting into; that it must know its competitors, its potential buyers, and its network of distribution; that it must understand the past and the present if it hopes to succeed in the future. Commercial Research also showed companies with layers of managers how they could grasp the intricacies of an ever-growing marketplace and function more efficiently as a result. Information was more reliable and more profitable than intuition, Curtis argued. As companies increasingly bought into that idea, they began forming their own research departments, turning a lone company's experiment into a new profession and into a cultural phenomenon that still guides companies large and small in their quest for a piece of the consumer marketplace.

Making It—Finally

Parlin called the emergence of market research "an age of adventure." If Curtis Publishing had not started Commercial Research when it did, "sooner or later somebody else would have done so," he said in 1936. Even so, he said, he was not sure that Commercial Research was part of the company's long-term plans until early 1915, when Boyd placed a two-page advertisement for the division in the *Saturday Evening Post*. That ad was a follow-up to a two-week trip Parlin had made to Detroit, speaking to automakers about his recently completed report on the automobile industry. That ad built on previous promotions that Curtis had done, stressing the importance of knowledge of the marketplace. To succeed, manufacturers needed to understand consumers and their habits; they needed to know about their competitors and about what products and approaches had been tried in the past; they needed to know where their products stood in the marketplace. The problem was, the ad said, few businesses had access to such information. Curtis was making it available, though, by studying the nation's most important industries and applying "commonsense methods of analysis" to the information it gathered. The primary purpose of the research, the ad said, "is that advertising campaigns may be built on facts—not impressions, not haphazard guesses, not on prejudice, not on favoritism, but on facts."[42]

Parlin later said that when the ad appeared, he knew his position with the company was secure. Boyd's proclamation in the *Post* "put Commercial Research over." Later that year, the Division of Commercial Research was moved from Boston to the new Curtis Publishing Company building across from Independence Hall in Philadelphia. Once pushed to the margins, Commercial Research soon moved to the core of Curtis Publishing and its approach to advertising.[43] As it did, Parlin and his colleagues methodically began constructing a vision of the American consumer.

5

Barbarians, Farmers,
and Consumers

urtis Publishing Company began mailing out dozens of
questionnaires to readers of its publications in the 1910s.
Most were one- or two-page surveys about reading and
buying habits, along with form letters asking people to complete and
send back the enclosures. The replies that trickled in were often
personal and thoughtful, with notes attached or scrawled in the
margins of the surveys. "Four years ago last October my wife and
myself gave up city life for the country," a New York farmer wrote
in response to a survey for Curtis's farm magazine, *Country Gentleman,* in 1916. "We had an old horse, fifty chickens and $200. Today
we are on easy street—health fine—a good small farm. We would
not go back to New York City if they would make me mayor."[1]

Even among such personal disclosures, a long letter from
Nebraska that arrived at Curtis's Boston office in September 1917
stood out. The letter, attached to a questionnaire that the office had

This chapter was published in an earlier form as "From Barbarian Farmers to Yeoman
Consumers: Curtis Publishing Company and the Search for Rural America, 1910–
1930," *American Journalism* 22 (Fall 2005): 47–67.

mailed that summer, was written by a woman who farmed near Seward, in southeastern Nebraska. "I am pleased to realize that you, living in an age of electricity, are inclined to sympathize with us outer barbarians, of whom you confess you are ignorant, and conceive of us as still living in the age of coal oil stoves, etc.," the woman wrote. But many Nebraskans, like Easterners, she explained, used electricity to light their homes, cook their meals, wash and iron their clothes, grind their grain, pump their water, and even milk their cows. "Some of us also read on occasion," the woman said, writing that she and her husband subscribed to about a dozen periodicals and two daily newspapers. She said that she and other farmers also owned automobiles and not only traveled, but knew quite a bit more about the United States than the Curtis staff apparently did. "I regret that you people do not travel more in the hinterland of America," she wrote. "You would find it interesting. It is, as my husband says, a h--- of a fine country."[2]

The staff members in Boston forwarded the letter to Charles Coolidge Parlin at the Division of Commercial Research in Philadelphia. He saved it with his expanding files about rural America and referred to it frequently when he spoke about advertising. The letter represented, Parlin thought, one of Curtis Publishing's biggest problems. Parlin had lived in small towns in Wisconsin for years, so he had an understanding of and an affinity for such towns. And yet he and other Curtis employees, all of whom lived in or near such cities as Philadelphia, Boston, New York, Chicago, and San Francisco, were largely ignorant of rural America. They often considered people who lived on farms and in small towns to be hicks and hayseeds who had been left behind as technological progress propelled urban America to greater comfort and superior quality of life.

The problem was, Parlin began to realize, there were more than 50 million of these "barbarians," nearly half the country's population, an enormous untapped market that Curtis Publishing, which was based in Philadelphia, knew little about. After he began researching rural America, Parlin, like many others in the world of advertising, saw an opportunity on the farm. Curtis had recently acquired

Country Gentleman, and the company was eager to make it as finan-
cially successful as its two other national magazines, the *Post* and the
Journal. Parlin was clearly aligned with other marketers who thought
that national advertisers needed to pursue a truly national market,
one that had to include rural America, and his recognition of the
agricultural market's potential steered the Division of Commercial
Research toward rural America again and again in the 1910s and the
1920s, even as the United States was becoming increasingly urban.
He and others at Curtis took the nineteenth-century symbol of the
yeoman farmer and recast it in terms of consumption. In doing so,
they created an idealistic image of a new class of consumers, an image
that urban advertisers easily understood and willingly bought.

The Making of Rural Consumers

In many ways, American advertising's intense interest in rural America during the early twentieth century seems counterintuitive. The
farm population was still growing, but cities were growing much
faster, accounting for an ever-larger proportion of the U.S. population. Until the 1910s, more than half of Americans lived in rural
areas, which by definition of the census office included not only
farms but towns and villages of under 2,500. Urban population surpassed rural population for the first time with the 1920 census, and
rural America never regained the prominence it once had.[3]

Even so, America was a nation of competing ideals in the early
twentieth century, as Roderick Nash argues. On the one hand,
industrialization was often seen as a means of casting off the drudgery
of farm work and cities as a form of efficiency and progress. On the
other hand, Americans often clung to agrarian ideals and a longing
for a simpler life as they perceived an unwholesomeness, even a
wickedness, in the industrialized city.[4] As Gilman M. Ostrander
argues, Americans continued to idealize American agrarianism at the
turn of the twentieth century, and clung to Thomas Jefferson's
image of the yeoman farmer "who gained his moral bearings from
nature and who produced food for the people." Even so, he says,

industrialization was pushing aside the importance of the farm, and "the countryside had largely ceased to be associated with the idea of expanding opportunity."[5]

Those competing ideals took shape in the Country Life Movement, which encompassed a patchwork of rural issues between about 1900 and 1920. The movement, one of many during the Progressive Era, involved such things as improving rural health, roads, education, and farming practices. Some scholars see it as little more than manipulative social engineering, or pandering among people who feared the loss of the yeoman farmer and an idealized rural life; others see it as a generally successful attempt to improve rural life. At the heart of the movement, though, David Danbom writes, was a desire to improve the efficiency of farming so that American agriculture could meet the needs of a growing urban society. Reformers saw themselves as ensuring the economic and social survival of the nation by making sure that affordable food was readily available, a view that rural Americans often bristled at and considered condescending.[6]

Marketers like Parlin and his staff seemed to see only promise in rural America, though. And in many ways, their perceptions were accurate. The Homestead Act of 1862 transferred enormous amounts of government-owned land to public use, and land grants to the railroads after the Civil War added millions more acres to the public domain. Between 1870 and 1900, the amount of improved land held by American farmers increased by 225 million acres, six times more than in the previous 250 years. More important, gross farm income doubled during the first two decades of the twentieth century as increased demand, especially during World War I, pushed up the prices of crops and livestock (one of the very things Country Life reformers worried about).[7] The use of threshers, grain drills, binders, and other types of equipment made farmers more efficient, and the growth of markets in the United States and abroad spurred them to specialize and to produce more foodstuffs. "Now the object of farming is not primarily to make a living, but it is to make money," the *Cornell Countryman* wrote in 1904. "To this end it is to be conducted on the same business basis as any other producing industry."[8]

Many farmers did indeed make good money, even as others eked out only a meager existence, and marketers found plenty of opportunities in the countryside. Thomas Schlereth argues that rural Americans were as fascinated as urban Americans by the vast array of consumer goods that became available in the late nineteenth and early twentieth centuries, and often found their way into this world of consumption through mail order catalogs, country stores, and county fairs. Danbom writes that the catalogs of Montgomery Ward and Sears, Roebuck and Company helped define ideals of taste and "involved a degree of rural deference to urban standards." Daniel Boorstin places these catalogs among a wide array of "consumption communities," in which the things people bought became a means of commonality, even democracy. Richard Tedlow goes as far as saying that these catalogs were the most effective means of selling in rural America until television came of age in the 1950s. David Blanke, though, sees farmers' embrace of catalog merchandise as a shift in rural culture. He argues that in the nineteenth century, Midwestern farmers embraced consumerism as a collective act infused with "notions of virtue and responsibility." By the 1920s, he says, these communal values began to erode as farmers bought goods as a means of self-expression and individuality.[9]

Even so, the rural areas of the United States were harder to reach than urban areas, and until around 1910, they usually did not receive manufacturers' first considerations. As the Country Life Movement cast a spotlight on rural America, manufacturers worked hard to expand from regional markets to a national one. In 1911, the advertising trade journal *Printers' Ink* called rural America "The Country's Biggest Neglected Market." One farm publication went as far as boasting that the farms of Illinois represented the "World's Greatest Concentration of Buying Power." *Printers' Ink* challenged businesses to look beyond large cities, where they could scatter their products indiscriminately and succeed by "brute force of personal salesmanship," and to work harder at becoming true national distributors. If they did not, the journal said in an editorial, they "will look small in the years shortly to come, compared with the national advertiser who scientifically studies the whole national market."[10]

Pursuing the Farm Market

Parlin seemed to follow that advice as he went about researching rural America, on his own at first and later with a small staff. Much of his early research contained boosterish sales pitches for rural America, not only to advertisers but to Curtis staff members. Parlin piled up statistics about farms and small towns, showing that they were ripe for marketers. His first attempt at market research, in 1911, was a report on farm implements. He and his staff followed that with studies of *Country Gentleman* readership (1915 and 1916), "Farm Tractors" (1916), "The Farm Market" (1917), "The Merchandising of Tractors" (1917), "Stock Feed and Commercial Fertilizer" (1917), "An Agricultural Trading Center" (1920), "Sabetha: Two Years Later" (1922), "Rural Markets" (1924), and follow-up surveys of *Country Gentleman* readers in 1920, 1924, and 1925.[11] "The lifting of the farm market to a new plane of earning and to a better appreciation of good merchandise seems to us the most encouraging factor not only for 1920 but for years to come," Parlin boasted at the time, calling the farm market "the greatest of all domestic markets."[12]

His interest in that market was clear in most of the research he conducted. In a study of department stores in 1912, for instance, Parlin estimated that towns of 2,500 or fewer people accounted for 21.5 percent of the dry goods business nationwide. He said that his figures understated the financial power of rural areas, though, because people tended to do half of their trading in urban areas, something made possible by the automobile.[13] In an exhaustive study two years later, Parlin said that the automobile was rapidly becoming a necessity for farmers, for business and social reasons. It allowed them to visit neighbors more easily, and to go more frequently to nearby towns and cities for repair of machinery, for groceries, and for entertainment. The work horses could be left to rest and, Parlin wrote, "in an hour, an errand in the city has been attended to, and man and beast return refreshed to work." He estimated that about 500,000 farmers owned automobiles in 1914 and that about 2,500,000 farmers were good prospects for cars.[14]

The automobile, though, was only one of many influences on rural life. The telephone likewise increased communication and interaction between farmers and city dwellers. Rural Free Delivery increased farmers' access to and reading of magazines and newspapers. Consolidated schools improved education for rural students, and better trained teachers showed how to make life easier through such courses as "domestic science" and "manual training." Land-grant colleges and county agents educated farmers about new methods of production, harvesting, and marketing.[15] If farmers were broadening their perspective on life, then so, too, were rural communities. As roads improved, downtown shopping districts drew people from a wider area. Stores did more business and were able to stock a broader range of products, much as their counterparts in metropolitan areas did. Many small stores expanded, as did many small towns where they were located. Land values increased, adding even further to rural prosperity in many parts of the United States. "The farming sections present the largest virgin market for automobiles," Parlin wrote in 1914, "for the farmers have both the need and ability to buy."[16]

Reaching the Leaders

In his analysis of the farm market, though, Parlin said that the way farmers approached purchases was different from that of their city cousins, and he sought to explain the spread of consumer products with a sort of copycat, or trickle-down, theory, what communications researchers would later call the two-step flow. For instance, in 1917 Parlin said that selling tractors was not a matter of selling every farmer at once—as was the general approach in mass marketing—but rather of "selling those farmers in every community who set the pace in farm methods." Persuading these farmers also required persuasion of "those who help them make their judgments," primarily bankers, lawyers, children, and agricultural extension agents. One Midwest merchant explained it this way to Parlin:

> For several years I have owned a farm. I hired an expert from the agricultural college to put in the first field of alfalfa in

the neighborhood. Other farmers and their sons looked on and said sarcastically, "College alfalfa." Within three years most of my neighbors had put in alfalfa, and all were exceedingly careful to put it in the same way. I was the first farmer in the neighborhood to paint my fences white. Within a short time, most of the fences in the neighborhood were painted white. I bought the first gasoline engine to pump water. Within a short time gasoline engines were in use on most of the farms in the neighborhood.[17]

The problem of reaching any group of people, especially in rural areas or small towns, was largely a problem of reaching the leaders, Parlin wrote in 1918. "The retail merchant says: 'I carry what my customers want.' Analyzed, he means that he carries what a relatively small number of *leading* customers want." If the merchant could satisfy those customers, he could please the rest. "A few people in every community are aggressive, know what they want, and insist upon getting it," Parlin said. Most of the others meekly took what was handed out to them, he added. That made it imperative that merchants reach those leadership families. He compared product sales to politics, saying that a politician knew that the way to get votes in the poorer districts was to win over ward leaders, not to try to earn the votes one by one. It was the same with advertising, he said. "The net of it is that advertising pioneers to those families who in turn pioneer in purchases. Following the pioneers come the masses of purchasers of all income groups."[18]

This idea of leading farmers toward consumption was made easier by the emergence of the Cooperative Extension Service of the U.S. Department of Agriculture, and Parlin's philosophy of identifying "pioneer" buyers borrowed from the success of county extension agents. Through land-grant universities, the agents worked with farmers—both men and women—and their children, providing advice and instruction on everything from safe methods of canning vegetables to sanitary ways of preparing meals to more efficient ways of planting and harvesting grain. Agricultural extension offices originated in Texas in 1902, became popular in the South, and then spread rapidly to other areas through the Smith-Lever Act of 1914. By the early 1920s, there were more than 1,000 home demonstration agents and 3,000 county extension agents throughout the United States.[19]

Although the agents were part of a Progressive Era notion of societal improvement and efficiency and were closely tied to the Country Life Movement, one of their most lasting effects was in teaching farm families how to consume. "The education of tomorrow's buyers is being done by the extension service work, among the juveniles of the farm family," the J. Walter Thompson agency wrote in 1924. That year, Thompson's New York office sent a representative to home extension conferences in Ithaca and Buffalo, New York, and reported that "the educational work being done by these organizations is tending to create more uniformly intelligent standards of consumer judgment," something that Thompson saw as aiding the "educational" work of advertisers. At a "better kitchens" demonstration, Hoosier cabinets were given away as prizes, and the Thompson representative reported that "great interest has been aroused. Many of the women kept the cabinet in the parlor until all of their neighbors had inspected it."[20]

Curtis Publishing likewise recognized the value of home extension agents and women's clubs in promoting consumer products. In 1925, staff members from *Country Gentleman* assisted the General Federation of Women's Clubs in a national census of equipment in farm homes, taking note of window screens, sewing and washing machines, vacuum cleaners, refrigerators, home lighting, house heating systems, and other appliances and modernizations. Curtis told its staff members that it expected the survey to "give us a cross section of rural homes throughout the land, with a mass of information that will be of almost inestimable value to those manufacturers whose products are of a labor-saving or comfort-making character."[21]

A "Typical" Town

One of Curtis's most ambitious undertakings was a study of what it deemed a "typical" farm town of 1920. It drew on the methods of rural sociology, which emerged with the Country Life Movement, and produced such works as *An American Town, Quaker Hill,* and *A Hoosier Village* around 1910. It was also an early example of the emerging field of community studies, or sociometrics, a technique used by social scientists to explore the social and psychological interconnections of a community. Biologists, ecologists, economists, jurists, social workers, and others used similar techniques to—as one scholar has said—see what communities are, "how they work, how to use them or change them." Perhaps the most famous such research was the study of Muncy, Indiana, or *Middletown,* by Robert and Helen Lynd.[22]

In Curtis's study, a team of more than a dozen representatives from the company's Advertising Department descended upon Sabetha, Kansas, in 1920. The representatives fanned out not only across Sabetha, in the northeastern part of the state, but to the nearby smaller towns of Morrill, Fairview, Berwick, Old Albany, and Price, and to farms in a 144-square-mile area in Nemaha and Brown Counties. They knocked on the doors of more than 1,300 residences—all but twenty in the area—and visited every business, asking questions, compiling questionnaires, and spending time observing how the community of 2,000 people and its trade area functioned. Their goal was to create a guide to the roles, actions, interactions, thinking, and philosophies that were shaping the United States into a consumer society. (See Figure 5.1.)

Sabetha was chosen as a typical agricultural community from among what Curtis identified as hundreds of "progressive" communities in Kansas, Nebraska, Illinois, Wisconsin, Iowa, and Missouri. It was not a major railroad junction, it had no factories, and the surrounding farm region was diversified. Many of its businesses were located in modern buildings, it had two and a half miles of paved streets, and it was one of the first towns in the state to put in street lights. The businesses in the town were dependent primarily on the trade of farmers in the region, and many of the people who lived in the community were retired farmers. Through interviews and observations, the company assembled a broad study of consumption—what is known in modern business parlance as a saturation survey[23]—one that tried to understand the importance of such

Figure 5.1   Curtis's investigation of Sabetha, Kansas, had an anthropological air as company representatives visited nearly every home, business, and farm in the area. Hughes Clothing, on Main Street, had a doctor's office above it.

factors as merchandising, national advertising, community leaders, brand names, and the automobile on purchases in a small farm town. Still at the center, not surprisingly, were Curtis magazines.

After visiting Sabetha, Parlin concluded that although circulation of Curtis magazines was sparse in the area, nine of ten community leaders, whose opinions were seen as essential to the spread of any consumer product, read Curtis magazines. The *Post,* the *Journal,* and

Country Gentleman reached these upper-class people—people who were "materially above the average" and had such conveniences as indoor bathrooms, vacuum cleaners, and automobiles. These people not only read the Curtis magazines, but they bought or asked for the products advertised in the magazines, Parlin said.

Merchants in Sabetha "studied the wants of the leaders; they stocked for others what these leaders selected for themselves," Parlin wrote, echoing his earlier conclusions about farm communities. By labeling Sabetha "typical" of Midwestern and Western farm communities, the company was able to claim the ability to generalize its findings to all farm communities, thereby creating further proof of the value of advertising in its magazines. "The three dimensions of Curtis circulation—large numbers, quality homes, and superior attention—enable a manufacturer through the pages of the Curtis publications to shape the thoughts of readers and dealers, and through them, of the masses who imitate," Parlin wrote. "The old idea that the farm is the market for cheap, unbranded merchandise is obsolete. The farm families of the Sabetha territory apparently have greater purchasing power than the families living in Sabetha itself, and the experience of merchants is that they are willing to spend it for high-grade branded goods. Today the manufacturer of high-grade merchandise can advantageously make a direct appeal to this new but very real farm market."[24]

In 1922, when Curtis returned to Sabetha for a follow-up study,[25] Parlin said that the original study "has proved to be a most valuable picture of the reading and buying habits of a typical rural community." Curtis used the Sabetha study as a guide for several other studies in the 1920s and 1930s as it gathered information about reading habits, buying habits, and product use.[26] These case studies, especially the study of Sabetha, were rich in detail—detail the company used to try to better understand the dynamics of the larger national marketplace. Such studies had a secondary benefit, though: They were much cheaper and less time consuming than the broad national surveys the company had done throughout the 1910s and 1920s, and by defining the smaller areas as "typical" or "average," the company could apply the results of the studies to areas nationwide. Similarly,

Parlin estimated that an advertiser could conduct a single-city study of its product distribution and sales methods for about $400. If research in one city resulted in information that saved money, he said, then it could easily be expanded into other cities.[27]

Competing Views

Scores of agencies and other companies followed Curtis's lead in the 1920s. The Sabetha reports were among at least two dozen in-depth studies that publishers, advertising agencies, universities, federal agencies, and businesses made of farm and small town life in the early 1920s. *Household Magazine, Woman's World, People's Popular Monthly,* and Meredith Publications, publisher of *Successful Farming* and *Better Homes and Gardens,* all surveyed their subscribers. J. Walter Thompson alone conducted at least four such studies between 1924 and 1926. One research agency went as far as publishing a series of books about rural villages.[28]

Thompson said it found Curtis's Sabetha study flawed because it concentrated on a single county rather than the many regional farming areas. Thompson said in 1925, for example, that it had identified eighteen distinct agricultural regions in which farming, rural, and small town life "present a fair degree of uniformity." It chose eleven counties that it said were representative of about two-thirds of the rural population and then, like Curtis Publishing, set out to visit every store and hundreds of farm homes in those counties. In doing so, it hoped to log, as Curtis had in Sabetha, what people read, what they bought, what the sales potential of the area was, and what sort of distribution and sales system would be needed to sell more products in the areas.[29]

After compiling information from two counties—Putnam in New York and Randolph in Indiana—about everything from farmers' preferences for rubber boots and overshoes to hair tonics, breads, soaps, and knit underwear, Thompson called its study "illuminating in the extreme." For the first time, the company said, it had a tangible basis for judging the way that urban lifestyles and tastes had spread to rural areas.[30] Paul T. Cherington of Thompson's New

York office noted that between 1900 and 1925, nearly 500,000 miles of good roads had been built in rural America, more than 3,500,000 farmers had bought automobiles, farm products had increased in value by a factor of four, 450,000 homes had been wired for electricity, and 640,000 had been equipped with running water. "These changes all represent modified habits of and capacity for consumption," Cherington wrote.[31]

Both Curtis and Thompson considered that type of information crucial. In the 1920s, Thompson distributed a memo to its staff each month about the rural market. In 1922, it told its clients not to overlook small towns, especially in Western states. In many cases, wrote George Pearson of Thompson's Chicago office, towns of 12,000 to 15,000 population were "commercially of greater importance" than densely populated urban areas, in part because they attracted consumers from a wide trading area. Curtis's internal publications from the 1920s also contained many observations about the farm market, analyzing, among other things, the effect of Prohibition on farmers, the economic outlook for agricultural areas, and changing consumer tastes of farm families. In 1924, Curtis declared the image of the hick farmer "as extinct as the dodo bird."[32]

Despite its potential, though, the rural market was difficult to reach, a problem that kept advertisers from pursuing that part of the nation as much as they would have liked. One reason was the lack of a dominant national medium. Newspapers were the medium of choice for most agencies and advertisers through the 1910s and into 1920s. By advertising in the largest city dailies, advertisers could easily reach an urban and suburban audience of hundreds of thousands, and even millions. Obtaining a similar exposure in rural areas was much more difficult. In 1916, J. Walter Thompson estimated that there were almost seven times as many weeklies (serving primarily rural areas) as dailies (serving urban areas), in addition to smaller monthlies, bimonthlies, semi-monthlies, and various other publications. Sorting through all those papers and selecting the ones worthy of national advertising, it said, would take a "superhuman" effort. The matter was made worse by the cost of the advertising.

The agency estimated that using country weeklies to reach the same size audience as the *Chicago Tribune* would cost six times more than the *Tribune*.[33] That is where Curtis had an advantage, and that is where Curtis sought to portray itself as the purveyor of the true national market, not only through the *Saturday Evening Post* but through its new magazine, *Country Gentleman*.

A New Curtis Magazine

Cyrus Curtis was intimately familiar with the farm periodical market, having started the *Tribune and Farmer* in 1879. He gave up that farm paper when he and his wife turned a section of the paper into the *Ladies' Home Journal* in 1883, but he began to see opportunity again and went shopping for a farm magazine in 1908. The farm periodical market had been growing steadily. Between 1875 and 1909, the number of general agricultural periodicals more than doubled, from about 70 to 180.[34] Despite that crowded field, Curtis had a vision of a new type of magazine, one modeled on the *Post*. That is, he wanted to create a national farm magazine devoted to the business aspects of agriculture.[35] In 1911, he bought *Country Gentleman*, which claimed to be the oldest farm publication in the United States. It had a subscriber list of only 25,000, and many of those had failed to pay for several years. For $100,000, Curtis essentially bought a name, but it was a name that he could build up through advertising, as he had done with the *Post*.

The magazine drew from both the staffs and the philosophies of the *Journal* (listening to readers) and the *Post* (emphasizing business). J. Clyde Marquis, the first editor, came from the *Journal*; Harry A. Thompson, its second editor, had been art director of the *Post*. Yet Thompson promised a publication with its own identity, one that would be broad enough to appeal to the entire family and the entire nation. "I do not want to talk about big features, but I want to make each number as full of stuff that will interest the farmer and his family as we can possibly make it," he told the advertising staff in 1913. The next year, in outlining the magazine's philosophies, the company said the mission of *Country Gentleman* was fourfold: to seek a national solution to the problems of agriculture; to pursue "a square deal" for farmers, in "recognition of the fact that whatever improves the situation of the man on the land is of universal benefit"; to improve the efficiency of farmers; and to improve social conditions and "standards of home-making" on the farm.[36]

Curtis spent more than $2 million on *Country Gentleman* before it turned a profit in 1917. Much of that money went to pay for the experts in farming that the company hired to write for the magazine, from officials in the Department of Agriculture and state experiment stations to college professors and business leaders. Curtis Publishing was so impressed by the Agriculture Department's investigative methods that it patterned the editorial operation of *Country Gentleman* after it. The Agriculture Department sent "men throughout the country to investigate and discover facts, to get the best material on the subject wherever they happen to be and to present the same to men in other states who have similar problems," Marquis said in 1915.[37]

A large portion of the magazine's early spending, though, went toward advertising, circulation, and marketing. (See Figure 5.2.) Between January and April of 1916, for example, the company spent $200,000 on twice-weekly advertisements in 185 newspapers in the Midwest and several farm publications, promoting *Country Gentleman* as a "progressive" farm paper and "the great national farm weekly" that provided "crisp, clear suggestions" about practical agricultural problems. The company used similar, frequent campaigns throughout the 1920s and 1930s, essentially embracing the very advertising strategy that the Thompson agency had dismissed as impossible.[38]

Creating a Savvy Consumer

Curtis Publishing's goal for *Country Gentleman* was clear from the start: to help turn the farmer into a business leader and thus create a more savvy consumer of advertised products. "Some people think that the chief end of farming is to put a seed into the ground, sit

Figure 5.2 Curtis promoted its farm magazine, *Country Gentleman,* extensively. It often used iconic images on the cover, as in this promotional issue from 1925.

down and watch it grow," Curtis wrote in a promotional pamphlet in 1913. "That side of farming can be found in books of poetical quotations and on foreclosed mortgages. The chief end of farming is profit. The farmer is no sentimental hero of a poem—though the poets have overworked him up to date. He is a business man like a manufacturer or a banker. He sows seed to reap dollars."[39]

Curtis also catered specifically to farm women with a section of the magazine called "Country Gentlewoman." In 1923, after a survey found that more women were reading the magazine than Curtis realized, the company hired an editor, Caroline B. King, to better develop the "Country Gentlewoman" section. Under King, whom Curtis called a "nationally known authority on cooking and homemaking," the magazine greatly increased the amount of material for women, focusing on such things as fashion, beauty, child care, interior decorating, and handicrafts. It further enhanced the section in the 1930s, essentially turning it into a magazine for women within the pages of *Country Gentleman*. It also created an organization of clubs for farm women, the Country Gentlewoman League, in effect forming a social organization linked to consumption of the magazine.[40]

Curtis drew on the growing importance of consumption of consumer products as it marketed *Country Gentleman* to advertisers in an elitist tone, saying that it was "a high-priced farm paper" that was "edited for farmers who are leaders in farm methods—whose thought and actions dominate farm progress in their localities." In 1923, Curtis told its staff members that the number of farms that *Country Gentleman* reached did not matter nearly as much as the wealth of those farms. Although the magazine's circulation did not parallel farm wealth, Curtis said, "it does undoubtedly reach a far greater percentage of the farmers in the wealthy counties than in the poor ones; it has been tending in this direction more or less for the past three or four years; and as our effort is very consciously directed to that end, it will continue to do so."[41]

In the memos Curtis sent to its staff members during the 1920s, the company stressed the practicality of *Country Gentleman,* and in 1929, Curtis said it took "particular pride" in the "popularizing of fundamental scientific research" through *Country Gentleman* and in assisting farmers in the move toward mechanization and electrification in the 1920s. It said that American farmers were by necessity broadening their view of the world, concerning themselves with such things as marketing, tariffs, foreign competition, and international trade, and that *Country Gentleman* was shifting its focus to help interpret those sorts of issues. "There is more to farm life than corn and hogs," Curtis wrote in 1924. "There is more in the *Country Gentleman* than corn and hogs. It is the rural weekly."[42]

Again, Curtis seemed to be fighting the perceptions of its staff members and the biases of advertisers and agencies. It was a conflict that would continue for years. The research kept telling the company that the farm market was full of opportunities. And yet staff members could not quite believe that themselves. The conflicts were apparent throughout the 1910s and 1920s. In promoting *Country Gentleman* in 1914, for example, the company asserted that American farming was "big business, and the market for farm products is more than nation-wide. Modern means of transportation bring remote points close together and make any section a market for any other section."[43] In its house organ a few months later, though, it told manufacturers that they did not need to worry too much about the rural population because the people to whom they had the easiest access lived in and around cities. "Commercial conditions depend largely upon density of population, which is necessary to the maintenance of considerable markets and of transportation facilities for moving products. Great buying power, therefore, is found in the denser districts—and a greater need for the majority of manufactured products."[44]

The Curtis magazine audiences also created a dilemma for the company. The *Post* and *Journal* were most popular in urban areas, with about half of their circulation in cities of 100,000 or more population. (See Table 5.1.) *Country Gentleman* was aimed at a rural audience, but lacked the prestige of either of the other two magazines.[45] If, as Curtis and others asserted, the rural and small town markets contained the largest portion of the country's wealth and purchased the largest amount of consumer goods, how effective could magazines like the *Post* really be?[46]

Table 5.1 U.S. Distribution of Curtis Magazines by Population, 1913, 1928

Population of Area	% of U.S. Population	*Journal* Readers	%	*Post* Readers	%	*Country Gentleman* Readers	%
		1913					
500,000 and over	12.5	211,667	13.3	330,443	16.9	34,067	13.3
100,000–500,000	9.6	246,141	15.4	334,953	17.2	34,858	13.6
25,000–100,000	8.9	274,345	17.2	346,787	17.8	37,784	14.8
10,000–25,000	6.1	176,988	11.1	202,644	10.4	28,966	11.3
2,500–10,000	9.2	273,691	17.2	297,026	15.2	42,392	16.6
Less than 2,500	53.7	411,559	25.8	438,614	22.5	77,473	30.3
TOTAL		1,594,391		1,950,467		255,540	
		1928					
100,000 and over	29.6	1,108,364	46.5	1,459,108	53.5	250,700	18.2
25,000–100,000	10.5	408,247	17.1	445,825	16.3	210,743	15.3
10,000–25,000	7.4	297,437	12.5	311,358	11.4	219,550	15.9
5,000–10,000	4.8	192,961	8.1	195,744	7.1	192,499	14.0
Less than 5,000	47.6	373,470	15.7	315,225	11.5	503,643	36.6
TOTAL		2,380,479		2,727,260		1,377,135	

Sources: "Distribution of Circulation in Cities" in "Circulation Data, 1915–1919"; "Distribution of Magazine Circulation in United States," Curtis *Bulletin* 103 (1928); *Fifteenth Census of the United States*, 1930; *Thirteenth Census of the United States*, 1910.

The company had another problem to overcome as well. In most cases, the small town market was controlled primarily by merchants. National advertising was considered to have little effect. "The small-town dealer sells on his personal word and on the reputation of the store, rather than on the reputation of the merchandise," one observer wrote in 1920. "He has a tighter hold on his customers' trade than the manufacturer can hope to secure thru all the general publicity at his command."[47]

Parlin identified this problem, too, in his early studies, and he and his colleagues worked hard to understand the distribution process. Much of advertising, Curtis Publishing told its customers, was not aimed at the consumer as much as it was at the shopkeeper, who could generate sales simply by stocking a product. It did little good to produce and advertise a product if that product was not available in stores.

Despite those problems, Curtis's strategy of cultivating an elite audience and of selling that audience to advertisers worked to a large degree, as *Country Gentleman* became the dominant farm publication of the 1920s. By 1918, it took in more advertising revenue—$1,505,022—than any other farm publication, accounting for 13 percent of the total revenue of the 63 farm publications tracked by the Advertising Record Company. Between 1915 and 1930, the magazine ranked no lower than thirteenth in advertising income among *all* national publications. It peaked at No. 7 in 1919, but throughout the 1920s, it outdistanced competitors like *Farm Journal* and *Successful Farming,* taking in hundreds of thousands of dollars in advertising from companies like Goodyear Tire & Rubber, U.S. Rubber, International Harvester, Moline Plow, and Thomas A. Edison Inc.[48]

Country Gentleman went over well with readers also. Circulation rose from about 30,000 in 1911 to 300,000 in 1914. The magazine was revamped in the mid-1920s and was switched from weekly to monthly publication. Curtis increased the quality of the magazine's paper stock, reduced the amount of "purely technical agricultural material," and increased the amount it paid its writers, boasting that it was creating "quality without counting the cost." In an attempt to broaden the magazine's circulation even more, Curtis dropped the price of *Country Gentleman* to $1 for three years. At that price, the national master of the National Grange told Curtis in 1926, "we have not a farmer anywhere, or an individual interested in rural problems, who cannot afford to take the paper." The circulation of *Country Gentleman* surpassed 1 million in 1925, reached 1.6 million in 1929, and grew to 2 million by 1939.[49]

An Elusive Market

Despite the emphasis that Curtis and other marketers placed on rural America in the early twentieth century, the farm market remained maddeningly elusive. Commodity prices plunged in 1920, remained flat through the 1920s, and nosedived during the Great Depression. What has been called the "golden age of agriculture" began to lose some of its glimmer, and Curtis itself said that the implement industry experienced "four disastrous years" between 1920 and 1924, "the darkest years in its history." And for all its success on the surface, *Country Gentleman* apparently struggled behind the scenes. By one account, the magazine was profitable in only twelve of the forty-five years that Curtis owned it, and its cumulative loss totaled about $15 million.[50] Curtis gave up on *Country Gentleman* in 1955, changing its name to *Better Farming* and then selling it to *Farm Journal* and *Town Journal*. It had more than 2,400,000 subscribers at the time.[51]

Rural Americans did indeed buy, though, as Parlin predicted. By the mid-1920s, Curtis Publishing said, farmers and city people had jumped into the same melting pot of consumption. "America had finally become homogenous," the company wrote in 1929, speaking of previous changes. "The people were all alike in dress, in language and, with minor differences, in thought and general reactions."[52] This common culture of consumption, though, helped make rural residents more comfortable in the cities and suburbs than they once had been. Even before the Depression wiped out many of the gains that farmers had made earlier in the century, the ranks of rural America were thinning. Between 1920 and 1930, the number of American farms declined by 160,000, and the percentage of the population in rural areas continued to shrink.[53] Parlin and his colleagues had found their market and perhaps even had a hand in creating it. And yet, for all the research, for all the millions of dollars in advertising they took in, they never seemed willing to say that they understood it. "The vital question as to how much these people could, or would, buy if urged has been difficult to answer," the J. Walter Thompson agency wrote of rural residents in 1926. "Nor is it answered yet."[54]

Rural America may have perplexed marketers at the time, but their persistence in studying it shows how central it was to their thinking. In their eyes, urban America seemed a much simpler place to understand and pursue, largely because of its concentration and growth. The population of rural America, on the other hand, was spread over a vast region and was, at least to the urban marketers, foreign. There were more mundane reasons that Curtis Publishing focused on rural America, though. With the company's acquisition of *Country Gentleman* in 1911, the advertising staff was expected to fill the new publication with advertising, and the circulation staff was expected to sell more magazines. They could not do that unless they understood what they were dealing with. Parlin's rural background also played a role. He had grown up in a small town in Wisconsin, and until he went to work for Curtis, had spent most of his adult life in small towns in the upper Midwest. His father had bought butter, eggs, and poultry from farmers and resold them in his small shop, and Parlin spoke nostalgically of the simple, idyllic lifestyle of nineteenth-century Wisconsin.[55] Even if Parlin's background gave him an affinity for rural America, he pursued those areas not because of affection, but because his research pointed him that way. Clearly there was money to be made in rural America, and Parlin sent the Curtis staff in pursuit of it.

Still, as Curtis and other marketers began to look at rural America, they seemed to see both visions of what could be and, perhaps more important, images of what the country as a whole had long been. Since its founding, the United States had worshiped the ideal of the yeoman farmer. That ideal was still strong in the early twentieth century, although the United States itself was changing, year by year, into a nation dominated by city people.[56] Even so, marketers saw in rural America not only the yeoman farmer, but also the yeoman consumer, a leader who had money to spend, who was willing to try new products, and who could help reset the moral compass of the masses and lead them into this new world of consumption.

In the end, rural America changed the way it looked at consumer goods, and marketers like Curtis cast aside many of their stereotypes and changed the way they looked at rural America. To them, this was all about creating new consumers, wherever they could be found. And yet the same narrow mindedness that Curtis and other companies harbored about farmers and farm communities took on an even stronger edge when race, class, and ethnicity were involved. For much of the consumer products world, color and class were not simply boundary lines; they were walls that conveniently blocked out what marketers considered the "worthless elements" of American society, leaving a white moneyed class in clear view. It was with that view that Parlin and his colleagues shaped the image of the ideal consumer.

6

Readers as Consumers

Do you know why we publish the Ladies' Home Journal? The editor thinks it is for the benefit of the American woman. That is an illusion, but a proper one for him to have. But I will tell you the publisher's reason. . . . To give you people who manufacture things that the American women want and buy a chance to tell them about your products.

—CYRUS CURTIS TO A GROUP OF ADVERTISERS

As Charles Coolidge Parlin researched department stores and textiles in 1913, he began to realize that many of the workings of the marketplace depended not so much on strategy and science as on whim. Distribution was certainly an important factor. So were such things as product availability, salesmanship, product displays, and advertising. He did his best to analyze those factors for Curtis Publishing and its advertisers and to point out weaknesses in business strategy and possibilities in the marketplace.

Not long after he began his work for Curtis, though, he began to see that those factors were meaningless if a product did not appeal to the consumer. Individual opinion mattered, but thousands of individual opinions mattered more. The success or failure of a product in the emerging national marketplace depended upon its steady mass appeal. "The consumer is king," Parlin said in his report on department stores. He later adopted the saying as part of a creed he

This chapter was published in an earlier form as "The Reader as Consumer: Curtis Publishing Company and Its Audience, 1910–1930," *Journalism History* 22 (Summer 1996): 46–55.

used to end speeches to manufacturers and trade groups. "The whim of the consumer makes and unmakes the manufacturers, the jobbers and the retailers," he said. "Whoever wins the confidence of the consumer wins the day; and whoever loses it, is lost."[1]

Parlin's creed was, Robert Bartels argues, an articulation of the notion that consumption was the "end and object of production," a rejection of the nineteenth century view of production as an end in itself and as a means of self-sufficiency. It was also part of an important rethinking of consumer behavior. Until the early twentieth century, most business executives and advertising practitioners considered the consumer self-interested but rational. With a growing acceptance of social science, especially psychology, their views shifted, and they began to consider the consumer as an irrational actor in the marketplace, someone guided more by emotion than by reason.[2] Parlin's motto also underscored a shift in thinking about the marketplace and the priorities of American business. The government, and to a lesser extent, business, had long collected statistics about everything from shipping and exports to the production of agricultural products and the output of mining operations. What they lacked, until the late 1920s, was detailed data about the nationwide consumption of consumer products. That is where Parlin's work fit in. As businesses were placing increasing emphasis on consumers and the need to tailor their products toward the masses, researchers like Parlin were recognizing the need to study those consumers.

Paying close attention to consumers had been a crucial part of the magazine world since the late nineteenth century, when publishers like Cyrus Curtis saw an opportunity in amassing audiences that advertisers would pay handsomely to reach. Curtis and his contemporaries promoted consumption as a dutiful act that aided the advertiser, who in turn aided the publisher, who in turn aided the reader. It was this type of circular process that thousands of Americans began to see as a wheel of progress, moving them toward greater comfort, status, and well-being individually and as a nation. To keep that wheel rolling toward greater profits for itself, though, Curtis Publishing had to hold the interest of readers and advertisers. The central element of doing that was information—reading matter for subscribers and data about those subscribers for advertisers.[3]

From the 1880s on, Curtis and his staff continually made a case that Curtis publications reached the elite of American society—people with culture and, most important, people with money.[4] The company told advertisers that Curtis publications, with their "high grade" artwork and printing, appealed only to "the intelligent, the earnest and the progressive." The *Ladies' Home Journal* was "designed for the home loving," while the *Saturday Evening Post* was "designed for the men and women who desire a wholesome, sane and entertaining treatment of modern life in fiction and in fact."[5] The *Post*'s editor, George Horace Lorimer, said that the *Post* appealed "to two classes of men: Men with income, and men who are going to have incomes, and the second is quite as important as the first to the advertiser."[6] With its farm magazine *Country Gentleman,* Curtis assured advertisers of "an *intelligent* audience, an *interested* hearing and a well-grounded *confidence*,"[7] and insisted that "the exceptional and constant increase in the wealth of these particular readers means that from season to season they will be more and more desirable customers for high-grade merchandise of many sorts."[8] Similarly, Curtis proclaimed its newspaper, *The Public Ledger,* the publication of the "intelligent masses," asking advertisers: "What *kind* of people do you wish to reach in Philadelphia?"[9]

Responding to Doubts

Even as the publisher of the two widest-circulating magazines of the 1910s and 1920s, though, Curtis Publishing could not escape the scrutiny of advertisers who wanted proof about its readership claims. Edward Bok, the editor of the *Journal,* noted in 1913 that his magazine had been criticized for being read by too many girls and not enough serious-minded women, although he discounted any such criticism as speculation, without offering any proof to back up his own claims.[10] Companies such as Peerless, Packard, and Pierce-Arrow automobiles were skeptical that buyers of their products read

Curtis publications, and they were, therefore, reluctant to buy Curtis advertising.[11] The advertising manager of the Thomas B. Jeffery Company, maker of Rambler Motor Cars, criticized magazines in general for crowing about their widespread circulations but failing to provide accurate information to back up their claims that their readers were really buyers.[12]

Advertising agencies also put pressure on publishers, demanding proof about publications' claims that their large audiences paid close attention to advertising. Publications had come to use large circulation figures as a sort of status symbol, demanding higher prices for advertising as circulation numbers rose. The identification of readers in mere numbers no longer seemed enough, though. Advertisers wanted to know who those readers were and what other publications they read. They wanted to know where the readers lived and the types of products they bought. Just as businesses increasingly sought information about markets and products, they likewise sought information about audiences and consumers. Advertisers and agencies also raised concerns that magazines, including those published by Curtis, failed to reach a unique audience. That is, readers tended to subscribe to more than one periodical. To advertisers who sought the widest possible audience at the lowest possible cost, such "duplication" was often seen as wasteful and inefficient. Why, advertisers asked, should they buy space in both the *Post* and the *Journal* if the same families subscribed to both magazines?[13]

To blunt such criticism and to provide proof that it reached both a mass and a class audience, Curtis began using its Division of Commercial Research to compile information about readers. Its early readership reports appear to be among the first of their kind conducted by an American publisher. Parlin conducted Curtis's first readership survey in 1916, and through the 1920s he and his colleagues expanded their use of audience studies. That research involved a process of definition that required both inclusion and exclusion, and helped Curtis carve a niche in the mass market. It also reinforced stereotypes of African Americans and immigrants, labeling them as outcasts in a culture built on the ability to buy. To Cyrus Curtis and his staff, readers were more than just an audience; they were a product in themselves, something that could be defined, packaged, and sold to advertisers. In the commercial publishing world at the turn of the century, readers became a valuable commodity.

"Mass" and "Class"

In the early twentieth century, Curtis Publishing often blurred the distinction between "class" and "mass" circulation as its subscription lists soared into the hundreds of thousands, and then into the millions. Its definition of "class," though, was often middle class—or, perhaps more appropriately, buying class. The target readership was often defined by the ownership of such things as homes, automobiles, typewriters, and telephones, or the availability of electricity or department-store charge accounts.[14] It sought to portray its publications as the choice of the well-to-do, but then broadened its definition of well-to-do to include everyone from "millionaire to mill worker"—essentially anyone who could be considered "a substantial citizen and a good customer for a worthy product."[15]

By 1915, Bok had begun defining the readers of the *Ladies' Home Journal* by income. He told the advertising staff that the magazine was directed primarily toward families with incomes of $1,200 to $3,000 (about $26,000 to $65,000 today[16]), and to a lesser extent toward those with incomes up to $5,000. Some people who made more money also read the magazine, he acknowledged. "We direct our attention, however, to the class from $1,200 to $3,000, because they are the families having the greatest need of help, and to whom we can be of greatest assistance."[17]

That "assistance," as several scholars have shown, often involved instructing people what to buy and how to buy. In the 1910s and 1920s, for instance, Curtis sold patterns of fashions featured in the *Journal,* offered blueprints for houses featured in the *Journal,* and worked with department stores to display and make available the ready-to-wear fashions the magazine showcased.[18] It addressed cleanliness, home decorating, and countless other areas involving the consumption of increasing numbers of consumer products. As Jennifer Scanlon writes, Bok had two visions of the *Journal's* audience:

women as caretakers of the home and women as consumers. At a time of enormous change in American society, she says, the *Journal* encouraged women "to read rather than act, to conform to middle-class mores rather than seek out new and possibly more revolutionary alternatives" in education, work, and household.[19]

Lorimer did not have nearly as precise a definition of readers of the *Post*, but he nonetheless had an idea of who his readers were. When circulation rose above three million for a few issues in 1927, Lorimer called it "honest circulation, clean circulation" free of cut-rate promotions. He said the *Post* "goes to the most intelligent and progressive audience in America—the backbone of the community's buying power."[20] The *Post*, in fact, came to symbolize the rise of the mass magazine in the early twentieth century. John Tebbel and Mary Ellen Zuckerman call it "the bible of middle-class America" in the early twentieth century, and Daniel Boorstin calls it "weekly fare for the great mass of Americans who considered themselves middle class." Jan Cohn calls it "one of America's great mass magazines—perhaps its greatest."[21]

A 1928 article by Leon Whipple, a writer and social critic, seems to sum up the general sentiments that have persisted into the twenty-first century about the appeal of the *Post*:

> Who reads the *Post*? Who looks in the mirror? Everybody—high-brow, low-brow, and mezzanine; the hardboiled business man and the soft-boiled leisure woman; the intelligenzia, often as a secret vice; Charles M. Schwab has subscribed for twelve years, Elbert Gary had for eighteen. The White House must take in a copy or two if it has a sense of gratitude. You read it—and I.[22]

Lorimer himself used to lurk near the newsstand at the Reading Railroad terminal in Philadelphia and see who bought the *Post*. He described those people as "the class of people you like to see—the prosperous business men and the young women who have positions with good firms."[23]

A Special Audience

Cyrus Curtis had made similar generalizations in the late nineteenth century. From the early 1880s, when he started the *Tribune and Farmer,* Curtis told advertisers that the readers of Curtis publications were something special. He stressed that the paper's "entire circulation was secured by newspaper advertising, consequently all our readers are peculiarly the very class who read and answer advertisements." He also promised advertisers that if their ads failed to produce results, "we shall neither expect nor solicit a continuance of your patronage."[24]

To attract subscribers, Curtis offered the paper at a discount, but only if buyers would sign a statement that they would "read and answer the Advertisements as far as they can conveniently do so." He sought to induce in readers a sense of responsibility toward his publication, toward advertisers, and toward buying in general, and he tried to create a sense of guilt in those who did not buy advertised products. He admitted that advertisements were scorned by many people, but he promised, in language that would later be repeated in promotional material for the *Ladies' Home Journal,* that *Tribune and Farmer* advertisements "are known to be reliable and may be answered with perfect safety." Advertisers, he told readers, were for the most part manufacturers and producers, and by answering ads, consumers could bypass the middleman. "So great a variety is advertised in our columns that one is almost sure to find something he needs, and having found it, should not hesitate to send for it, not only for his own profit but for ours also, as, by giving this paper at cost, we are obliged to look to advertisers for our profits, and must make it a good medium to secure patronage."[25]

That type of attention to the reader began to grow after the turn of the century as the consumer became ever more important in the success of Curtis Publishing Company. During Parlin's first several years at Curtis, as he conducted studies of agricultural implements, textiles, department stores, automobiles, and foodstuffs, he gathered anecdotal information about the readership of the *Post* and *Journal.*[26]

He did not attempt to conduct a full-fledged analysis of the readers of the two magazines, but instead talked with many merchants, jobbers, and manufacturers around the country about the content of the magazines and their perceptions of readers. He did not seem interested in finding out anything new about the magazines, but rather in confirming their importance to consumers and to businesses.[27] "Everybody reads the *Post,*" Parlin wrote, "not only the merchants and their buyers but the girls at the counter." He also wrote that department store managers considered both the *Journal* and the *Post* "authorities on quality," and they pored over the magazines to try to pick up tips for their newspaper advertising and to apply to their salesmanship.[28] He later compiled snippets of his interviews in a book for advertising representatives, and he urged representatives to familiarize themselves with the quotes before meeting with potential advertisers.[29]

Within a few years, as Parlin gained experience and confidence as a researcher, he moved the consumer to the forefront of Curtis Publishing's research projects.[30] His division still sought to define "markets." That is, he and his associates still attempted to chart the distribution and sales mechanisms of the growing volume of consumer goods in such businesses as food, textiles, farm machinery, and automobiles. That type of information was increasingly valuable and necessary as competition intensified nationally. Increasingly, though, the Division of Commercial Research sought to learn more about the consumer and to try to prove that the readers of Curtis magazines were a well-heeled, responsive audience that the progressive manufacturer could not do without. Like other publishers of magazines and newspapers, Curtis sought increasingly to define readers as consumers and to market those consumers as an audience for advertisers.[31]

Parlin conducted the company's first readership study in 1915 and 1916, a mail survey of 31,000 readers of the *Country Gentleman.* He followed that, in 1919 and 1920, with a study of the *Public Ledger* of Philadelphia. The two reports seem to be among the first full-fledged commercial readership surveys done by a U.S. publisher.[32] Although readership studies of the *Post* and *Journal* would later become a regular part of Curtis's research, the direction and control of those and other Curtis publications were left mostly to their editors.[33] The *Post* and the *Journal,* especially, were vastly successful, and the company saw no need to apply extensive research to the editorial formula of successful products. In fact, readership research as an editorial tool did not really catch on until the Great Depression, when editors and publishers were forced to look more closely at costs and space.[34] Curtis, under the guidance of Parlin, began to experiment with those types of studies years earlier.

Starting with the Farm Audience

The first *Country Gentleman* survey looked partly at reader wants, but as with nearly all Commercial Research studies, it was primarily aimed at gathering information for the Advertising Department. The purpose of the survey, Parlin wrote, "was to define the characteristics of these readers, their agricultural activities, their habits of buying, and their interest in *The Country Gentleman.*" The questions he asked helped define readers as people with money and land and with the ability to make major capital purchases—such things as tools and machinery. More than 90 percent lived within twenty-five miles of a trading center, indicating that they "can be cultivated for the sale of products having a distribution in city stores."[35] A follow-up survey in 1920 sought much the same information, but broke the survey into more geographic areas and identified the brands of products that readers bought. It also sought to determine why nonrural residents purchased *Country Gentleman.*[36] The next year, the company gathered feedback from readers by offering prize money for essays about "Why I Subscribe to the *Country Gentleman.*"[37] The company continued periodic audience analyses, conducting reader surveys in 1925, 1926, 1931, and 1940.[38]

The *Public Ledger* survey did not seek to define the newspaper's readership. Curtis did that itself in choosing whom it interviewed: primarily business leaders, political figures, labor leaders, professors, teachers, women considered to have community influence, and to a lesser extent, newspaper sellers and distributors.[39] The *Ledger,* which was created as a penny paper in 1836, had long had a reputation as a conservative newspaper with a devoted readership that was "all quality." Under the editorship of George W. Childs in the late 1800s, it became the primary newspaper of Philadelphia's elites. Cyrus Curtis hoped to build on that reputation. He bought the newspaper in 1913, created an afternoon edition the next year, and sought to turn the *Ledger* into a national daily that would enhance the image of Philadelphia.[40]

The primary aim of the *Ledger* survey was "to formulate concrete suggestions for the betterment" of the editorial product. How, in other words, could the newspaper attract more readers? As Parlin and his staff contemplated that question, they grounded their opinions in the workings of advertising, reflecting a shift, which had started in the nineteenth century, toward running newspapers more as commercial businesses than as political organs. The success of the advertising columns depended to a great extent on the success of the editorial columns. If a newspaper could not attract readers, it could not attract advertisers, and if it did not have advertisers, it could not afford to pay for news coverage. It seemed probable, Parlin wrote, "that serious losses in advertising or circulation whenever they occur are apt to reflect unsound editorial policies; for, what in the long run is best for one department must be best for all." He advised the *Ledger* staff to concentrate on three things: becoming a city booster, improving the accuracy of local news, and avoiding sensationalism.

He also urged the two newspapers to follow a unified editorial policy and to be less aggressive in taking on public officials and in taking unpopular stands on controversial issues in editorials and news stories. It was advice that clearly conflicted with journalistic ideals, but showed how the values of advertising had begun to encroach on the values of journalism.[41] In other words, he offered the same advice to the newspapers that he offered to the manufacturers of consumer goods: provide a quality product consistently and do so without offending buyers. Journalism was a commodity that could be shaped and packaged just like any other commodity. The trick was to win enough market share to achieve profitability. Parlin urged going after the "right" market, the readers with money—the type of consumers that advertisers most desired. A consistent, conservative, and thoughtful editorial policy would do just that, he wrote.[42]

How much of that advice the editors took is not known. Curtis Publishing and its newspaper company spared no expense with the *Ledger,* though, spending millions on news coverage, starting a national syndicate, and buying four competing newspapers. It also constructed an enormous, state-of-the-art office building and printing plant next to the Curtis Publishing Company building in 1925, offered free classified advertising for a time, and often operated the newspaper at a loss. None of it was enough. Both the morning and evening editions faltered during the Depression. In 1934, the morning and Sunday *Ledgers* merged with the *Philadelphia Inquirer,* which carried the *Ledger* name on its nameplate until the 1970s. The evening edition folded in 1942.[43]

"Advertising Land"

Increasingly in the early twentieth century, the world of advertising worked with such an idealized notion of audience that nearly everything except consumption was discounted. In 1915, a copywriter admonished his colleagues for living in a fantasy world he called "Advertising Land." In Advertising Land, people sat at home and waited eagerly for the arrival of the next issue of *Marvelous Monthly.* The young women of the family all clipped coupons and kept their hope chests stuffed with free samples and brochures about buying wedding rings on credit. Their brothers walked around in a daze, saying little but "U-m-m-m, it's good!" The mother of the family eagerly thumbed through the magazine's advertising, crying out: "Here is the very thing we have been needing." She and a neighbor later chat excitedly about a new campaign for Scotch Marmalade. Her husband, having already read the magazine, is busy writing away for a free booklet that will tell him how to increase his profits, one of several booklets he sends away for each month. The writer of the satire, F. R. Feland, wondered whether his profession had not lost touch with the people it was trying to reach. "Is this country of ours really a country or is it the pipe dream of a tired copy writer?" he asked. "Are citizens real people or are they cloud shapes, formed in the drifting smoke of a commercial artist's cigarette?"[44]

Gradually, advertisers began to demand more than just idealized notions of audience, and readership surveys emerged as a means to help identify the subscribers of publications.[45] These surveys were extensions of circulation data that advertisers and agencies began to scrutinize as readership of popular magazines and newspapers soared in the late nineteenth century—data that were themselves extensions of simple lists of publications that agencies kept.

With no uniform means of proving—or even calculating—circulation, unscrupulous publishers felt free to inflate their numbers by hundreds or even thousands.[46] The most confident publications began offering independent circulation audits to satisfy their wary customers. As early as the late 1880s, Curtis Publishing encouraged advertisers to visit its office in Philadelphia and conduct their own audit of the *Ladies' Home Journal.* Other magazines, such as *Century,* *Harper's,* and *Scribner's,* initially resisted audits, with editors and publishers saying they did not think figures alone could represent the true "quality" of their circulations. "Common law does not compel the publisher to state his circulation, but the law of sense will not allow the advertiser to buy his advertising uncounted and unaccounted for," Nathaniel C. Fowler, author of one of the early reference books on advertising, said in 1897.[47] Publications gradually began to adopt that point of view, and by the early 1910s, organizations such as the Audit Bureau of Circulations verified circulation figures for advertisers.[48]

Circulation statistics alone, though, began to seem like a shallow means of judging a market, especially as advertising costs rose and the choices of media grew. Around the turn of the century, individual advertising agencies began to devise ways of collecting statistical audience data. Among the most influential was the Chicago agency run by John Mahin. His monthly *Mahin's Magazine* began to show advertisers the value of demographic research and how such factors as population shifts, employment trends, and income variations could affect an area's sales potential and could be used in planning an advertising campaign.[49]

Others also began experimenting with audience studies. Walter Dill Scott, a professor at Northwestern University and a writer for *Mahin's Magazine,* surveyed Chicago daily newspaper readers for his book *Psychology of Advertising* in 1908. In 1911, R. O. Eastman of the Kellogg's breakfast food company conducted his first study of magazine readers—a post card survey for about fifty members of the Association of National Advertising Managers.[50] That same year, the advertising agent George Batten chose 100 homes in a Wisconsin town of 3,000 people and conducted interviews to find out what periodicals they read.[51]

Curtis Takes a Cue

In late 1913, Eastman told the Curtis advertising staff of a second readership survey he had directed earlier that year. The survey was backed by more than sixty companies that, like Kellogg's, wanted "to know what we are buying." That is, they wanted to know more about magazines' readers, especially how much duplication of circulation there was among the dozens of popular magazines. Eastman compared an advertising purchase to a purchase of coal, which was analyzed to determine its heating and power potential. "We cannot buy advertising that way, unfortunately," he said, "but we ought to work toward that point—of buying and selling advertising by its heat units, by its power units, by what it will do."

The survey Eastman had directed consisted of a house-to-house canvass of 16,894 homes in 209 cities and forty states. He said that such surveys were just a beginning. "Advertising is a force," he said, "a wonderful, powerful, tremendous force, but it has not been weighted, measured or gauged. Not only that; we have not found, we have not devised, the weights and measures or the gauge wherewith to weigh, measure and gauge it. The first rudiments of the thing are before us."[52]

Curtis took the hint from Eastman and other advertisers. The company first provided a detailed breakdown of its circulation in 1919, and through the 1920s and 1930s, it continued to expand its analyses of circulation, correlating Curtis circulation with such things as income tax returns, number of wage earners, value of products sold in an area, and the number of passenger cars (both Fords and non-Fords). It mined the 1920 census for information about rent and other indicators of income. It also used its own research to further its claims of superiority over competing publications.[53] (See Chapter 7.)

The company expanded the market analyses of its readership each year, providing circulation figures by cities and counties, along with consumption information about each. It also tried to justify the cost of advertising in its publications, showing how a page in the *Post* or *Journal* cost more than an ad in other magazines but reached more people, thus offering a lower cost per reader. It also began to compile information to rebut arguments that few women read the *Post* (although its target audience was still men), and that the magazine had grown so large—it often exceeded two hundred pages in the late 1920s—that readership of advertisements had declined.[54] In 1928, the company interviewed residents of more than 28,000 homes in Watertown, New York, to determine not only which magazines people of the community bought, but more important, what magazines they actually *read*.[55] "Advertisers pay for circulation," the company wrote in 1925. "But any part of the circulation of a magazine that doesn't produce *readers* is waste. The most profitable magazine to an advertiser is the magazine whose number of readers is highest in proportion to its circulation. That is why advertising volume tends to parallel 'number of readers' rather than 'quantity of circulation.'"[56]

A Closer Look at the *Post*

Worrying about the effect of movies, radio, automobiles, and competing magazines, Curtis began looking more substantively at readership of the *Post* in the mid-1920s. In 1922, the company cross-checked the subscriber lists of the *Post,* the *Journal,* and *Country Gentleman* from Ohio, Iowa, and New York to show that the duplication of subscribers among the magazines was small.[57] That same year, it surveyed *Post* readers and asked them to name the other magazines they read, trying to determine how much duplication there was between *Post* subscribers and subscribers of competing publications. It continued to narrow the market analyses of its read ership, providing circulation figures by towns and counties, along with consumption information about each.[58]

In 1925, the company sent staff members to four towns, where they called upon mostly men in offices and homes, drugstores, and groceries "to obtain something rather definite as to the intensity with which the *Post* was being read." Two years later, Curtis told its advertising staff that the best way to respond to advertiser doubts about readership was to cite circulation, which had surpassed three million for some issues. The company also railed against competitors who cited "figures showing newsstand sales of ONE issue, with phrases that paint a brilliant picture of reader-hordes, pantingly trampling on each other's necks in their anxiety to buy. . . . But for week-in-and-week-out, all-the-year-through DEMAND, we can submit *facts* that enable us safely to challenge any publication to come within Big-Bertha range of the *Post*." The first broad study of *Post* readership seems to have been done in 1930 and was fol-lowed up in 1936 and 1939.[59]

In the 1930 study, Curtis said that certain basic things were known about all publications: total circulation, advertising volume, the class of advertising published, and physical appearance. Several lesser-known things were just as important, though, Curtis argued: how long a magazine was kept in a home, how many readers it had per copy, how readership was broken down by sex and occupation, and whether advertising was read. "There is no standard of measure-ment by which the biggest factor in publishing may be reckoned— the extent to which its columns are valued by the reader," the company wrote. Curtis used that survey, as it had earlier surveys, to argue that each copy of the *Post* was read by 3.84 people and that the magazine reached a disproportionate percentage of high-income people (claims backed by advertising agency studies such as the one in Table 6.1). For instance, a group made up of executives, profes-sionals, merchants and shopkeepers, and retired people accounted for 69.62 percent of readers but only 11.89 percent of the population.

Table 6.1   Sample of a Readership Study

In late 1926, Daniel Starch, director of the Department of Research of the American Association of Advertising Agencies, released a readership analysis of 74 magazines. The study was based on personal interviews in 20,000 homes in 37 cities and towns.

According to Curtis Publishing, advertisers looked not at how a magazine's circulation was distributed by class (columns marked % of Circulation below), but rather the percentage of each class that the publication reached. For example, 5.8% of the *Post*'s circulation went to people in class AA, but of all people in class AA, the *Post* reached 50.3%. In this survey, the *Post* reached a larger percentage of homes in the first three classes than any other magazine. It was fifth in group C, eighteenth in D. The *Journal* ranked fourth in group AA, second in A, B, and C, and fourth in D.

"Class" Circulation Breakdown of *Post* and *Journal*, 1926

Class	% of Total	% of Income	% of *Post* Circulation	% Reached by *Post*	% of *Journal* Circulation	% Reached by *Journal*
AA	1.2	7.6	5.8	50.3	2.8	22.1
A	6.6	18.1	20.2	31.3	14.0	19.8
B	46.8	47.8	49.8	10.9	53.5	10.7
C	38.8	24.1	23.3	6.1	27.7	6.7
D	6.6	2.4	0.9	1.3	2.0	2.8

People represented in each group:

Class AA   Incomes of $10,000 and over. Business executives and owners of large businesses, some judges, military officers of higher ranks.

Class A   Incomes of $5,000 to $10,000. Business executives and owners of slightly smaller businesses, judges, military officers, professors at larger universities.

Class B   Incomes of $2,000 to $5,000. Business executives and owners of smaller businesses, department heads and managers, high-grade clerical workers, some skilled workers, some military officers, teachers in the upper salary groups, and professional men.

Class C   Incomes of $1,000 to $2,000. Heads of small businesses, small retailers, skilled and semi-skilled workers, clerical workers, and elementary teachers.

Class D   Incomes of below $1,000. Domestic servants, unskilled laborers.

Sources: "An Analysis of the Occupations and Incomes of the Subscribers and Buyers of Magazines," and "Eastman Circulation Figures," Curtis *Bulletin* 80 (November 12, 1926).

A second group made up of salesmen, skilled trades, office clerical, agriculture, and students accounted for 28.89 percent of readers and 54.55 percent of the population. A third group of public service employees, unskilled labor, and domestic and personal service occupations accounted for only 1.49 percent of readers but 33.56 percent of the population.[60]

The next year, Curtis translated its estimates into consumption, saying that the *Post*'s nearly 3 million copies were read each week by 11.4 million people who ate 239.4 million meals and had 220,000 birthdays and more than 120,000 anniversaries, marriages, or engagements. It prepared for those readers an imaginary meal of oyster stew, rolls, butter, coffee, ice cream, and cake, estimating that it would require 60 million oysters, 11.4 million rolls, 236,000 pounds of butter, 228,000 pounds of coffee, 1.9 million quarts of ice cream, and 570,000 cakes. "Discount this as you will," the company wrote. "It's a market."[61]

The company seemingly saw no hypocrisy in sticking to its claims of an elite readership even after cutting the price of the *Journal* twice in the early 1920s, to nearly half its price of the late 1910s. The second price cut, from $1.50 to $1.10 a year in 1923—a dime more than Curtis had charged in 1890[62]—came as competing magazines had begun to chip away at the *Journal*'s share of the market. Curtis seemed to see the biggest threat coming from *Pictorial Review,* which in 1926 began claiming a circulation larger than the *Journal*'s. Curtis dismissed the claim, but said that even if it were true, the *Journal* was superior because its subscribers paid full price in advance; its circulation was highest in the best markets; the women who read it were leaders in their communities; and it had a history that had endeared it "into the minds and hearts of American women and created for it a confidence in its character that makes" the *Journal* unique and dominant among women's publications. That is, it continued to claim only an elite readership, the type that advertisers most sought.[63]

A Process of Exclusion

When Eastman told the Curtis advertising staff about his survey of magazine readership in 1913, he said he did not have enough money or manpower to conduct a random survey of the country. Instead, he had to define those areas that he thought would yield the most useful information, and he focused the survey "where the magazine-reading classes were," which primarily was "where the buying power of the country lay." The survey takers were instructed to get information about every English-language publication that people read, as well as demographic information about a town or community and about the income group of the readers, from the upper class and upper middle class to the lower middle class ("the common people") and the "lowest class of people that have the magazine-reading habit," excluding such people as "the Slavs and Armenians and the illiterates."[64]

At Curtis, the stated intention for mapping circulation was to help manufacturers determine the potential for their products, but the comparisons were also clearly aimed at helping Curtis magazines maintain their reputation as invaluable sales tools. As such, as in Eastman's survey, there was a common denominator in nearly all of the company's market studies, as well as in its promotional and sales materials: exclusion. Publishers like Curtis were interested in reaching a growing middle class, a middle class that they saw as a homogenous group of white, and usually native-born, Americans whose genetic makeup and inherent abilities were assumed to have allowed them to rise to prosperity. These elites were seen as different and disparate from the lower classes (the "shawl" class, as Parlin called them). Because of that, Curtis rejected from its target audience both blacks and immigrants from Eastern Europe, the type of people that Parlin considered "worthless elements" and that the company considered to have "lowered tastes."[65] At one point, Curtis even tried to make a case that its readers were truly at the top of the evolutionary ladder. "To the illiterate, the slovenly, the foreign-speaking, the shiftless, the improvident, the appeal [of the *Journal*] is of no moment—or, at least, not enough to warrant purchase," the company said in an advertisement in 1912. "Those who can't read, those who won't read, and those who can't afford to read are automatically excluded."[66] (See Figures 6.1 and 6.2.)

Segregation and discrimination were widespread in American business of the time, and they were firmly embedded in the corporate culture of Curtis. The company employed many African Americans in the 1920s, but an employee newsletter showed them holding such jobs as lamp cleaners, snow shovelers, stewards, custodians,

Due to the cost of $2.00 per year

and

because a reader's intelligence
must be higher than a 14-year old
average there are millions of potential radio listeners who are
not reached by The Saturday Evening
Post -

25 PER CENT

14,204,149
FOREIGN BORN

10,951,000
UNEMPLOYED

11,891,143
NEGROES

Figure 6.1   In promoting the "quality" of its readership, Curtis drew on stereotypes of blacks and immigrants, sometimes even using labels like "sub-normal" in referring to their ability to buy consumer products.

or similar positions. Each spring when the company sponsored an annual Curtis Day celebration for its more than 4,000 workers, white employees gathered at the Curtis Country Club in Cheltenham, north of Philadelphia, and were treated to a parade and a circus, part of a full day of festivities. Black employees, dressed in their

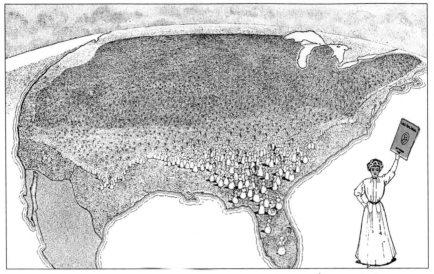

EVERY TENTH WOMAN IN THE UNITED STATES *BUYS* THE LADIES' HOME JOURNAL

Figure 6.2 Curtis portrayed its readers as white, educated, attentive, and well-to-do, characteristics it saw as defining an ideal buying class.

Sunday best, gathered at nearby Willow Grove Park, where they had sack races and watched the company's Negro baseball squad. Through the 1930s, the company's advertising and circulation departments never crossed the color line. African Americans were not included in the company's research into markets and consumer products, and circulation agents were directed away from areas inhabited by blacks and recent immigrants.[67]

A Divisive Mindset

Money, literacy, and education had for years been measures of worth in American society, but the divisiveness of class intensified with the growth of a consumer society at the turn of the century. At the same time that advertisers and publishers sought to tap into and promote a new middle class, they used the methods of social science to exclude and marginalize those who failed to share in the rewards of modern industrial capitalism. "As a whole, the colored peoples have fewer wants, lower standards of living, little material prosperity and are not generally responsive to the same influences as the whites," Curtis Publishing wrote in a primer on using census data in 1914.[68] The next year, Barton W. Currie, a *Country Gentleman* writer and editor, told the advertising staff that to understand the magazine's audience, "we must begin by eliminating the illiterate and peasant type, and the foreign type who do not read English papers."[69]

For the most part, that meant avoiding much of the South, with its large numbers of African Americans and its "shiftless white class." The company backed up its position with its research, saying in 1928, for instance, that Connecticut had a smaller population than South Carolina, but nearly six times the number of income tax returns and five times the bank deposits. New Jersey had less than twice the population of Arkansas but nine times the number of income tax returns and seven times the number of homes with electric lights.[70] And, as I have showed in other research, the *Post* and the *Journal* had far lower circulations in the South than they did in other regions, an analysis that fits with David Nord's finding that working class Southerners in the late nineteenth century spent considerably less on reading material than people who lived in New England and the Middle Atlantic states.[71]

Researchers, who themselves were primarily white and urban, saw consumers as white and urban as well, at least until farmers gained some cachet in the late 1910s and early 1920s, as I have shown in Chapter 5. In estimating the trading populations of important U.S. cities, Parlin and an assistant, Henry Youker, said they had eliminated African Americans from all their counts. "Negroes, of course, buy some dry goods but the elimination of all Negroes about offsets the subnormal portion of both races," they wrote. In the department store study, Parlin wrote of the South, "The large Negro population throughout the section is sub-normal in its purchasing power, and there is also a shiftless white class which is of little value in a mercantile proposition, so that the trading power as compared with that of the northern section, is best represented by the white population only." In a later study of food products, they echoed the Constitution's count of each slave as three-fifths a person, eliminating half of an area's black population in an effort to make "buying power comparable in other sections."[72]

In 1922, the company reiterated its desire to reach "worth-while white families." In developing a market index in 1923, the Advertising Department explained that because among blacks and the foreign-born there was a high percentage of illiteracy "and relatively low average of buying power, it seemed fair to base a market index primarily on native whites; but of the native whites some are ignorant and some lack the means to buy merchandise of their choice. Hence it seemed that perhaps it would be fairest to take one-half of the native whites as an index." In other words, those people who could and did consume regularly were considered among the valuable and the elite. Those who did not, or could not, were considered deficient, unable to improve themselves and their quality of life through spending. The idea was circular: Those who consumed succeeded, and those who succeeded consumed. Those who did not consume were cast aside like the packaging on the new name-brand products.[73]

In Parlin's case, this view that anyone but a white Anglo-Saxon was inferior seems to have come partly from a belief in a genetic and ethnic hierarchy, a common view of the era perpetuated and even promoted by American universities.[74] Parlin once wrote that Jews had an "innate brilliance," while blacks were "naturally indolent,"[75] a view that seemed to be shared by the Curtis advertising and circulation staffs. A Curtis sales superintendent once ridiculed the circulation methods of a competitor because a solicitor for the magazine sought subscribers in African American neighborhoods: "He says that they are not supposed to solicit Negroes, but that some he collects from 'look like Negroes' to him. He refers to Mulattoes who live in the Negro sections, and as you know . . . they are classed as Negroes in every way and are no more intelligent. He could not recall how many of this class he has to visit, but said there are 'a few.' However, these few Mulattoes together with the white trash make up about 75 percent of the subscribers."[76] That line of thinking suggests that even if blacks of the time had been on equal footing with whites economically, the color line would still have run deep. Just as Curtis employees sought to attract an economic elite to the company's magazines, they believed in a white cultural elite that was duty bound to steer the masses toward "proper" behavior and collective salvation.[77]

The tools of inclusion and exclusion that Curtis used in defining consumers were important to the arguments it made. By excluding large segments of the population and by defining the primary audience of consumer products as families instead of individuals, it could create a smaller target audience and increase the percentage of the audience its magazines reached, thereby giving the impression of higher efficiency. That is, by excluding blacks and the foreign-born, it could reduce the U.S. population in the 1910s from about 100 million individuals to about 15 million native-born white families, about 9 million of whom lived in the cities and suburbs—what, in 1914, it considered the "accessible" areas of the country. Curtis then cut that 9 million to 4.6 million by factoring in incomes, saying that advertisers should target families earning $1,000 or more annually.[78]

By defining its target audience and by narrowing the range of people it tried to reach, Curtis used an early form of niche marketing, targeting not the whole of the population but only those most likely to buy a product. A market, in Curtis's terms, was only a fraction of the entire population. "The job is to find out how large that minority is—and how to reach that fraction without wasting money and effort on the unavailable majority," the company wrote in its house organ in 1914. In marketing a product, it urged manufacturers to ask themselves three questions: How many people could use the product? How many of those people could afford to buy the product? How many of those people could profitably be reached by both advertising and mass distribution? "No product can support intensive selling effort in every nook and cranny of the nation," the company said. "The expense would be prohibitive. The problem is to determine what to reject—what classes of the population, what geographical sections, what avenues of trade—then to concentrate selling effort on the rest. This demands, above all, careful study of the population figures."[79]

Reconsidering Immigrants

Although the company did not include recent immigrants in the same class as native-born Americans in the 1910s, 1920s, and 1930s, its perception of immigrants changed considerably in the early 1920s after the Division of Commercial Research made a study of the Pilsen district of Chicago. Parlin described the Pilsen area as populated by Bohemians, Poles, Magyars, Swedes, and other nationalities, "each with a racial consciousness. This district is not only foreign itself; it is surrounded by districts only less foreign than itself." The company sold few magazines in the area, yet the researchers found that Pilsen residents bought just as many nationally advertised canned goods as did residents of such affluent areas as Jackson Park and Evanston.

That discovery was initially startling, but Parlin and his associates formulated a theory to explain it. They reasoned that immigrants first shopped at stores that stocked products from their home countries, but then gravitated toward branded goods to make themselves feel more American. Word about advertised products spread by word of mouth through the streets, Parlin wrote. Someone in a neighborhood might read a magazine and then pass information on to a friend. Or a child or an acquaintance might work in another section of town and bring back news about products they had seen others use. "Upon the mind of the American, accustomed every hour to learn from the printed page, the manufacturer's message quickly registers an impression. Upon the mind of the laborer, accustomed to heeding only verbal orders, the spoken word is potent," Parlin said. "The foreign laborer is trained to heed what people say. He buys, for the most part, what someone tells him to buy. The advertising medium that reaches him is the spoken recommendation of his neighbors."[80]

The important observation, regardless of the explanation, was that immigrants did indeed buy. The people in the foreign districts were still discounted to a great degree, defined in disparaging terms, in part because they did not read Curtis magazines. They could not be valued nearly as much as those in the affluent sections of town who were loyal subscribers. The old biases and fears about foreigners did not disappear when Curtis Publishing discovered that they actually bought consumer goods, but in the eyes of Parlin and his associates, immigrants were seen in a slightly better light. They consumed, and better yet, they consumed advertised goods. That, in Curtis's view, made them a little less foreign and a little more American.

Elevating Women

Even as Curtis marginalized African Americans and immigrants, it tried to elevate the importance of women. As publisher of the country's leading women's magazine, it sought to establish women as the decision makers in the purchasing of everything from women's and men's clothing to food and automobiles.[81] Parlin noted that the modern department store catered to women and that many women "have come to consider the spending of money not as a privilege, but as a serious economic duty worthy of careful thought and effort." Most women were discriminating shoppers who constantly compared goods to find the best value. The way women shopped for various goods had a tremendous effect on the dynamics of the marketplace, he wrote, and manufacturers needed to take note.[82]

Women, because of the influence they held over personal and family purchases, held positions of economic power in a consumer society. A man, on the other hand, was portrayed as "notoriously a poor buyer of personal things" and "too easy to please." Men were seen as more likely to buy only things they needed and then only from familiar and usually convenient places that allowed them to make their purchases quickly. Women, on the other hand, were considered better judges of merchandise, especially clothing. They asked for advertised brands and had "a distinct loyalty to brands which they have found satisfactory."[83]

Curtis used such portrayals to stress the importance of advertising in the *Journal*. "The *Journal*'s advocacy of great public and social movements, its brilliant interpretation of passing events, its whole constructive service to American womanhood, have automatically drawn to it the women who think, the fine, up-to-date women who take responsibilities and exercise them effectively," the company said in an advertisement in 1915. Similarly, Parlin noted in 1920,

World War I had helped break down social barriers that had held women back from business and industry, and the *Public Ledger* needed to do more to win the support of female readers. "This is a formative period in woman's thought," he wrote. "While woman's interests are expanding from the purely domestic to a national and worldwide vision there is a chance, such as never before, presented to the newspapers of the country to win a new clientele of serious readers."[84]

Men were hardly irrelevant, though. In fact, Parlin said that automobiles, whose advertising created a solid, growing core of *Post* advertising, had turned men into shoppers for the first time. The high cost of automobiles, he said, forced men to look more closely at the product they were buying, rather than simply turning the decision over to their wives as they often did. He portrayed automobile buyers as both savvy and extravagant. By the early 1910s, he said, they had some experience with mechanical equipment and were not as easy to fool as they had been when cars were first sold more than a decade earlier. Even so, they were willing to spend hundreds and even thousands of dollars for a machine they did not really need. That is where research came in. Parlin said the goal of commercial research was to find the "underlying principles on which merchandising is founded." To do that, researchers needed to study "the psychology of the consumer," or the "philosophy of buying."[85]

Parlin and his staff built on that thinking through the 1910s and 1920s and began to focus not just on defining consumers but on helping advertisers *find* them. As many businesses struggled in the early 1920s, Curtis began promoting a sales method that it said would make companies more productive and more efficient as they moved into the national marketplace. And yet, even as Curtis helped its customers look outward, it decided that the best way to do that was by looking inward—at its own audiences.

7

Chasing the Consumer,
Protecting the Company

As the United States economy started moving out of a post war depression in the early 1920s, Charles Coolidge Parlin predicted good times ahead. Bank transactions reached near-record levels in 1923. Railroads were hauling record numbers of freight cars. Cities were building houses, office towers, and roads. Farming was starting to bounce back after two difficult years. The number of income tax returns more than doubled between 1917 and 1921. Advertising revenue was growing healthily. The number of high school students had increased by a factor of five since 1890. More education meant that more workers had an ability to earn higher salaries (and, indeed, employment and wages were up, he said). It also meant the country had more people interested in reading, which, he said, turned them into more discriminating buyers. All that would lead to more customers for American business in the 1920s, Parlin claimed.

The question was, how could businesses find those customers reliably? The U.S. marketplace had truly become national, Parlin said, and a manufacturer could no longer circulate its goods in the Northeast and claim to "cover America." If it did, it was missing out on millions of dollars in potential sales. Neither could companies that wanted to increase sales simply place advertisements, throw their products out indiscriminately, and expect revenues to grow. They had to know whom they were selling to and where to send their sales representatives. Those who did not were simply wasting their money.[1]

Parlin's message resonated at a time when "efficiency" had become a prime goal of American business. For years, businesses had grappled with ways to find and keep customers. And yet, that pursuit of the customer took on a new urgency in the 1920s as the United States heartily embraced a modern consumer economy and companies jostled in an increasingly crowded marketplace to sell ever more consumer products. After World War I ended, American business saw just how fragile America's new consumer-oriented economy could be. A sudden and continuing drop in demand for consumer products from the summer of 1920 until the spring of 1922 was the first prolonged depression that businesses had faced since the early 1890s, and mass marketers and large industrial corporations were caught by surprise. The Armour family lost control of its meat packing business. Julius Rosenwald saved Sears, Roebuck and Company from defaulting on payments to suppliers by infusing the business with money from the family fortune. General Motors was forced to write down the value of its inventory by more than $83 million in 1921 and 1922. Magazines such as *Collier's, Everybody's,* and *Scientific American* lost two-thirds or more of their advertising lineage. Curtis Publishing fared better but still saw its annual revenues fall by one-fourth between 1920 and 1921, from $50 million to $38 million.[2]

The depression jarred businesses into recognizing the need for better economic indicators, a better means of forecasting demand and, in turn, stabilizing the capitalist business system. One of the central means they used was market research, which spread like wildfire through government, business, and academia. By the mid-1920s, the J. Walter Thompson advertising agency, which had one of the most sophisticated operations of the era, was conducting up to eighteen research projects a month.[3] The federal government, which had long been the source of statistics about society, trade, and business, redoubled its efforts in the 1920s, publishing a long-sought-after census of distribution from 1929 to 1932, and emphasizing its role in "fact engineering."[4] After World War I, the United States finally began "to realize the importance of knowing something about the vast field of merchandising," Parlin said in 1931.[5] As one manufacturer noted, research "is in the air. Everyone is being investigated."[6]

A Shift in Focus

This abundance of research and information about the marketplace allowed Curtis Publishing to change the emphasis of its research work in the 1920s. Although the Division of Commercial Research continued to investigate industries on a broad scale—it updated its studies of automobiles and department stores, for instance, and undertook extensive studies of Prohibition and the radio and airline industries—it increasingly turned its efforts to helping businesses increase sales by pointing them to the "right" areas. In doing so, it tried to align itself with companies and salesmen around the United States by holding out its detailed analysis of circulation, census data, and other statistics as a means of identifying markets ripe for selling. For instance, Parlin and his colleagues spent several years analyzing major cities block by block, issuing color-coded maps that identified areas with the highest incomes, the highest property values, and the largest concentration of Curtis publication sales—the homes most able and likely to buy an increasing array of consumer products. It also began issuing yearly reports on the volume and makeup of advertisers in the *Post,* the *Journal,* and *Country Gentleman,* attempting to show that the largest advertisers achieved the greatest success. Those efforts, which consumed much of the energies of the Division of Commercial Research in the mid-1920s and into the 1930s, reflected a subtle shift that grew more dramatic in the 1940s. That is, the division began to pull back from broad investigations of industry and marketplace and to concentrate on the promotion, positioning, and reinforcement of Curtis publications. Parlin and his staff continued their original mission of analyzing trade and commerce, but they also worked their way into the public relations business. Increasingly, Commercial Research became not only a creator of market research, but the company's chief means of marketing.

The reasons behind that shift lay partly in the increasingly competitive media marketplace of the 1920s. Although no magazine came close to matching the *Post*'s circulation or advertising revenues in the 1920s and early 1930s, the *Journal* increasingly lost market share to such publications as *Good Housekeeping, Woman's Home Companion,* and *McCall's,* especially after Edward Bok stepped down as the *Journal*'s editor in 1920. Competition came from other media as well. Newspapers pulled in a shrinking but still dominant share of national advertising in the 1920s, and radio began to attract the attention and the imagination of consumer goods manufacturers, who lavished large amounts of money on their own programming. That created a challenge for Curtis Publishing, which increasingly used both quantitative and qualitative analysis to promote and defend magazine advertising, to bolster the move toward branded products, and to position its magazines as the premiere media for reaching the consuming public. Even as it liberally dispensed advice about the nature of the marketplace and the techniques of selling, though, the Division of Commercial Research began concentrating its efforts on the workings of its most important customer: Curtis Publishing Company.

In Defense of Advertising

The advertising that formed the backbone of Curtis's publishing empire had long had critics. Many businesses rebelled against the idea of spending tens or hundreds of thousands of dollars to promote their products in national magazines. Many retailers doubted that magazine ads intended for a national audience helped bring in their local customers. And, as Charles McGovern shows, during the Great Depression consumer groups became increasingly vocal and even called for federal laws to ensure the veracity of advertising.[7] The magazine and advertising industries fought back, of course, and at Curtis, the job of defending advertising often fell to Parlin. Although he was not the only person to act as spokesman for Curtis Publishing, he was perhaps the most thoughtful and the most articulate. His booming voice played well in convention halls, and as he interpreted various aspects of the Curtis operation, he used his debating skills to build an argument that drew a generally favorable response in the business world.

Elements of that argument changed slightly during his twenty-six years at Curtis Publishing, but the core message and the central philosophy stayed essentially the same. It went something like this: Advertising was a form of education, a means for manufacturers to inform people about their products—information that consumers wanted to know and needed to know to make their lives better. "If we believe in education, we must believe in advertising, for advertising only gives information to people," Parlin wrote in 1926. Such "education" worked in conjunction with old-fashioned word-of-mouth publicity: friends, neighbors, and family members recommending products to one another. Advertising could do something that word-of-mouth publicity could not, though: It could reach millions of people at the same time, and it could repeat the manufacturer's message week after week.

Advertising was, in effect, a form of religion. It was "the great force that goes out to prepare the market." Like the Gospel, it could be continually repeated, reinforcing people's belief in a product they had purchased. In a marketplace that relied on repeat sales, that was as important as winning over—converting—new customers. "You know that the most important thing for any manufacturer is to hold the market he has; the hardest market to sell is the market a man has once had and then lost, so that it is of supreme importance to keep sold those people who are users of your product," Parlin told a group of perfume makers in 1921.[8]

Parlin told companies that one of the big benefits of advertising was the pride it instilled in employees. In 1924, he gave ice cream manufacturers this step-by-step list on how to do that: say the words of the advertising copy; study the message; put a copy in a prominent place in the factory; and tell workers that their labors must match the rhetoric. "In that way you will get help out of your own organization to make your product better without additional expense to yourself," Parlin said. "Out of that cooperation you will build your business."[9] In Curtis's case, the same line of thinking held true with its sales formulas. They not only assisted advertisers, but they became a means of promoting Curtis as an authority on the marketplace and as a company that depended upon the knowledge of its employees.

Consumption and Progress

Parlin built his philosophy of buying on the idea that people were constantly looking for a reason to purchase more goods to better themselves—to progress, in other words. They made major purchases, though, only when they were sure that prices would not go lower. They would not buy a new automobile if they were sure the dealer would drop prices in a few months. They would not buy new clothes if they were sure that a department store would soon have a sale. "People do not buy on declining prices," Parlin said. "They only buy when there is a degree of stability or an upward turn of the market which gives them reason to believe that nothing will be gained by waiting longer, and that they might as well buy and cover themselves at the existing price." He likewise saw mass psychology at work in trends in the housing market. "Somebody decides that the time has come for him to build and he starts to build, and his neighbor who has long had building plans in his pocket, decides he will build, and so on. Out of that you are apt to get sooner or later a mass movement leading to a very considerable building program."[10]

In Parlin's view of advertising and marketing, the consumer was malleable, but certainly not stupid. The advertised product was doomed if it did not live up to its claims. That is, an advertised product, because of the increased attention it received, had to be of superior quality. Parlin liked to tell the story of the man who made pies of cheap ingredients and then advertised them as the best pies in the land. When swarms of people showed up at his door, he hung out a sign saying he was sold out, even though he had not sold a one, because he knew that his pies were of poor quality and that he could fool the public only once. "It is too dangerous to advertise shoddy merchandise," Parlin said. "The light of publicity would focus attention on the poor merchandise and the brand would enable consumers to avoid it." Only "by winning recognition for his quality can a quality manufacturer hope to maintain his markets."[11]

Two Cultures

In articulating a philosophy of advertising, Parlin sought to place the values of the new consumer culture on equal footing with those of a producer culture. Both valued saving, ambition, and hard work. The only difference, in Parlin's view, was that workers of the twentieth century applied their savings to products that would improve life and thus keep people working to sustain the things they valued. "Who would be bold enough to say that life is not better worth living when a man gets an ambition to possess an automobile or a talking machine or a radio or a vacuum cleaner, and applies the energies that may be necessary to earn the thing he desires?" Parlin asked "That the desire for these things has not impoverished the country can be readily demonstrated by the vast increase in wealth in individual deposits in the bank. That it has not seriously diverted funds from worthwhile things of the older type may be demonstrated by the great increase of students in our colleges and high schools."[12]

The logic in that argument, if not sound, was at least consistent with other circular arguments that Parlin made about advertising, and indicated deep confidence in the Darwinian notion of natural selection applied to a capitalist economy. In 1926, when a critic challenged his unabashed optimism about advertising, Parlin answered mostly with facts and figures. If manufacturers were "lukewarm" about advertising, he asked, why had spending on advertising risen from $30 million to $130 million between 1915 and 1925? If manufacturers were skeptical about the *Post,* then why did nearly half of all advertising revenue in the thirty-two leading publications go to the *Post*? Parlin was not above dismissing research, though, if it fit his need. He brushed aside two laboratory studies that purported to show that the more pages a publication had, the less effective its advertising was, saying that the power of Curtis magazines "have thus far eluded laboratory tests. Twenty-five years of consistent editorial policy which wins the confidence of the American public and which causes its pages to wield editorial influence and to build markets for advertisers builds something into a publication that cannot be measured by a line rule or judged by the ease with which a magazine is handled."[13]

By 1929, Parlin and his colleagues had even come up with a formula for determining the power of advertising: "Power or Force in advertising equals Size of Space times Circulation times Number of Appearances."[14] In other words, success could not be criticized.

Chasing the Consumer

Even as Parlin and Curtis Publishing staunchly defended advertising, they made it clear that advertising was only part of a much larger picture. Advertising, in Parlin's view, could be used to encourage consumers to take that important first step and ask for a specific product. Under this idea of pulling the consumer, the reasoning went, manufacturers could change attitude and behavior if they would advertise their products persistently. Advertising alone could *prepare* a market, Curtis argued, but advertising alone could not *sell* a market. That was up to manufacturers, salesmen, and retailers. Consumers needed to be sold on new products, of course, but so did retailers. If the products were not stocked on store shelves, no amount of advertising, no means of promotion could sell more consumer goods. So Curtis encouraged salesmen to use the sales pitches made in advertisements in the *Post,* the *Journal,* or *Country Gentlemen* to sway retailers to stock products. "Around every insertion build a sales story," the company advised in 1922. "The more capable the man the more strongly your advertising story will appeal to him."[15]

Curtis did far more than just promote the idea of "educating" retailers and consumers. In the 1920s, it created a sales tool based on its portrayal of readers as loyal consumers. This tool took the form of a series of statistical books intended to help businesses home in on the areas that held the most sales potential and that helped them set sales goals for those areas. The intent was threefold: to provide a service that would lure and keep advertisers by emphasizing Curtis's expertise in the consumer market; to remind advertisers of the reach and the audience of the Curtis magazines; and to portray Curtis advertising as clusters of local advertising that could compete against newspapers, rather than as something with a distant, national scattershot delivery.

In 1920, the company issued the first of its *Curtis Circulation* books, in which it broke down its circulation figures into increasingly smaller units of analysis. That first book, based on circulation data from 1919, was little more than a listing of magazine circulation by states, counties, and cities, and by number of subscription copies and direct-sale copies, along with population figures for all U.S. counties and for cities of various sizes. The intent seemed little more than to put Curtis on record as having updated and printed its circulation records, emphasizing to advertisers and agencies the honesty and accuracy of its readership claims.[16]

In 1921 the company went into much more detail and for the first time held up the distribution of Curtis magazines as a tool for measuring sales goals of consumer products. In that book, it listed for each state the number of personal income tax returns for individuals with incomes of more than $1,000, the combined circulation for all three Curtis magazines, and the combined cost of one black and white page of advertising, "distributed among the states in proportion to the circulation within each state."[17] The company plotted its circulation on a national map, shading large areas, including New England, the Middle Atlantic states, the Midwest, Texas and Oklahoma, and the Pacific Coast states. The Rocky Mountain states were excluded, as was the South, because the company had comparatively little circulation in those areas.

Curtis said the shaded area accounted for 59 percent of the states, 74 percent of the population of the country, 86 percent of income tax returns, and 81 percent of its magazine circulation. It also said that in the shaded area could be found large percentages of everything from drugstores to automobile registrations to department store sales—all things intended to correlate Curtis readers with consumption. "Where total Curtis Circulation is high in proportion to population it is safe to assume surplus sales opportunity," the company wrote, "and conversely, where total Curtis Circulation is low in proportion to population, it is a fair indication that the community is subnormal in its purchasing power."[18]

Experimentation and Rejection

Under Parlin's leadership, the company had tried unsuccessfully for more than a year to create an index of sales potential based on such statistics as population, income tax returns, and automobile registrations. At one point, it thought it had found an answer in taking one-half of the native white population of an area as a trade index. It abandoned that idea after company executives decided it was too complex, and that company representatives would have to continually explain how they had arrived at their calculations. It decided that the number of income tax returns in an area was ineffective as well, because it did not account for variances in cost of living. For instance, someone with a $2,000 salary in a small Illinois town could afford far more luxuries than a person making the same amount in Chicago. It argued that an index based on the number of automobiles emphasized rural areas over urban areas because rural residents considered automobiles necessities, while those in urban areas often did not need cars.[19]

After discarding each of those measures as flawed, Parlin and his staff settled on using Curtis circulation. It was an imperfect measure, they admitted, but it nonetheless offered a starting point for companies that had no other measure of current sales territories or had no means to judge the potential of new territory. Its simplicity was another strong point. By beginning with Curtis sales figures and taking into account such factors as a company's sales from previous years, the ability of its sales staff, and the general economic conditions of an area, a company could determine the sales potential of its product, the Curtis staff reasoned. "In the end, the answer for the sales organization has not been arrived at by a purely statistical method, but it is a specific basis arrived at by common sense judgment, which is always a safer and saner thing upon which to build a market," Parlin said.[20]

In 1922, Curtis cast aside any public doubts about the sales guide and declared that its circulation "parallels sales opportunity. It furnishes a measuring rod by which a manufacturer may determine his sales opportunity." By using the information in *Curtis Circulation,* the company said, a manufacturer could "judge the adequacy of his own distribution." The company, for the first time, offered extensive advice to salesmen of consumer products, telling them that their two primary problems were getting a new line introduced and gaining better cooperation from merchants. In effect, Curtis was proclaiming itself *the* authority on the consumer marketplace, and by trying to strengthen the link between advertising and sales, it furthered its own cause by suggesting that salesmen use the *Post* and the *Journal* as textbooks.[21] (See Figures 7.1 and 7.2.)

Curtis grew so confident in its approach that at one point, when automobile statistics it had bought for *Sales Quotas* were found to be incorrect, it said the error did not matter. Rather, it only reinforced its assertion that Curtis circulation was a more reliable predictor of sales than any other statistic. "The more inaccurate any other line of statistics is shown to be the less possible it becomes as a market index and by comparison the better is Curtis Circulation," the company told its employees in 1923.[22]

Testimonials that Curtis solicited from several businesses indicated that its sales system could work quite well. In one case, it said that the Bradley Knitting Company had increased its sales volume by nearly a million dollars by using the Curtis quota plan. "Probably the most important feature of the whole quota scheme is the effect on the morale of the sales organization," Bradley's general manager, Bradley Tyrell, wrote in a letter that Curtis solicited in 1924. The Corona Typewriter Company called *Post* circulation "perfect distribution," when compared with potential Corona customers. Another company that Curtis identified only as "the oldest and most outstanding manufacturer in a particular industry" said it was at first doubtful of using Curtis's plan because it saw no correlation between magazine circulation and its product. After trying Curtis's quota

Figure 7.1 Ads for *Ladies' Home Journal* and other Curtis publications emphasized the magazines' appeal in "worth-while homes," meaning those that were owned by whites who had money to spend on consumer products.

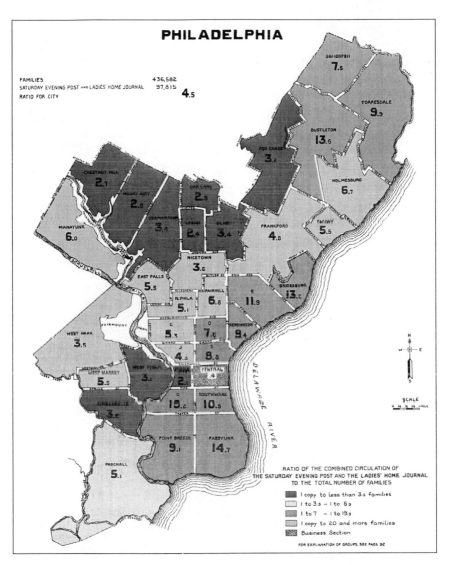

Figure 7.2 In the 1920s, Curtis began promoting the combined circulation of its magazines as a means of finding buyers of consumer products. Maps such as this one of Philadelphia delineated sections of cities by zones. The darkest areas (what the company sometimes called the Red Zone) had the highest readership rates for Curtis magazines and thus, the company argued, manufacturers would have the best luck selling new consumer products there.

system, though, it called the approach "an absolutely reliable index figure." In another case, Curtis even accompanied a business's salesmen into the field, showing them how to use the quota books and reporting sales that far exceeded the manufacturer's expectations.[23]

By 1925, more than fifty manufacturers had set sales quotas based on circulation of Curtis magazines. By mid-1927, that number had risen to 321 companies, including Log Cabin Products, Parker Pen, Carnation Milk Products, Swift & Company, the Home Appliance Corporation, Coleman Lamp, the Moline Chemical Company, Corona Typewriter, Apco Manufacturing, and Lever Brothers. The company continued to publish these types of sales guides into the early 1960s.[24]

Chasing the Competition

In issuing its books on circulation and population, Curtis was playing catch-up, of sorts, with such competitors as *Woman's World* (which guaranteed that it could, with "mathematical certainty," show advertisers how to better reach the farm market)[25] and with such advertising agencies as J. Walter Thompson (which had challenged publications in 1914 to issue just such information). As early as 1904, Thompson had compiled a list of towns over 2,500 population so that a client could see how much sales territory he had covered. In 1912, the company repackaged census figures in *Population and Its Distribution,* a book it updated several times in the ensuing two decades. It urged its clients to set sales quotas based on the information the book provided about such things as state-by-state population and location of retail stores. "Today the biggest word in the Dictionary of Selling is Quota," the company wrote. "How much business should a given salesman or territory produce? Find the answer—fix the quota—and your first big step toward increased sales is taken." In 1922, the company offered a $1,500 prize to anyone who could move beyond mere population figures and create an index of purchasing power for communities around the country, saying that "an accurate knowledge of markets for products is fundamental in the formulation of business policies."[26]

The idea behind that index and the other sales and quota measures put forth by Thompson, Curtis, and organizations like The 100,000 Group of American Cities[27] was to help—and attract—customers, but there was a certain amount of prestige involved, with various advertising agencies and publications vying to become the definitive authority on consumer sales. As competition among publications and other businesses grew, companies strove to set themselves and their products apart from the pack. Just as important, many companies were, for the first time, bypassing wholesalers and jobbers and taking their products directly to retailers. Having no sales experience, they were essentially starting from scratch with retail sales. They did not know territories, they did not know techniques, and they did not know what to expect in the national marketplace. That national market was too broad and too obscure to work effectively as a whole. The only way to confront such a large market was to break it into smaller markets that could be worked aggressively with sales and distribution strategies. So the broad national markets came to be seen as a collection of local markets, and that is how Curtis portrayed its information about them—a change in initiative and strategy that the company said had helped the Curtis staff target its advertising sales efforts much more specifically.

Curtis had another important reason for producing materials to help salespersons: self-defense. Advertising was important for opening doors, or as Parlin said, "the power to build a market opportunity." If a sales force did not pursue its market aggressively and follow up on the advertising, though, advertising would fail. "Whether that opportunity will be gathered in or not depends upon the efficiency of the sales forces, upon whom devolves the problem of selling it." He gave the example of two companies that bought the same amount of space in the *Post*. One, he said, had become the leader in its industry; the other had gone into in bankruptcy. "So far as we know, the only real difference in those two firms was that in one case the sales organization went ahead aggressively to sell the advertising, and in the other case the firm left it to the advertising to sell the goods for them."[28] Such assertions offered an important hedge against the critics of advertising. When a product failed, advertising—and in turn, the Curtis magazines—could not be fully blamed. That hedge offered representatives the ability to continue to sell more and more advertising because blame for failure could always be placed elsewhere.

Concern About Newspapers

Because of its size and success, Curtis Publishing saw itself as *the* purveyor of a mass market. The *Post,* certainly, reached more people than any other single publication in the 1920s and 1930s, and yet more and more national advertisers were drawn to newspapers' ability to reach people in their local markets. At the turn of the twentieth century, magazines accounted for about 60 percent of national advertising, but by World War I the figure had dropped to about 50 percent, and it moved even lower as newspapers and radio flexed their muscle in the ensuing years.[29] By 1929, newspapers' share of national advertising had risen to about 54 percent, compared with 42 percent for magazines and 4 percent for radio. Ten years later, the advertising split among the three media had shifted even more, with 37.7 percent of national advertising going to newspapers, 35 percent to magazines and 27.3 percent to radio.[30] (See Table 7.1.)

As Curtis began to feel the pinch of competition, it shifted the way it portrayed its audiences. In the early 1910s, it had represented the enormity of its magazine circulation in pictorial form, showing that the circulation of one issue of the *Journal* would create three stacks as high as Mount Shasta. In the 1920s, it moved away from that idea of a voluminous national market and instead portrayed its

Table 7.1   Where Advertisers Spent Their Money

	Percentage of Total Spending on Each Medium				
	1900	WWI	1929	1935	1939
Newspapers	40	50	54	50	37.7
Magazines	60	50	42	35.5	35
Radio	—	—	4	14.5	27.3

Source: Edwin Emery and Henry Ladd Smith, *The Press and America* (Englewood Cliffs, NJ: Prentice-Hall, 1954), 402, 660, 666.

magazine circulation as an unprecedented collection of local markets. Advertising in Curtis magazines, the company said, was "local advertising conducted *simultaneously* in every city and in every county of the United States. But it is more than local advertising, for it carries into each locality the consciousness of the national prestige of the manufacturer's merchandise. . . . Curtis Publications therefore . . . are powerful national media, because they are universal local media."[31]

The logic behind that strategy is easily seen in a testimonial from a Procter & Gamble salesman, who was a loyal user of Curtis's *Sales Opportunities* as he went about pitching such products as Ivory soap and Crisco shortening. "I never use the term 'national' when I speak of our magazine advertising," the salesman wrote in the P&G house organ in 1926. "I think that the word 'local' is much better." He said the dealer was interested only in his own customers, between 50 and 250 housewives who bought products from him regularly. "Why, then," the P&G salesman asked, "should I tell him how we are trying to reach the other one hundred and ten million? He doesn't care. Why should he? They don't bring any profit into his pockets, do they?" But, the salesman wrote, by showing a dealer how many customers in his area read Curtis publications—and, by extension, the advertising for the nationally branded products in his store—the dealer would definitely take notice. "Believe me, the dealer will forget about his dinner or the baseball score if you can show him that we are spending money to tell the housewives in his own town—his own customers—about the soap he buys from us to sell to these customers."[32]

The next year, Curtis distributed another testimonial it said proved the *Post* superior to newspapers. In that testimonial, the president of an unidentified Curtis advertiser said that the reason his firm advertised in the *Post* and only the *Post* was that newspaper advertising was too expensive. Newspapers could generate short-term sales, but that would only create animosity among salesmen and jobbers after that increase inevitably subsided. He also cited the case of a Buffalo drug jobber who did more than twice as much business in the smaller towns around Buffalo than he did in Buffalo itself. That was not unusual, the official said, and that was a prime reason for sticking with the *Post*. "The great problem of any advertiser is to get people to ask for his product. That is difficult enough under the most favorable circumstances. Our chances of creating good customers among a thousand *Post* readers are several times as good as they would be among a thousand newspaper readers."[33]

What Curtis did not mention was that even as it attempted to discount the effectiveness of newspaper advertising, it used newspaper advertising extensively in its campaigns to attract new readers. In the 1920s, the company routinely spent $75,000 to $100,000 each month advertising its three magazines in newspapers around the country. Even as it tried to diminish their importance in national advertising, the company again and again gave newspapers the ultimate vote of confidence: It gave them money.[34]

Success and Concern

Throughout the 1920s, the *Post* and the *Journal* ranked first and second in advertising revenue among all American magazines, and combined, its magazines accounted for more than 40 percent of the magazine revenue generated by up to seventy competing publications. (See Tables 7.2, 7.3, and 7.4.) In 1923, the company reported that gross ad revenue for the *Post,* the *Journal,* and *Country Gentleman* had reached $50,948,513, a gain of 21.8 percent over 1922. By 1927, advertising revenue for the *Post* alone surpassed $53 million. That was more than the magazine's combined advertising revenue from 1897 to 1914. For the three Curtis magazines that year, advertising revenue exceeded $70 million for the first time.[35] In 1924, *Post* and *Journal* circulation stood at 2,500,000 each, and *Country Gentleman* circulation hovered at 900,000. By 1929, *Post* circulation had exceeded 3 million for some issues, *Journal* circulation was still about 2.5 million, and *Country Gentleman* circulation had exceeded 1.6 million.[36]

Despite its grand successes, Curtis began to see its dominance of the magazine field, especially the women's field, weaken during the 1920s. In 1921, the *Journal* accounted for 40 percent of the advertis-

Table 7.2   Ad Revenues for *Saturday Evening Post, Ladies' Home Journal,* and Nearest Competitors

Year	Competitor	Ad Revenue ($)
1911	*Post*	5,635,342
	Total for 7 other weeklies*	1,886,389
	Journal	2,082,142
	Total for 12 other women's magazines**	4,733,494
1915	*Post*	8,523,836
	Total for 7 other weeklies*	3,194,139
	Journal	2,342,296
	Total for 10 other women's magazines**	4,870,608
1921	*Post*	25,404,687
	Journal	10,370,829
	Literary Digest	7,414,518
1924	*Post*	39,935,825
	Journal	13,657,392
	Literary Digest	7,800,000
1927	*Post*	53,144,987
	Journal	16,627,363
	Good Housekeeping	8,977,705
1928	*Post*	48,661,580
	Journal	16,617,968
	Good Housekeeping	10,124,643
1931	*Post*	35,942,312
	Journal	12,861,530
	Good Housekeeping	9,587,391

Collier's, Life, Literary Digest, Outlook, Every Week, Leslie's, Youth's Companion, Christian Herald.

**Butterick Quarterly, Delineator, Good Housekeeping, Housekeeper* (1911), *Ladies' World, McCall's, Pictorial Review, Quarterly Style Book* (1911), *Woman's Home Companion, Woman's World, Designer, Woman's Magazine.*

Sources: *Leading Advertisers—1932;* "Summary of Lines and Revenue from 1892 to Date," Curtis *Bulletin* 35 (Dec. 26, 1923); "Leading Advertisers, 1911–1916."

ing revenue generated by the six leading women's magazines. By 1930, that amount had slipped to 26.5 percent, and by 1933 had dropped to 23 percent. *Country Gentleman,* despite its top-ranked circulation and advertising revenue among farm publications, achieved only sporadic profitability. And the *Post,* though easily in a class by itself in both circulation and advertising, was increasingly threatened by radio and newspapers in the late 1920s. Its revenue stalled in 1928, rose again in 1929, and then plunged in the Depression.[37]

Table 7.3   Ranking of Selected Magazines by Advertising Income, 1915–1930

	'15	'16	'17	'18	'19	'20	'21	'22	'23	'24	'25	'26	'27	'28	'29	'30
*Post	1	1	1	1	1	1	1	1	1	1	1	1	1	1	1	1
Journal	2	2	2	2	2	3	2	2	2	2	2	2	2	2	2	2
*Literary Digest	4	4	4	3	3	2	3	3	3	3	3	3	4	6	5	7
*Collier's	3	3	3	4	5	6	12	18	17	14	14	13	14	12	7	5
Pictorial Review	7	5	5	5	4	4	5	4	4	4	6	6	7	8	8	8
Woman's Home Companion	6	7	6	6	6	5	4	5	5	5	4	5	5	4	4	4
American	32	24	16	9	9	7	6	6	6	6	7	7	8	9	10	11
Good Housekeeping	19	11	12	11	11	10	7	7	7	7	5	4	3	3	3	3
McCall's	11	14	14	12	12	13	10	8	8	8	8	8	9	7	6	6
Country Gentleman	13	13	9	7	7	8	8	9	9	9	11	11	10	10	11	13
Delineator	8	9	8	10	13	12	11	10	11	10	12	14	12	11	12	9
Cosmopolitan	5	6	7	15	14	14	13	11	12	12	9	10	11	13	13	12
Vogue	9	8	11	17	15	15	14	12	10	11	10	12	13	14	15	15
Farm Journal	18	19	18	13	10	11	16	13	14	15	15	17	18	19	24	26
Successful Farming	14	12	13	33	18	17	17	14	13	13	16	16	16	18	22	23
Redbook	54	53	49	16	17	18	16	15	15	18	20	20	20	22	28	34
Popular Mechanics	16	10	10	37	31	27	23	16	20	20	22	21	21	20	25	27
National Geographic	—	33	31	22	21	21	21	17	16	17	18	18	17	16	18	21
Woman's World	12	17	17	22	21	21	21	20	21	22	21	22	22	24	31	29
*Liberty	—	—	—	—	—	—	—	—	—	32	13	9	6	5	9	10
True Story	—	—	—	—	—	—	—	—	—	—	—	—	—	—	14	14
*Time	—	—	—	—	—	—	—	—	—	—	—	—	—	—	23	16
*Better H&G	—	—	—	—	—	—	—	—	—	—	—	—	—	—	16	17
*New Yorker	—	—	—	—	—	—	—	—	—	—	—	—	24	23	20	20
Household	—	—	—	—	—	—	—	—	—	—	—	—	—	—	26	24
Harper's Bazaar	38	23	24	23	30	26	25	23	22	19	19	19	19	17	19	19
House & Garden	63	63	60	60	60	56	35	25	18	16	17	15	15	15	17	18
Life	22	25	30	29	24	20	24	33	35	37	36	35	35	—	—	—

*Asterisk denotes weekly. Underlining denotes Curtis magazines.

Sources: Leading Advertisers—1932; Curtis "Dope Book"; Leading Advertisers, 1911–1916; Leading Advertisers, 1917; "The Advertising Department," Curtis Bulletin 25 (May 23, 1923).

Even as the Curtis magazines had their ups and downs, though, Commercial Research seemed only to grow. Few of the financial and operational records from Commercial Research have survived, but the available material shows a considerable growth in both size and status within the company. In 1915, the staff of Commercial

Table 7.4   *Post*'s and *Journal*'s Shares of Advertising Expenditures among Comparable Magazines, 1915–1922

Post, Relative to Other Weekly Magazines				
	Post		All Other Weeklies	
Year	Advertising Revenue ($)	% of Total	Advertising Revenue ($)	% of Total
1911	5,635,342	75.0	1,886,389	25.0
1912	7,168,730	76.0	2,259,376	24.0
1913	8,191,934	78.0	2,271,740	22.0
1914	8,389,032	77.6	2,419,314	22.4
1915	8,361,324	72.1	3,229,920	27.9
1916	12,171,629	68.6	5,569,152	31.4
1917	16,747,393	70.1	7,158,194	29.9
1918	17,713,865	66.7	8,842,462	33.3
1919	28,515,636	67.7	13,632,131	32.3
1920	36,006,730	64.9	19,432,239	35.1
1921	25,104,774	72.4	9,582,104	27.6
1922	27,564,784	77.8	7,858,497	22.2

Journal, Relative to Other Women's Magazines				
	Journal		All Other Women's Magazines	
Year	Advertising Revenue ($)	% of Total	Advertising Revenue ($)	% of Total
1911	2,082,142	30.5	4,733,494	69.5
1912	2,366,668	31.3	5,190,237	68.7
1913	2,312,664	31.5	5,023,323	68.5
1914	2,273,680	30.5	5,182,797	69.5
1915	2,462,712	33.9	4,796,626	66.1
1916	3,041,108	28.3	7,721,814	71.7
1917	4,647,815	34.4	8,848,218	65.6
1918	5,723,274	37.2	9,669,353	62.8
1919	8,508,649	36.0	15,137,048	64.0
1920	11,116,094	33.0	22,522,057	67.0
1921	10,281,183	37.0	17,483,440	63.0
1922	11,063,744	38.6	17,592,272	61.4

Sources: "Total Expenditures by Groups of Publications, Curtis *Bulletin* 25 (May 23,1923); "Tables Showing Advertising Investments of Leading Advertisers Using $10,000 and Over in 30 Publications," 1916.

Research consisted of Parlin and two other men who assisted him directly in trade investigations, along with an office staff that varied from ten to thirty people. By the early 1930s, the division had grown to about ninety field workers and had a full-time office staff of about one hundred. When he was hired in 1911, Parlin was paid $5,000 a year, slightly more than an advertising representative with a few years' experience. By late 1919, Parlin had become one of a small group of employee stockholders, and his annual salary of $14,000 was $2,000 above those of the managers of the Philadelphia and Boston advertising offices.[38] He was also part of a group of men from the Advertising Department who met regularly with the company's board of directors and provided economic analyses and predictions.[39]

As the importance of Commercial Research grew, so did the amount of work it produced. It continually funneled information to the advertising and circulation staffs, showing the positioning of Curtis publications and emphasizing their dominance in the marketplace. In 1922, the division began producing a weekly newsletter called the *Bulletin* for members of the advertising, editorial, and circulation departments.[40] The weekly briefings contained news about the company, its competitors, and its customers; about research done by Curtis, the federal government, and other businesses; and about features and articles in the *Post,* the *Journal,* and *Country Gentleman.* It charted circulation and promoted and explained sales techniques, and in general served as a means of crowing about the advantages and success of Curtis advertising. These *Bulletins* contained everything from letters of praise from readers to contents of the magazines to circulation sales methods of the Curtis magazines and their competitors. The intent seemed to be to prepare the advertising and circulation staffs to answer criticisms or doubts from customers and to provide information that staff members could use when making sales.

The briefings reinforced and added to a sales kit—a loose-leaf binder of printed and typescript material known internally as the Dope Book—that Commercial Research assembled in the early 1920s.[41] The book contained such material as cost-versus-circulation comparisons of advertising in the *Post, Journal, Country Gentleman,* and their nearest competitors; comparisons of total advertising revenue in seventy-two popular magazines; and charts of Curtis's total advertising revenue over the previous eight years, equating its growing revenues with success.

A Means of Persuasion

The Dope Book gave company representatives pages and pages of material on which to base their sales arguments and to market Curtis publications to advertisers, retailers, sales agents, and readers. Its aim also seemed to be to unify the thinking, direction, and arguments of Curtis staff members at a time of enormous growth (Curtis employed more than 4,000 people in the early 1920s) and labor strife (the company settled a divisive pressroom strike in 1920).[42] The promotional and sales material, in essence, became a means of increasing company morale and productivity and creating a collective identity.[43] "We are all associated in one big organization, and I like to believe that we have a mutual interest in its affairs and in its welfare," Cyrus Curtis wrote in another internal publication, *Curtis Folks*, in 1921. "The magazine can be made a means of keeping us in touch with each other and a medium for keeping before all members of the Curtis family matters in which we have a common interest. This means cooperation, 'team-work' and mutual confidence and understanding."[44]

The internal reports and the Dope Book were just a small part of Commercial Research's work, though. The division produced at least eleven broad-scale trade reports in 1920, four in 1921, three in 1922, three in 1923, seven in 1924, four in 1925, three in 1926, and nine combined in 1928 and 1929.[45] Those were just the reports the company made public. No record exists of smaller, proprietary reports the company did for individual advertisers, although those private reports may have outnumbered the larger market investigations by a considerable amount. Parlin said in 1922 that the research staff at Curtis kept busy on many small projects spurred by manufacturers' queries: One manufacturer, for instance, wanted to prove during World War I that alarm clocks were an "essential" product that should be free of restrictions. Another manufacturer wanted to know the number of square feet of roofing used on various sorts of buildings, and still another requested help in estimating the American market for shaving cream. "No matter what questions the letters ask, each of them receives careful individual attention, and an effort is made to secure the exact information desired and also to furnish collateral information of significance," Parlin said.[46]

In one month in 1922, the division produced more than 150 charts (on everything from Curtis circulation to the growth of income in various regions of the country), answered 108 inquiries, and produced four to seven research reports. "The aim of Commercial Research is to obtain information and then to use it so that manufacturers can do a more profitable business and can become stronger advertisers in Curtis publications," Parlin said. "There is always something new to be attempted in this work and the amount to be learned is limitless. Commercial Research is to the advertising and merchandising side of industry what chemical research is to the manufacturing side of business. Its field is boundless. It will always have ahead of it new and practical problems to investigate and solve."[47]

In running the Division of Commercial Research, Parlin kept on the road constantly. When he was not interviewing people for research reports, he represented Curtis Publishing at meetings around the country. He estimated that in 1921 alone, he attended 170 meetings of conferences, advertisers, associations, or boards of directors, and between 1915 and 1930, he spoke with more than fifty cooperative associations, such groups as raisin growers and hardware dealers. His speeches from the 1920s and 1930s indicate a busy schedule of traveling and public appearances before such groups as the Conference of Paint and Varnish Advertising Men, the National Piano Manufacturers Association, the American Face Brick Association, the Boston Conference on Retail Distribution, and the New York Council of the American Association of Advertising Agencies. Those speeches were usually based on his latest research, although they increasingly emphasized the changes that had taken place in the United States in the 1920s in such areas as education and merchandising, and how those changes affected advertising and selling.[48] They also began to reflect an important shift in the role of Commercial Research in the 1920s. Increasingly, Parlin and his division assumed a more visible role in advertising and in public relations. Despite an inauspicious start, Commercial Research established itself as a pillar of the country's top magazine publisher.

Possibilities and Pitfalls

Regardless of its standing, Commercial Research had its limits. Parlin and his staff could tour the country, pore over government and industry statistics, get a clear handle on the national marketplace, and even make well-founded predictions about the directions of industries and the American economy. They were hardly omnipotent, though. The quest for reliable information had transformed American business and industry in the early twentieth century, paving the way for ever more reliable tools of fact gathering and prediction. And yet, even reliable information had its limits—human limits. That is easily seen in Curtis's study of the radio industry in 1925.

Parlin and his colleagues offered an intriguing look at the fast-growing radio industry, tracing its emergence, its appeal, and its potential in the American business world. As radio took root, they said, it caught the American imagination more than any product since the automobile: "The thought that the very room in which one sits is filled with music from distant cities and that any of this may be made audible gave a thrill to a world that thought it had grown blasé to invention and to entertainment." Because of the excitement that radio generated, people were willing to spend substantial sums of money for receivers, creating what Curtis called "a more universal market than any product of like cost" ever had. "Many who buy only one thing above subsistence will choose the radio," the company wrote.[49] And yet, they said, radio was anything but fleeting, and manufacturers and retailers needed to take note. Radio "touched a universal longing," Curtis said, and that longing would only grow.

The company said radio fit awkwardly into the retail landscape. It was a unique product, and sets were sold as part of electrical goods, music, sporting goods, and even hardware. Businesses that sold other goods took on radio as a sideline. As radio caught on, the company said, an increasing number of manufacturers and sellers jumped into the game. By 1924, a glut in the number of sets forced companies to sell the remaining sets at a discount to make way for the newer models. That made people who had paid full price earlier angry, and as production continued to increase in 1925, made for a likely repeat of the earlier scenario. To alleviate further problems, Curtis advised manufacturers to limit production and to intensify sales efforts in colder months, when people stayed indoors more and sought out entertainment.

The company predicted that the ability to service radio sets would play an important role in shaping the retail market. Many businesses that took radio on as a sideline knew nothing about repairing the sets they sold. Nor did they want to deal with the burden of repair. A retailer who could provide good service was very likely to thrive, the company said, and it singled out the sellers of musical instruments and phonographs as the best fit for radio sets. "Opportunity today knocks at the door of every good music dealer to become an outstanding radio dealer in his town," Curtis wrote. It also pointed out the potential for selling such things as speakers, tubes, and batteries, and pointed out the potential problems of accepting trade-ins on older models, as the automobile industry had done. Curtis said the days of easy money in radio sales were over, and it predicted that the radio industry would soon begin consolidation, just as the automobile and agricultural implement industries had. It said that strong brand recognition would become ever more important. As always, Curtis saw advertising playing a crucial role, and indeed, the *Post* and *Country Gentleman* had already become prime vehicles for the advertising of radio sets.

In compiling the report, Parlin and his staff conducted 1,500 interviews in 225 cities, and performed their usual in-depth analysis of an important retail field. For all their work, though, Parlin and his staff missed a crucial factor that would haunt Curtis Publishing in the 1930s: radio's rise as a competitor for advertising. Although the total amount of advertising revenue for *all* radio programs in 1929 was less than the amount taken in by the *Post* that year, the ad volume for radio increased by a factor of ten—from $4 million to $40 million in just two years, from 1927 to 1929. By the end of the 1930s, radio had captured a quarter of the national advertising market, and was leaching away millions of dollars that otherwise might have gone to Curtis magazines.[50]

Even if Parlin had seen the threat that radio would eventually bring, the information would have done little good. No amount of information, even for a behemoth like Curtis, could push back a cultural force. Market research could help companies see many things that might not otherwise be apparent. It could broaden their view and help them proceed with added confidence. It could not see and predict everything, though. As important as market research had become by the 1930s, it could never be an unfailing oracle.

8

The Legacy of
Commercial Research

You may ask, "What is the greatest accomplishment of Commercial Research in twenty-five years?" The greatest accomplishment is the putting over of Mr. Latshaw's concept that in the minds of men are ideas, not yet written down in books, that are the answers to most, if not all, of sales problems. Twenty-five years ago the men had no information—and wanted none. Today, every man is eager to take any information that comes fresh from the field, and will go out and supplement it with work of his own.

—CHARLES COOLIDGE PARLIN, 1936

As Curtis Publishing and its advertisers looked for ways to survive the Great Depression, the company intensified its work in market research. During the 1930s, Parlin's division conducted surveys in such areas as private brands, the life insurance and construction industries, household appliances, and home furnishings, and it updated studies of the automobile industry and the farm market. It also continued to find innovative ways of acquiring information, studying brand loyalty in food products with a survey of home pantries and an analysis of trash in Philadelphia neighborhoods. The division still did not provide any direct revenue, but the company did not back away from what Parlin called a "spirit of research—a belief on the part of salesmen that accurate information is obtainable, a belief that the answer to many of their problems can be found by inquiries in the field."[1]

In the late 1930s, Parlin said he was sure that Commercial Research had made "a noteworthy contribution to our industrial life." When he arrived at Curtis in 1911, he said, the advertising industry still lacked any "working tools." By the late 1930s, it had acquired many of those tools—several forms of qualitative and quantitative research and analysis—and had learned the value of applying the information it collected and analyzed to many types of business problems. Information alone could not guarantee success, however, Parlin said. "Research material is a help to constructive thinking but is not a crutch to lean on with weak faith or lazy thinking. In other words, research material is a good supplement to, but a poor substitute for, original thinking."[2]

Parlin provided much original thinking as he helped shape the Division of Commercial Research during the 1910s, 1920s, and 1930s. The division began to draw the attention of advertisers, advertising agencies, and others as it gathered and analyzed scarce information about the activity of commercial business, especially such things as product sales in individual stores, cities, counties, and states. It analyzed the inner workings of important industries, and it provided a map, of sorts, of the consumer culture that was beginning to take shape in American society. Just as important, Curtis Publishing promoted—through speeches, advertising, house organs, and company-printed books and pamphlets—the work that Parlin and his associates did, making a case that businesses could and should use market information to plan their sales strategies in both the short term and the long term.

Parlin went a step further than that, though, as Samuel B. Eckert recognized several years after Parlin's death. In delivering the Charles Coolidge Parlin Memorial Lecture in 1950, Eckert, executive vice president of the Sun Oil Company, said that Parlin's creed, "the consumer is king," had a deeper meaning than most people realized. "Today we should understand his words to mean that the consumer must have confidence not only in our products but also in the business system which creates those products. When we view his words in that light they take on new and increased significance."[3] In other words, Parlin's work provided a means of enhancing the legitimacy of American capitalism among the citizenry and engaging the consumers who had become so central to the business world.

Despite all the emphasis that Parlin and his colleagues at Curtis placed on consumers, they did not seem to subscribe to the idea of consumer sovereignty, an economic concept that emerged in the mid-1930s and that was much debated throughout the century. Under that line of thinking, consumers use their free will to make rational, independent decisions about the products they buy. Those decisions, in turn, regulate production of goods.[4] Parlin certainly suggested that affluent consumers—those he considered community leaders—had a great deal of sovereignty. Under his philosophy, though, even those consumers could be swayed with the right information and the right product. Once those leaders were won over, others would follow like sheep. Parlin also embraced facets of consumer sovereignty in his "philosophy of buying," the categorization of purchases into convenience goods, emergency goods, and shopping goods, and in his insistence that the consumer is king. That slogan contained other elements, though:

> The whim of the consumer makes and unmakes the manufacturers, the jobbers and the retailers. Whoever wins the confidence of the consumer wins the day; and whoever loses it, is lost.

So the powerful consumer acts on whim, not rationality, and though some consumers may make sovereign decisions, most simply follow along. Such complexities and contradictions filled Parlin's work, and his career highlights the tensions that emerged between scholarly researchers and practitioners: He had no interest in distilling the workings of the economy into overarching, long-term theories. Rather, he applied his findings and observations in ways he thought would sell more advertising and more consumer products. The ideas were not nearly as important as the outcomes.

Parlin's applied approach to business problems helped him become an important figure within Curtis Publishing Company. He began his career on the periphery of the Advertising Department but gradually gained the confidence of his colleagues, of Curtis's business customers, and of his superiors. As his work proved increasingly useful, his opinions and views carried more weight within Curtis Publishing until, during the 1920s, his voice became indistinguishable from Curtis's corporate voice. Parlin and his division did not set company policy, but because of the trust they earned and the value that others placed in their work, they became a crucial means by which Curtis legitimized itself in the eyes of advertisers.[5] Parlin's department became a think tank, of sorts, a place in which ideas could be turned into strategy and ideology. Through the publications that the Division of Commercial Research produced, members of management and the advertising and circulation departments were able to seize upon the words and ideas of Parlin and his associates and assimilate them into their own thinking. Commercial Research became a clearinghouse for material that Curtis employees used in promoting not only their own departments, but the company, advertising, research, and business in general.

A Change of Direction

That was not the original intent of Commercial Research, but it was the direction that Parlin steered the division as his acceptance of and involvement in advertising grew. When Parlin joined the company in 1911, he had no experience in advertising, and during his early career, he emphasized the need to maintain his objectivity. That meant separating himself from his coworkers in the Advertising Department. As late as 1915, he expressed his desire for distance from his colleagues, telling the National Dry Goods Association: "I am not an advertising man and desire to avoid advertising in discussing this subject."[6] By the early 1920s, though, he not only called himself "an advertising man," but he became a central spokesman for Curtis Publishing, emphasizing the importance of advertising in the economic success of nearly all businesses. His point of view changed from one of "neutral" investigator to active salesman. Caught up in the world of advertising, he became not only a convert, but a preacher. He ministered to congregations of manufacturers and associations, telling them about the great potential of the marketplace and about the even greater potential of advertising. He gradually became not only a gatherer of facts and figures and an interpreter of the marketplace, but an ambassador to the business world for Curtis's Advertising Department. He bridged the gap between those who based advertising and merchandising decisions on "common sense" and those who wanted to infuse those decisions with the methods and respect of science. By equating knowledge with profit, he advocated a new means of doing business, one based on study and interpretation rather than on faith and gut instinct.[7] As the marketing historian Robert Bartels notes, Parlin helped introduce science into business management and helped make "commercial fact-finding a profession."[8]

In short, the move toward market research was a step toward modernity. It relied on a belief in science to transcend the guesswork and the uncertainty of the past.[9] Science was a means not only of understanding the world but of overcoming it. In scientific method, Curtis saw a means of throwing a lasso around advertisers and leading them in the direction that Curtis wanted. It was not an outward means of coercion, but Curtis's approach took advertisers into its confidence and made them a part of a system of scarce information. They became involved—as insiders, not outsiders. So by stressing the "scientific" evidence that was shared on the inside, Curtis made them believe they could hold sway on the outside (the world of consumers and sales of consumer products). It was, in a sense, a self-fulfilling prophecy. The use of research did not guarantee the success of a product, but it did allow a manufacturer to proceed more boldly with distribution and promotion, which increased the chances that the product would sell. But Parlin was right about consumers. A product that failed to live up to buyers' expectations or that failed to meet a need or desire in the first place had little chance of survival, no matter the amount of research or advertising. In this intricate dance in the consumer marketplace, whim played a central role, and no amount of research could change that.

A Change in Business Strategy

In many ways, the changes that took place within Curtis Publishing Company during the early twentieth century mirrored the transformation of American business in a modern industrial society that was trying to keep up with urban growth; that was coming to understand itself as a nation, not just clusters of regions; that was defining itself by the products and services it consumed; and that was increasingly turning to specialization and bureaucratization to help cope with the changes at hand. American capitalism was moving beyond a regional bent and entering an era of controlled risk, managed growth, and expansion nationally, and expectations of continual growth in profit. Market research quickly moved to the center of such a philosophy, especially as American businesses engaged in a power struggle for a greater share of, and even domination of, the national marketplace.[10]

In Curtis's case, its research also helped it maintain contact with other businesses and with its customers—both advertisers and readers. Through a policy of public service, it catered to both as it first carved a niche in the world of publishing and then increased the influence it had in the marketplace. One of the central means it did that was by using information it gathered about such things as production, distribution, sales, and readership. By knowing and understanding competitors, and then customers, it was better able to chart a course in the modern business world. Through its magazines—which had some of the highest circulations and easily the highest advertising revenues of their era—Curtis disseminated information to millions of people each week and each month. Through its market research division, it took a broader view, gathering information that better prepared it for understanding those readers and for understanding the thousands of current and potential advertisers.[11]

Commercial Research did nothing to prove that advertising in the *Post* or the *Journal* was effective in selling products or changing people's attitudes. (Parlin's main argument was circular: Advertising worked because if it did not work, businesses would not be queuing up to buy space in the *Post* and the *Journal*. In other words, advertising worked because no one could prove it did not work.) But it did answer the critics of advertising by broadening the argument about the role and effectiveness of product promotion. Parlin and others within Curtis Publishing took manufacturers' doubts about advertising, recast them into the broader context of merchandising, and turned them into doubts about the way a manufacturer did business. That made advertising—and in turn, Curtis publications—more difficult to turn down. With the assistance of its market studies, Curtis portrayed advertising not as the chain needed to hoist products into prominence, but as a single, although important, link in that chain. Advertising could not succeed unless the other links—from the distribution system to the sales staff to the quality of a product—were also strong. Advertising might prepare people to buy, but the real power lay in the hands of manufacturers' salesmen and in the local merchants who stocked and sold the goods, Curtis argued. Advertising, Parlin said, provided nothing more than an opportunity for an honest business to get its message before the eyes of the American public, and with it, to portray an image of how things could be in this new world of consumer products. It was a narrow view, but one that offered members of the Curtis advertising staff a certain amount of protection from critics and from any doubts they might have had about their own jobs and their own product. In their view, they were simply working toward the betterment of society by serving their customers. In the broader sense, though, Curtis's main interests were far more selfish: It sought power—over competitors, audiences, and the world of advertising—that it could leverage into profit. It called this effort "paternalism," and it sought to make the Curtis standard the standard for all of advertising. It saw itself as the leader, certainly, but it also saw itself as part of a larger "family." As the head of that family, its role was to see that everyone succeeded, and it thought the best way to do that was to pass on the wisdom it had gained.

A Form of Progressivism

Commercial Research was created at the height of the Progressive Era, and through the 1920s it was guided through Progressive notions of societal betterment. It proceeded in a way that separated it from other, more traditional means of Progressivism. Parlin did not work directly with the poor as Jane Addams did. He was not interested in rooting out governmental corruption or breaking up trusts as the muckraking journalists did. He did not try to make government more responsive through the promotion of initiative and referendum. Rather, Parlin and other Curtis executives used the company's money, power, prestige, and prominence to build up businesses that advertised, to build up advertising as a profession and an industry, and to spread the idea that consumption was necessary for the prosperity of the country. The "reform" they sought to effect was economic reform, a change in the way people viewed and acted on advertising and consumption.[12] They did that in part by drawing on another touchstone of Progressivism: education.

Throughout his career at Curtis Publishing Company, Parlin argued that advertising was merely "education" and that a consumer society was simply an evolved form of a producer society. In doing so, he and others in the advertising business used important cultural symbols to stifle widespread criticism about the promotion of consumer products. Education and thrift were both valued and valuable. They were means of increasing one's standard of living, and they inspired hard work. The notion of "quality" was based on the idea of honesty, repeat sales, and even permanence among businesses. That is, advertising could build not only notoriety but also respect if the advertiser was honest. By tying such elements to advertising, Parlin attempted to yank promotion from the humbug of P. T. Barnum and place it into the hands of Benjamin Franklin, strip it of the baggage of "waste" and cover it in the protective layer of "progress." "If it be argued that advertising for 'luxuries' has increased desires for merchandise one could be without, what are such luxuries?" Parlin asked rhetorically in 1926. The implication was that luxuries had become necessities, and that consumption, fueled by advertising, should be considered the norm. "If we believe in a constantly advancing civilization," Curtis Publishing said in 1914, "if we believe that people ought to keep on trying to live a little better and have a little more comfort and a little more ambition, then we must believe that whatever shows people the way and rouses their ambition to possess—and to improve in order to possess—is a public service. Advertising does that."

The marketplace and readership studies that Curtis conducted also defined for Curtis managers, employees, and advertisers the favored participants in the marketplace: Urban whites were favored, as long as they were born in the United States. Women were, as were farmers after they purchased automobiles. Blacks in any region were not. Neither were Eastern European immigrants, at least not initially—not until Curtis studied their buying habits and found that they, like the rest of the country, were using primarily nationally advertised products. Even then, they were discounted as imitators, as illiterates who did not understand the true value of advertised products but bought them anyway in an effort to become "more American." At the same time that advertisers and publishers like Curtis sought to tap into and promote a new middle class, they used the methods of social science to exclude and marginalize those who failed to share in the rewards of modern industrial capitalism. The culture of consumption created or eliminated opportunity, depending on the amount of money a person had to spend, and increasingly audiences that had once been viewed as members of a democratic society were seen in terms of their ability to "cast votes" with their dollars.[13] Those who could and did consume frequently were wooed and welcomed. Those who did not or could not were scorned, or as in the case of Curtis's market studies, simply excluded. The mass market that Curtis magazines symbolized in the early twentieth century was clearly a white market, and if Curtis's claims are to be believed, a mostly upper-class white market.[14]

From an economic standpoint, Curtis's positioning made sense. To companies like soap manufacturers, which wanted to reach as wide an audience as possible, Curtis stressed the millions of readers its magazines reached—the largest print audiences available during the first four decades of the twentieth century.[15] To the makers of pianos or automobiles, who had fewer products to sell and who needed to reach people with money, Curtis stressed the "quality" of its circulation—an affluent group of readers who paid full price for the magazines, responded to advertising, and bought brand-name products. In both cases, it used readership studies and statistics from Commercial Research and the federal government to try to prove to manufacturers and advertising agencies that Curtis publications were the best media for their advertising dollars because they reached the people most likely to buy. This differed from much of the work of the agencies themselves, which had begun studying consumer psychology at least ten years before Curtis created Commercial Research. And yet, the purpose was similar: Agencies used their psychological studies to help turn physical characteristics of products into objects of desire. William Leiss, Stephen Kline, and Sut Jhally give the example of soap, which has a chemical composition that gives it a distinctive smell and texture. Marketers add cultural characteristics that make that soap masculine or feminine, refined or tough, creating storylines in which consumers can place themselves. Curtis did exactly that with the statistics it gathered, the audience studies it did, and the market research it published. In many cases, Curtis found that businesses did not know how to interpret statistics or did not trust the initial research Parlin did. By placing its work into a storyline, though, Curtis turned its audience, its information, and its advertising into means of achieving greater sales and greater wealth. That push to the heart of capitalism eroded resistance and created desire for new means of doing business. It also reinforced consumer culture's ties to the experimental and the new, as market research itself continually tried new techniques of gathering information—information that had to be updated continually. In attempting to show trends and changes over time, though, Parlin and his colleagues added an element of historical continuity to their work, much as advertisements used social symbols that tied past, present, and future together. Advertising gave birth to market research, and as a result, market research assumed many of the characteristics of advertising.[16]

From a social standpoint, Curtis's positioning amounted to a reinforcement of racial and ethnic stereotypes, and its writings and actions foreshadowed the exclusionary tendencies that the United States followed through much of the twentieth century. Although a substantial number of literate black elites embraced consumption as a way of displaying status and success after the Civil War, blacks faced large hurdles in joining a consumer society because, as Jason Chambers points out, under slavery, blacks themselves were considered property. Curtis was hardly alone in espousing business strategies that excluded blacks, immigrants, and whites who could not read. It rode with the economic tides of the times, and breaking away from cultural norms in the business and publishing worlds could have cost it millions of dollars in lost advertising and lost subscription income. Not until the 1940s did mainstream marketers pursue black customers in a systematic way. Curtis Publishing alone was not responsible for racism, of course; nor could it alone have stopped it. Rather, the company was one more voice—an important voice—in perpetuating attitudes that hindered participation of blacks and recent immigrants not only in business but in American society.[17]

And yet, as Curtis promoted exclusionary stereotypes on the outside, on the inside its actions proved contradictory and, if not progressive, then certainly humane. The company showed no ambitions of crossing the color line in the hiring of executives or in welcoming black employees as guests to its country club. It did show respect toward those employees, though, in setting up annual events for them and in writing about them in its internal publications. Pictures and short articles, like those profiling a black exterminator named "Rat-Trap Elmer" and a black cuspidor cleaner named Walter Jones, can certainly be seen as a way to reinforce the position of blacks in menial jobs. At the same time, such articles celebrated the men's abilities and the company's reliance on them. And the act of writing about black employees respectfully and publishing many photographs of them showed a laudable acceptance of blacks, something that Parlin and other executives lacked in the work they circulated to the business world. It was easy to write off a large swath of nameless, faceless "others," as the company did in its business materials. It was far harder to do that with flesh-and-blood human beings who worked in the same building.[18]

Promoting Consumption

Throughout his career at Curtis, Parlin pushed the idea that the widespread buying of consumer goods was the direction the United States needed to move, and he went as far as to take his case to Washington during the Depression. He spent two years as a representative of the National Publishers Association, lobbying primarily against the Copeland Bill, which would have put the oversight of advertising into the hands of the Food and Drug Administration instead of the Federal Trade Commission, and would have established a system of standards and grading for food— standards that Parlin said would have had a chilling effect on advertising. Although he reluctantly accepted some of the government regulation put into place during the New Deal, he said that any sort of business regulation needed to be scarce. A system of business unfettered by rules and regulations would benefit rich and poor alike, he said, because it would promote increased consumption. "The best opportunity, as I see it, is to go ahead, encourage industry to produce ever greater volumes of merchandise that they may have more to distribute," Parlin said during the Depression. "If but few cars were produced, the wealthy will have them. If pork is scarce only the well-to-do can afford it, but if there be an abundance of motor cars, they are bound to sell into wide markets, and if there be an abundance of pork, most of those who wish may have it."[19]

A free-wheeling world of business and advertising, in Parlin's view, was the best way to encourage a democratic means of national progress, a betterment of the masses through the same sort of trickle-down means he had identified in Sabetha, Kansas, in 1920.[20] Similarly, Parlin said that the "desire to possess" was the cure for the economic slump that had settled on the United States in the 1930s, because the desire to possess created a desire to work, and a "desire on the part of the many to work is the one sound foundation for national prosperity."[21] Consumption, in the view of Parlin and his colleagues, was clearly the yardstick for measuring self-worth and societal advancement, even during the Depression. As consumption of consumer products became ever more important to the economy, and as officials and researchers sought ways to revive the economy during the Depression, government and social researchers embraced that idea as well.[22] And as advertising proliferated on radio and then on television, Americans increasingly embraced just such a view, expanding a cultural force that continues to define American society today.

Flexibility through Success

Throughout the 1920s and 1930s, Parlin and his staff used the tools of their research continually to try to prove the value of advertising.[23] Their case was, on the surface, successful. Through the 1930s, the *Post* and the *Journal* remained the two dominant advertising vehicles for national manufacturers, an accomplishment that Curtis management credited in part to Commercial Research.[24] Early in the Depression, with profits sliding, the company gave Parlin's division an even more important vote of confidence, maintaining its budget and staff, even though it generated no revenue.[25] During the early 1940s, a few years after Parlin had left, Commercial Research became an autonomous department with a status equal to that of the advertising, circulation, and editorial departments. Parlin's successor, Donald Hobart, began to report directly to the company president, rather than to the head of the Advertising Department, as Parlin had done.[26] "Research is already performing an important service for industry," Parlin said in 1931. "In the future it will perform a much greater service. Competition is becoming more keen. Less can safely be left to chance; more must be founded on accurate information." It was a message that more and more businesses, including Curtis, took to heart.

Just how much of Curtis Publishing's success in the early twentieth century can be attributed to the use of market research is impossible to say. Too many other variables worked in conjunction with

market research, everything from the popularity of the editorial matter of the *Post* and the *Journal* to the widespread use of promotion to
the personalities of the people involved in selling the advertising.
Curtis's success, though, which helped the company grow large and
profitable, allowed it to pursue its philosophy of service and paternalism and to experiment with such ventures as Commercial Research.
The millions of dollars of profit produced by the *Journal* and the *Post*
gave the company the flexibility to see new ventures through many
years of unprofitable times—a flexibility that most smaller companies did not have. The company held a unique position in publishing
and advertising during the first four decades of the twentieth century, and it had the respect and name recognition necessary to get
manufacturers to provide information that was often carefully
guarded. The type of research and planning that Parlin and his staff
advocated eventually became known as dynamic marketing: The
marketplace and the consumers that made up that marketplace were
constantly changing. A manufacturer, Parlin used to say, was selling
a parade, not a standing army. The basis for understanding that
parade of consumers was marketplace information, and in that sense,
the system that evolved during the early twentieth century was one
of dynamic information. Marketplace information and understanding were constantly becoming outdated. New studies and new
information led to new theories and new philosophies. Knowledge
was dynamic, not static. "Commercial research, like the writing of
history, will go on forever," Parlin said in 1931. "Every day, thoughts
are changing and new market problems are created. . . . As corporations grow larger and as the decisions begin to involve large sums
of money, commercial research seems to become imperative."[27]

This need to comprehend change, along with the growing link
between knowledge, decision making, and money, drove the expansion of market research through the early twentieth century, and it
continues to be one of the defining elements of the "information
society" or "information age" of the twenty-first century. Although
both of those phrases have become amorphous descriptions for the
overabundance of often useless data available today, they are telling
in that they indicate that true information—material that is in some

way instructive, helpful, or useful—is a valued cultural product of modern American society.[28] Market research was not the originator of the information explosion that began in the mid-1900s and accelerated into the 2000s, but it was certainly an important precursor. Market information empowered those willing to seek it out and shape it to their needs, and those with the power of respected information had a greater ability to gain greater wealth.

It is unlikely that the commercial information Curtis gathered helped it or any other business truly *control* the marketplace. There were simply too many other factors involved. Market information could help businesses spot trends and understand competitors; it could help them direct supply to meet demand in areas where demand was high. It could not and did not formulate policy or make decisions to act. Nor could it account for such things as financial panics, the responses of competitors, or the outbreak of war. Market and readership studies provided feedback about consumers and helped companies tailor their products, their advertising, and their sales approaches; it could not and did not predict precisely how consumers would respond. It could not control their actions. "In a time of depression," Parlin said in 1931,

> statistics show that the world is headed for the bow-wows, and a projection of curves leads quickly to the nether regions. Yet out in the field conditions are not half so bad as the statistics indicate. Folks are still alive. They work, they eat, they play, they grumble a bit, they sigh for better days—but they are not dead—they do not intend to die right away. Ambition continues to assert itself; courage struggles to come back; the promise of better times is somewhere in the hearts of men. Markets are there for the man who studies folks and their wants and, through study of folks, learns how to advertise his products to win the favor of live people.[29]

Despite the promises—and the promise—market research was as fallible as the people who had nurtured it. It was—and is—a truly a human endeavor.

Epilogue

arlin retired from Curtis Publishing in 1937 and moved to
Florida from the Germantown section of Philadelphia. He
traveled extensively after leaving the company, and in 1939
he asked to go back to work part time as a spokesman for Curtis
Publishing. The company agreed, and during the ensuing three
years, Parlin represented Curtis at several meetings and conventions.
He grew increasingly reflective and philosophical about his career
and about advertising. His speeches from the time show a man coming to grips with the end of his life, feeling the need to justify the
nearly thirty years he had spent in research and advertising.[1]

In one of his last speeches, Parlin relied on one of his familiar
themes: that of change. He told the Florida State Bankers Association:

> Change is inevitable. Change is the law of God. In all the
> universe only change is permanent. . . . Yet underlying
> unending change, there are eternal verities such as man's
> faith in God, man's faith in himself and his fellow men, and
> eternal aspirations to nobler thoughts and better living to
> which men must adhere unless civilization is to return to

chaos. Change is to be accepted not merely because it is change but because it evolves toward what we hope will be better standards.[2]

Parlin died the next year at age seventy. His contributions to market research and to advertising were memorialized in 1945, when the Philadelphia chapter of the American Marketing Association established the Charles Coolidge Parlin Memorial Award— an award that is still presented today—and in 1953, when Parlin was elected to the Advertising Hall of Fame. In 1950, Donald Hobart, Parlin's successor at Curtis, dedicated his book *Marketing Research Practice* to Parlin, "whose vision made marketing research possible, whose insight kept it simple, whose integrity kept it honest and sincere."[3]

"To say that knowledge is power is trite but it is true," Parlin said in 1914. "Knowledge is the foundation of modern merchandising, and as competition grows more intense, it becomes more apparent that the manufacturer must know in order to succeed."[4]

As with many of Parlin's observations, that still holds true today.

Notes

INTRODUCTION

1. "Testimonial Dinner to Mr. Charles Coolidge Parlin," Curtis Publishing Company papers, Rare Book and Manuscript Library, Van Pelt Library, University of Pennsylvania (hereafter cited as CP), Box 149, Folder 92; and "Honor Parlin as Founder of Commercial Research," *Advertising Age*, June 1, 1936, CP Box 148, Folder 91.

2. "Testimonial Dinner"; on Curtis and his editors, see Frank Luther Mott, *A History of American Magazines*, vol. 4 (Cambridge, MA: Harvard University Press, 1957), 671–716.

3. "Testimonial Dinner."

4. Wroe Alderson, "Charles Coolidge Parlin, 1872–1942," in *Pioneers in Marketing*, ed. John S. Wright and Parks B. Dimsdale Jr. (Atlanta: School of Business Administration, Georgia State University, 1974), 103–105; Henry Assael, ed., *The Collected Works of C. C. Parlin* (New York: Arno Press, 1978); Peter F. Drucker, "Marketing and Economic Development," in *Marketing Classics: A Selection of Influential Articles*, ed. Ben M. Enis and Keith K. Cox (Boston: Allyn and Bacon, 1969), 26–36; and Stanley C. Hollander, "Some Notes on the Difficulty of Identifying the Marketing Thought Contributions of the 'Early Institutionalists,'" in *Theoretical Developments in Marketing*, ed. Charles W. Lamb Jr. and Patrick M. Dunne (Chicago: American Marketing Association, 1980), 45–46. Paul Converse calls Parlin "one of the leading developers of marketing research." See Converse, *The Beginning of Marketing Thought in the United States* (New York: Arno, 1978; reprint of 1959 ed.), 36; and Converse, "The Development of the

Science of Marketing—An Exploratory Survey," *Journal of Marketing* 10 (July 1945): 14–23; and Coleman Harwell Wells, "Remapping America: Market Research and American Society, 1900–1940," Ph.D. dissertation, University of Virginia, 1999, especially chapter 4.

5. Donald Hobart's *Marketing Research Practice* provides perhaps the most useful starting point for the research of Curtis's market research. Hobart succeeded Parlin in 1938 as manager of the Division of Commercial Research. Also see Hobart's introduction to *Digests of Principal Research Department Studies,* vols. 1 and 2 (Philadelphia: Curtis Publishing Company, 1946); Alderson, "Charles Coolidge Parlin, 1872–1942"; Paul D. Converse, *Fifty Years of Marketing in Retrospect* (New York: Arno, 1978; reprint of 1959 ed.), 36–38; Frank Edson Parlin, *The Descendants of Nicholas Parlin* (Cambridge, MA, 1913), 209–210; and Charles Coolidge Parlin and Daisy Blackwood Parlin, *The Parlins: Incidents Trivial and Otherwise in the Lives of Charles Coolidge Parlin and Daisy Blackwood Parlin,* vol. 1 (Philadelphia, 1931).

6. Professionals and scholars alike have credited Parlin with developing many of the techniques of early market research. Stanley Hollander has written that historians of marketing thought have paid Parlin "due homage." See Hollander, "Some Notes on the Difficulty of Identifying the Marketing Thought Contributions of the 'Early Institutionalists'"; also see "Testimonial Dinner"; Alderson, "Charles Coolidge Parlin, 1872–1942"; Assael, *The Collected Works of C. C. Parlin*; and Drucker, "Marketing and Economic Development."

7. John Tebbel and Mary Ellen Zuckerman, *The Magazine in America, 1741–1990* (New York: Oxford University Press, 1991), 73–97; Darwin Payne, "The Age of Mass Magazines," in *The Media in America,* ed. William David Sloan, James G. Stovall, and James D. Startt (Worthington, OH: Publishing Horizons, 1989), chapter 16; Frank Luther Mott, *American Journalism: A History of Newspapers in the United States Through 250 Years, 1690 to 1940* (New York: Macmillan, 1947), 512, 591, 655–659; and Mott, *A History of American Magazines,* vol. 2, 432–436; vol. 4, 536–555, 671–716.

8. See, for instance, Mary Ellen Zuckerman, *A History of Popular Women's Magazines in the United States, 1792–1995* (Westport, CT: Greenwood Press, 1998); Carolyn Kitch, "The American Woman Series: Gender and Class in the *Ladies' Home Journal,* 1897," *Journalism and Mass Communication Quarterly* 75 (Summer 1998): 243–262; Maureen Honey, "Images of Women in the *Saturday Evening Post,* 1931–36," *Journal of Popular Culture* (Fall 1976): 352–358; Patricke Johns-Heine and Hans H. Garth, "Values in Mass-Periodical Fiction, 1921–1940," *Public Opinion Quarterly* (Spring 1949): 105–113; Mary Ellen Waller-Zuckerman, "Marketing the Women's Journals, 1873–1900," *Business and Economic History* 18 (Fall 1989): 99–108; and Michael Dennis Hummel, "The Attitudes of Edward Bok and the *Ladies' Home Journal* Toward Woman's Role in Society, 1889–1919," Ph.D. dissertation, North Texas State University, 1982.

9. Jennifer Scanlon, *Inarticulate Longings: The "Ladies' Home Journal," Gender and the Promises of Consumer Culture* (New York: Routledge, 1995); Helen

Damon-Moore, *Magazines for the Millions: Gender and Commerce in the "Ladies' Home Journal" and the "Saturday Evening Post," 1880–1910* (Albany: State University of New York Press, 1994); Christopher P. Wilson, "The Rhetoric of Consumption: Mass Market Magazines and the Demise of the Gentle Reader, 1880–1920," in *The Culture of Consumption: Critical Essays in American History, 1880–1980,* ed. Richard Wightman Fox and T. J. Jackson Lears (New York: Pantheon, 1983), 40–64; T. J. Jackson Lears, "From Salvation to Self-Realization: Advertising and the Therapeutic Roots of the Consumer Culture, 1880–1930," in *The Culture of Consumption,* 3–38; Bonnie J. Fox, "Selling the Mechanized Household: 70 Years of Ads in *Ladies' Home Journal,*" *Gender & Society* 4 (1990): 25–40; William Leiss, Stephen Kline, and Sut Jhally, *Social Communication in Advertising: Persons, Products, and Images of Well-Being* (New York: Methuen, 1986); Rosalind H. Williams, *Dream Worlds: Mass Consumption in Late Nineteenth-Century France* (Berkeley: University of California Press, 1982); Martha Johnson Feldmann, "Never Underestimate Empowerment through Consumption: Women and Advertising in the *Ladies' Home Journal* from the 1880s through the 1920s," Ph.D. dissertation, Memphis State University, 1991; and Richard W. Pollay, "Thank the Editors for the Buyological Urge: American Magazines, Advertising and the Promotion of the Consumer Culture, 1920–1980," in *Marketing in the Long Run: Proceedings of the Second Workshop on Historical Research in Marketing,* ed. Stanley C. Hollander and Terence Nevett (East Lansing: Michigan State University, 1985). For a cogent overview on the study of consumption history, see Susan Strasser, "Making Consumption Conspicuous: Transgressive Topics Go Mainstream," *Technology and Culture* 43 (2002): 755–770.

10. See, for instance, Salme Harju Steinberg, *Reformer in the Marketplace: Edward Bok and the "Ladies' Home Journal"* (Baton Rouge: Louisiana State University Press, 1979), xvii; John Tebbel, *George Horace Lorimer and the "Saturday Evening Post"* (Garden City, NY: Doubleday, 1948); Jan Cohn, *Creating America: George Horace Lorimer and the "Saturday Evening Post"* (Pittsburgh: University of Pittsburgh Press, 1989); Edward W. Bok, *The Americanization of Edward Bok* (New York: Charles Scribner's Sons, 1920); Bok, *A Man from Maine* (New York: Charles Scribner's Sons, 1923); Bok, *Twice Thirty* (New York: Charles Scribner's Sons, 1925); Walter Fuller, *The Life and Times of Cyrus H. K. Curtis* (New York: Newcomen Society of England, American Branch, 1948); Kenneth Stewart and John Tebbel, *Makers of Modern Journalism* (New York: Prentice-Hall, 1952); and James Playsted Wood, *The Story of Advertising* (New York: Ronald Press, 1958).

11. Otto Friedrich, *Decline and Fall* (New York: Harper & Row, 1970); and Joseph C. Goulden, *The Curtis Caper* (New York, 1965).

12. Tebbel and Zuckerman, *The Magazine in America,* 93–96.

13. I am oversimplifying here to emphasize a point. No part of a publication can be seen as completely independent of the others. The editorial work, although generating no direct revenue, becomes the product that is sold. That product, though, relies on distribution and sales. And only with an established circulation can a publication draw steady advertising. The advertising department, because it

concentrates on generating income and on maintaining the financial success of a company, can be seen as the most powerful component in a publication's economic well-being. As Richard Pollay notes, magazines are too often seen only as "a commercial literary form," with advertising just a byproduct created by the need for revenue. A better way, he says, would be to "recognize the business of magazine publishing as delivering the audience as its product to advertisers as its consumers. The editorial process is merely the mechanism by which the product, the audience, is produced." See Pollay, "Thank the Editors for the Buyological Urge." Gerald Baldasty makes a similar observation in his study of nineteenth century newspapers. He looks at how news changed from a political to a commercial product that reflected "the financial requirements of the newspaper organization, the vision of its producers and the day-to-day exigencies of production in the nineteenth century. . . . When news is seen, quite properly, as a manufactured product, it becomes even more compelling to examine the assumptions or agendas behind it." See Baldasty, *The Commercialization of News in the Nineteenth Century* (Madison: University of Wisconsin Press, 1992).

14. I am not holding Curtis up as an archetype. The way Curtis reacted to change was unique. I am simply pointing out that other businesses faced similar broad changes. It is impossible to show how each reacted, but it is possible to show how a few, or one—Curtis in this case—did.

15. I am using the term *information* to mean facts, figures, or other data that fulfill a need or can be applied to a problem, with the result being a perceived gain, often monetary, on the part of the user. Information in this sense has a utilitarian function in that it can help an individual or a company make a decision. It differs from *knowledge* and *understanding,* both of which can be gained from information but require greater intellectual application and context. For instance, Curtis collected *information* about markets: such things as volume of sales in a region or the types of products carried by a department store. Only by analyzing that information and putting it into the context of other information—about sales nationally, or the types of products carried by all department stores—could the company achieve greater *understanding* or purport to have *knowledge* of the marketplace.

16. James R. Beniger, *The Control Revolution: Technological and Economic Origins of the Information Society* (Cambridge, MA: Harvard University Press, 1986), 21.

17. Robert Bartels, *The Development of Marketing Thought* (Homewood, IL: Richard D. Irwin, 1962), chapter 7; Steven A. Sass, *The Pragmatic Imagination: A History of the Wharton School, 1881–1981* (Philadelphia: University of Pennsylvania Press, 1982), 174; William Leach, *Land of Desire: Merchants, Power and the Rise of a New American Culture* (New York: Pantheon, 1993), 155–163; Eric Clark, *The Want Makers* (New York: Viking, 1989), 61–64; and Donald M. Hobart, ed., *Marketing Research Practice* (New York: Ronald Press, 1950), 9.

18. Clark, *The Want Makers,* 61–64; and Lini S. Kadaba, "Seeing the Two Faces of Philadelphia," *Philadelphia Inquirer,* October 1, 1995, G1–G2.

19. Steven Lubar, *Infoculture* (Boston: Houghton Mifflin, 1993), 1–6, 290.

20. Thomas A. Stapleford says that even government research projects were held back because of the projected costs. See Stapleford, "Market Visions: Expenditure Surveys, Market Research, and Economic Planning in the New Deal," *Journal of American History* 94 (September 2004): 418–444.

21. Although the *Post* circulation reached 2 million in 1913, it dropped below 2 million the next year and did not reach 2 million again until 1919. See *Advertising in the Saturday Evening Post, 1926* (Philadelphia: Curtis Publishing Company, 1927), CP Box 125.

22. *Leading Advertisers—1932* (Philadelphia: Curtis Publishing Company, 1932).

23. "Salient Facts," Curtis *Bulletin* 38 (February 6, 1924). All totals are based on advertisers spending more than $10,000 per year.

24. "Total Advertising Revenue—1928 in 40 Farm Publications," Curtis *Bulletin* 108 (February 1929). That year, *Country Gentleman* brought in $4,739,024; followed by *Successful Farming* with $1,564,366; *Farm Journal* with $1,431,937; and *Capper's Farmer* with $1,091,492. The total advertising income for the top forty farm publications was $23,132,317; "Expenditures of Advertisers," Curtis *Bulletin* 25 (May 23, 1923)

25. "Total Advertising—1928 in 64 Publications," Curtis *Bulletin* 107 (January 1929); "The Year 1928," Curtis *Bulletin* 107 (January 1929); "Rank of Ten Leading Publications," Curtis *Bulletin* 59 (March 25, 1925); "Total Advertising—1926," Curtis *Bulletin* 83 (January 21, 1927); and Charles Coolidge Parlin, "National Advertising and Selling," typescript, March 25, 1928, CP Box 149, Folder 75.

26. Jackson Lears, *Fables of Abundance: A Cultural History of Advertising in America* (New York: Basic Books, 1994); Roland Marchand, *Advertising the American Dream* (Berkeley: University of California Press, 1985); Daniel Pope, *The Making of Modern Advertising* (New York: Basic Books, 1983); and Stuart Ewen, *Captains of Consciousness: Advertising and the Social Roots of the Consumer Culture* (New York: McGraw-Hill, 1976).

27. See, for instance, Charles McGovern, "Sold American: Inventing the Consumer, 1890–1940," Ph.D. dissertation, Harvard University, 1993; and McGovern's subsequent book, *Sold American: Consumption and Citizenship, 1890–1945* (Chapel Hill: University of North Carolina Press, 2006); and Wells, "Remapping America."

28. See A. L. Kroeber and Clyde Kluckhohn, *Culture: A Critical Review of Concepts and Definitions* (New York: Vintage, n.d.; reprint of 1952 ed.), 164–168.

29. Robert Darnton, *The Kiss of Lamourette: Reflections in Cultural History* (New York: W. W. Norton, 1990); George Cotkin, *Reluctant Modernism: American Thought and Culture, 1880–1900* (New York: Twayne, 1992), chapter 5; James W. Carey, *Communication as Culture: Essays on Media and Society* (Boston: Unwin Hyman, 1988); Carey, "The Problem of Journalism History," *Journalism History* 1 (Spring 1974): 3–5, 27; Warren I. Susman, *Culture as History: The Transformation of American Society in the Twentieth Century* (New York: Pantheon, 1984); and

Peggy J. Kreshel, "Advertising Research in the Pre-Depression Years: A Cultural History," *Journal of Current Issues and Research in Advertising* 15 (Spring 1993): 59–75.

30. The Curtis Papers consist of nearly two hundred boxes of material, including company correspondence, in-house publications, copies of more than fifty research reports, more than one hundred speeches by Charles Coolidge Parlin, minutes of some of Curtis's in-house advertising conferences, company histories, memorabilia, and various other material related to the company, the Division of Commercial Research, and to the *Saturday Evening Post, Ladies' Home Journal,* and *Country Gentleman* magazines. As Roland Marchand writes, the archival sources for the history of American advertising before World War II are spotty. Much inside material from advertising agencies and businesses has been destroyed. This amplifies the importance of such archival material as the Curtis Publishing Company papers, which are housed in the Rare Book and Manuscript Library at the University of Pennsylvania. See Marchand, *Advertising the American Dream,* 419–421.

31. The Curtis Archives in Indianapolis primarily handles requests for use of material from the heyday of the *Saturday Evening Post.* Some early records, including a considerable amount of the correspondence of Cyrus Curtis, the company's board of directors' minutes, and some of the published work of Commercial Research, are also housed there.

32. This follows the thinking of Peggy Kreshel, who asks in her research: "What *meanings* have been assigned to those practices we have come to label advertising research? In short, how has research 'made sense' from the standpoint of the actors involved?" See Kreshel, "Advertising Research in the Pre-Depression Years." Rosalind Williams does an excellent job of describing the techniques of cultural and intellectual history as including "an alertness to figurative language, to allusions and overtones, to how people express themselves as well as what they express, in order to discern patterns of response that have a collective validity." See *Dream Worlds,* 7. I also agree with Sam Wineburg's assertion that "the goal of historical study should be to teach us what we *cannot* see, to acquaint us with the congenital blurriness of our vision." See Wineburg, *Historical Thinking and Other Unnatural Acts* (Philadelphia: Temple University Press, 2001), 17.

33. I have tried to follow a philosophy similar to that of Sally Foreman Griffith in her study of William Allen White. See Griffith, *Home Town News: William Allen White and the Emporia Gazette* (New York: Oxford, 1989), 9.

34. Susan Strasser, *Satisfaction Guaranteed: The Making of the American Mass Market* (New York: Pantheon, 1989), 18.

35. Ronald A. Fullerton calls the changes that took place at the turn of the twentieth century "truly revolutionary." At the same time, he and other scholars reject the notion of a revolution in marketing. Rather, Fullerton proposes a model of "simultaneous dramatic change, incremental change, and continuity." That model allows for periods of rapid change but also diminishes the idea of distinct producer and consumer eras. See Fullerton, "How Modern Is Modern Marketing?

Marketing's Evolution and the Myth of the 'Production Era,'" *Journal of Marketing* 52 (January 1988): 108–125. Also see D. G. Brian Jones and Alan J. Richardson, "The Myth of the Marketing Revolution," *Journal of Macromarketing* 27 (March 2007): 15–24; and Stanley C. Hollander, "The Marketing Concept: A Déjà Vu," in *Marketing Management: Technology as a Social Process*, ed. George Fisk (New York: Praeger, 1986), 3–29. I examine this phenomenon in more detail in Ward, "Capitalism, Early Market Research, and the Creation of the American Consumer," *Journal of Historical Research in Marketing* 1 (2009): 200–223.

CHAPTER 1. A NEW ERA OF BUSINESS

1. Latshaw has been credited with coming up with the idea for Curtis's Division of Commercial Research. See comments by Latshaw and others in "Testimonial Dinner." Also see Hobart, *Marketing Research Practice*, chapter 1; and Bartels, *The Development of Marketing Thought*, 108.

2. "Ninth Annual Conference of the Advertising Department of Curtis Publishing Company," typescript, January 7–10, 1913, 18–80, CP Box 16; "Tenth Annual Conference of the Advertising Department of The Curtis Publishing Company," typescript, October 29–31, 1913, 8–13, CP Box 17; "Testimonial Dinner," 13–20; and Alfred D. Chandler Jr., *The Visible Hand: The Managerial Revolution in American Business* (Cambridge, MA: Harvard University Press, 1977).

3. *National Advertising: The Modern Selling-Force* (Philadelphia: Curtis Publishing Company, c. 1912), 3, CP Box 151, Folder 130. In that book, Curtis wrote: "Not so many years ago, most business men were inclined to look upon advertising as akin to speculation in 'wildcat' copper mines. Closing their eyes, they flung their money into the gamble, and waited for the fates to decide."

4. "Testimonial Dinner," 17–20; "Minutes of the Seventh Annual Conference," typescript, 1910, CP Box 15; Charles Coolidge Parlin, "Commercial Research," *Curtis Folks* 11 (September 1922): 4–5, CP Box 154, Folder 149. For an example of the argument that retailers used against advertising, see H. E. Whalen, "The Dealer Attitude Toward Advertised Goods," *Printers' Ink* (hereafter cited as *PI*), April 13, 1911, 38–40.

5. Earnest Elmo Calkins and Ralph Holden, *Modern Advertising* (New York: D. Appleton and Company, 1905), 14; *The Curtis Advertising Code*, 1912, 5; Curtis Publishing Company, Board of Directors Minutes, 1901, Curtis Archives, Indianapolis; Hugh A. O'Donnell, "Random Shots At Advertising," *PI*, March 2, 1911, 76.

6. "Ninth Annual Conference," 28–30, 59–61.

7. The distinction between sellers and merchandisers is subtle but important. By sellers, I mean those who primarily followed the practices prevalent in an industrial society. A product was offered for sale, a price was negotiated, and a sale was made. Merchandisers emerged in a business climate that was much more competitive.

8. Although Curtis Publishing was not the government, its size and influence in the advertising world provided it with a stature similar to a governmental agency. On changes during the Progressive Era, see Richard Hofstadter, *The Age of Reform* (New York: Vintage, 1955), 9–11.

9. Some of the first periodicals in America used "advertiser" in their names. For instance, the *Pennsylvania Packet and Daily Advertiser*, founded in 1784 in Philadelphia, was the first daily newspaper in America. Another prominent example was the *Boston Daily Advertiser*, edited at one time by Nathan Hale. See Willard G. Bleyer, *Main Currents in the History of American Journalism* (Boston: Houghton Mifflin, 1927), 101, 143.

10. Harvey Green, *The Uncertainty of Everyday Life, 1915–1945* (New York: HarperCollins, 1992), 6–7; George E. Mowry, *The Urban Nation, 1920–1960* (New York: Hill and Wang, 1968), 6–7; and Simon J. Bronner, ed., *Consuming Visions: Accumulation and Display of Goods in America, 1880–1920* (New York: W. W. Norton, 1989).

11. "A.N.P.A. Considers Important Question," *PI*, May 4, 1911, 78–79; Strasser, *Satisfaction Guaranteed*; and Earnest Elmo Calkins, *The Business of Advertising* (New York: D. Appleton, 1916), 183.

12. Edwin Emery and Henry Ladd Smith, *The Press and America* (Englewood Cliffs, NJ: Prentice-Hall, 1954), 402; T. J. Jackson Lears, "Some Versions of Fantasy: Toward a Cultural History of American Advertising, 1880–1930," *Prospects* 9 (1984): 349–405; Pope, *The Making of Modern Advertising*, 6; and Tebbel and Zuckerman, *The Magazine in America*, 141.

13. Mott, *A History of American Magazines*, vol. 4, 536–555.

14. Zuckerman, *A History of Popular Women's Magazines in the United States*, 3. She lists the others as *Delineator*, *McCall's*, *Woman's Home Companion*, *Good Housekeeping*, and *Pictorial Review*.

15. Zuckerman, *A History of Popular Women's Magazines*, 33.

16. *The Thompson Red Book on Advertising* (New York: J. Walter Thompson Company, 1899).

17. Mott, *A History of American Magazines*, vol. 2, 432–436 and vol. 4, 21, 536–555, 671–716; Tebbel and Zuckerman, *The Magazine in America*, 73–97; Darwin Payne, "The Age of Mass Magazines," in *The Media in America*, ed. William David Sloan, James G. Stovall, and James D. Startt (Worthington, OH: Publishing Horizons, 1989), chapter 16; "Ninth Annual Conference," 2–6; "Tables Showing Advertising Investments of Leading Advertisers Using $10,000 and Over in 30 Publications," 1916, CP Box 120; and Bok, *A Man from Maine*, 158–160.

18. Bok, *A Man from Maine*, 115–120, 220–221; "The Story of a Magazine," *Chautauquan Advertising Supplement*, 1890, CP Box 167; "The *Ladies' Home Journal*, the *Saturday Evening Post* and the New Building for the Curtis Publishing Company," October 1908 (reprinted from *Profitable Advertising*), CP Box 151, Folder 129; "Advertising Faith of Cyrus Curtis and How He Keeps It," *PI*, January 22, 1914, 57–68; Curtis Publishing Company, Board of Directors Minutes,

1900–1930, Curtis Archives, Indianapolis; "Advertising for Circulation," Curtis *Bulletin* 8 (September 28, 1922); and "More Newspaper Advertising This Spring," Curtis *Bulletin* 19 (February 28, 1923).

19. In 1900, a full-page advertisement in the *Journal,* which had a circulation of about 900,000, sold for $4,000. By 1913, circulation had nearly doubled—to 1,700,000—and the advertising rate had risen a third, to about $5,300 a page. The same page in the *Post* rose from about $1,150 a page in 1900 to $5,300 in 1913. I calculated the total for 1900 based on the rate of $1.75 an agate line in 1900. The line rate had risen to $8 a line in 1913. I based the calculation on Calkins and Holden's figures for the *Ladies' Home Journal* in 1905. Then, the *Journal's* line rate was $6; the page rate, $4,000. See Calkins and Holden, *Modern Advertising,* 71–72, 120–121; "Minutes of the Seventh Annual Conference," 30–31; and "Tables Showing Advertising Investments of Leading Advertisers."

20. *The Curtis Advertising Code,* 1912 and 1914; "A New Five-Cent Publication," *Obiter Dicta* 3 (July–August 1913): 3–4; "A Far Western Office" and "Curtis Service," *Obiter Dicta* 4 (September–October 1913): 3–4, 21–25; *Selling Forces* (Philadelphia: Curtis Publishing Company, 1913), 225–228; Bok, *A Man from Maine,* 183–190, 197–212; "Cyrus Curtis in Daily Field," *The Fourth Estate,* January 4, 1913, 2; "New Daily Paper in Philadelphia," *The Fourth Estate,* September 12, 1914, 3; "Evening *Ledger* in Philadelphia," *The Fourth Estate,* September 12, 1914, 2; "Ninth Annual Conference," 1–7; "The Proposition," advertisement, *PI,* August 28, 1913, 40; and Curtis Board of Directors Minutes, January and March 1914, Curtis Archives, Indianapolis.

21. Bok, *A Man from Maine,* 183–190; "The *Ladies' Home Journal,* the *Saturday Evening Post* and the New Building for the Curtis Publishing Company"; and *Selling Forces,* 227–228.

22. "Ninth Annual Conference," 8–35.

23. Beniger, *The Control Revolution,* v–viii, 17–32.

24. "Ninth Annual Conference," 25–35.

25. "Ninth Annual Conference," 35–80.

26. *The Curtis Advertising Code,* 1912 and 1914, 6–7; *Selling Forces,* 38–40; "Ninth Annual Conference," 1–2, 28–32; "Censorship," *Obiter Dicta* 2 (June 1913): 6–14; and "Curtis Service," *Obiter Dicta* 4 (September–October 1913): 21–25.

27. Bok, *A Man from Maine,* 107–132.

28. Bok, *A Man from Maine,* 107–132; and "The Story of a Magazine."

29. Bok, *A Man from Maine,* 97–103, 137–144, 215–218.

30. Leach, *Land of Desire,* 112–117.

31. Pope, *The Making of Modern Advertising,* 142–143.

32. Quoted in Pope, *The Making of Modern Advertising,* 144.

33. *National Advertising: The Modern Selling-Force.*

34. A. B. Freeman, "Advertising 'Agency' a Misnomer," *PI,* July 20, 1911, 132, 134–136. Also see Calkins and Holden, *Modern Advertising,* 165; Charles W. Hurd, "What an Agency Means to an Advertiser," *PI,* July 20, 1911, 108, 111–112.

35. Quentin J. Schultze, "The Rise of a Professional Ideology in the Early Advertising Business, 1900–1917," in *Proceedings of the Annual Conference of the American Academy of Advertising,* ed. Keith Hunt (Provo, UT: Institute of Business Management, Brigham Young University, 1981).

36. Lears, "Some Versions of Fantasy"; *The Curtis Advertising Code,* 1912 and 1914.

37. "Ninth Annual Conference," 85–103; "Tables Showing Advertising Investments of Leading Advertisers Using $10,000 and Over in 30 Publications," 1916, CP Boxes 119, 120, 121; *Advertising Charts, 1915–1923* (Philadelphia: Curtis Publishing Company, 1924), 19.

38. *National Advertising,* 24–28.

39. Converse, *Fifty Years of Marketing in Retrospect,* 7; and Charles Coolidge Parlin, "Department Store Lines: Textiles," vol. B, chapter 10.

40. McGovern, "Sold American," especially 82–100.

41. "The New Curtis Terms With Advertising Agents," *Obiter Dicta* 3 (July–August 1913): 5–9; *Selling Forces,* chapter 5.

42. *The Curtis Advertising Code,* 1912, 6–7.

43. "Ninth Annual Conference," 30, 80–84.

44. *The Curtis Advertising Code,* 1912; and *Selling Forces,* 38–40.

45. "Ninth Annual Conference," 1–2, 28–32; *The Curtis Advertising Code,* 1912 and 1914, 6–7; *Obiter Dicta* 2 (June 1913): 6–14; *Obiter Dicta* 4 (September–October 1913): 21–25; and *Selling Forces,* 36–40.

46. See, for example, "The Value of the Fittest," *PI,* May 30, 1912, 23; "Natural Selection," *PI,* July 11, 1912, 21; "Circulation of the *Public Ledger,*" *PI,* May 21, 1914, 11; "The *Ladies' Home Journal* for October—A Real Demand," *PI,* October 15, 1914, 14–15; "Woman's Keenest Interest," *PI,* January 7, 1915, 21; "Increasing Responsiveness," *PI,* February 4, 1915, 14–15; "13,312 Samples in 30 Days," *PI,* February 18, 1915, 19; "Developing Advertising," *PI,* March 4, 1915, 14–15; "87 Per Cent. Re-Orders," *PI,* April 15, 1915, 14–15; "100 Commodities Advertised in One Issue," *PI,* April 22, 1915, 22–23; "The Stability of Advertising," *PI,* August 5, 1915, 14–15; and "The Open Secret of the *Journal,*" *PI,* September 16, 1915, 33–36.

47. "Safeguards of Success," *PI,* February 26, 1914, 21; "My Goods Are Different," *PI,* March 12, 1914, 21; "The Price of Publicity," *PI,* March 19, 1914, 21; "$30,000 Worth of Faith in Advertising," *PI,* January 14, 1915, 19; "Developing Advertising," *PI,* March 4, 1915, 14–15; "Developing Advertising on the Pacific Coast," *PI,* March 18, 1915; "An Advertising Campaign," *PI,* July 1, 1915, 14–15; "Advertising and the High Cost of Living," *Obiter Dicta* 3 (July–August 1913): 23–28; "Who Pays For Advertising?" *Obiter Dicta* 4 (September–October 1913): 9–11; "A New Book on Advertising," *Obiter Dicta* 4 (September–October 1913): 33–34; and "Advertising and Luxuries," *Obiter Dicta* 6 (January 1914): 18–21.

48. "Advertising Faith of Cyrus Curtis and How He Keeps It."

49. *The District Agent as a Sales Promoter* (Philadelphia: Curtis Publishing Company, 1911), 3–5, 28–33, 185.

50. These ratios, the company said, included the total population of "men, women and children, literate and illiterate, of all races and all nationalities." In other calculations, the company was less generous toward blacks and recent immigrants, often excluding them from figures on the size of a consumer market. (See Chapter 5.) *The District Agent,* 12–13, 218–224.

51. *The District Agent,* 12–13, 218–224; and "Where Trade Is Brisk," *PI,* May 27, 1915, 17–20.

52. I develop this argument in more detail in "The Geography of the *Ladies' Home Journal*: An Analysis of a Magazine's Audience, 1911–1955," *Journalism History* 34 (Spring 2008): 2–14.

53. "Curtis Service," *Obiter Dicta* 4 (September–October 1913): 21–25; and "Minutes of the Seventh Annual Conference," 2–6, 10–18, 47–48.

54. "Minutes of the Seventh Annual Conference," 10–18.

55. "Minutes of the Seventh Annual Conference," 2–3, 10–47.

56. Latshaw recounts the formation of the Division of Commercial Research in "Testimonial Dinner," 13–20. Also see Hobart, *Marketing Research Practice,* chapter 1; and Bartels, *The Development of Marketing Thought,* 108.

CHAPTER 2. AN UNLIKELY LEADER

1. "Testimonial Dinner," CP Box 149, File 92.

2. "Testimonial Dinner," 33–34.

3. Curtis Board of Directors Minutes, July 1911, Curtis Archives, Indianapolis.

4. "Testimonial Dinner," 29. Also see Charles Coolidge Parlin, "What Commercial Research Is Doing for Manufacturers," typescript, September 14, 1931, CP Box 149, Folder 82.

5. "Testimonial Dinner," 13–20; and *The Parlins,* 101–104, 215, 249–250.

6. "Testimonial Dinner," 13–20, 30–37.

7. "Testimonial Dinner," 39.

8. "Testimonial Dinner," 39–43.

9. Bok, *A Man from Maine,* 144–145, 184–190.

10. "Testimonial Dinner," 39–43.

11. "Testimonial Dinner," 39–40.

12. *The Parlins,* 34–57; Alderson, "Charles Coolidge Parlin, 1872–1942"; and Frank Edson Parlin, *The Descendants of Nicholas Parlin,* 209–210.

13. *The Parlins,* 54, 85, 101–104.

14. *The Parlins,* 101–107; and Rick Tilman, *Thorstein Veblen and His Critics, 1891–1963* (Princeton, NJ: Princeton University Press, 1992), 308–309.

15. Charles Coolidge Parlin, "Agricultural Implements," typescript, 1911, 362, 114, CP Box 19.

16. I am primarily talking about the qualitative studies that Parlin did. They were by far the most numerous. But they were not the only types of studies he did. As early as 1912 and 1913, he conducted survey research for Curtis, although

those projects were generally less extensive than his qualitative work. See, for instance, Charles Coolidge Parlin, "Sewing in the Schools and Colleges of the United States," 1913, CP Box 26; and "An Inquiry Among Readers of the *Country Gentleman,*" vols. A and B, CP Boxes 46 and 47. For an overview of the research studies Curtis Publishing did through 1940, see *Digests of Principal Research Department Studies.* Volume 1 provides synopses of studies from 1911 to 1925. Volume 2 covers 1926 to 1940. The introduction by Donald M. Hobart in Volume 1 is especially helpful. Two subsequent volumes cover 1941 to 1945 and 1946 to 1949.

17. Hobart, *Marketing Research Practice,* 14–15, 37–39; "The Little Schoolmaster's Classroom," *PI,* January 26, 1911: 96–99; and Charles Coolidge Parlin, "Why and How a Manufacturer Should Make Trade Investigations," *PI,* October 22, 1914, 3–12, 74–80.

18. Parlin, "Why and How a Manufacturer Should Make Trade Investigations."

19. The poll was a tabulation of the opinions that merchants and manufacturers had about national advertising. See Parlin, "Department Store Lines: Textiles," vol. B, typescript, 1912, 184, CP Box 21.

20. "Ninth Annual Conference," 428–430; "Testimonial Dinner," 42–44; Charles Coolidge Parlin, untitled book chapter, CP Box 148, Folder 86; and Converse, *The Beginning of Marketing Thought,* 36–38.

21. *The Parlins,* chapter 24.

22. D. G. Brian Jones and David D. Monieson, "Early Development of the Philosophy of Marketing Thought," *Journal of Marketing* 54 (January 1990): 102–113.

23. Richard T. Ely, Ralph H. Hess, Charles K. Leith, and Thomas Nixon Carver, *The Foundations of National Prosperity* (New York: MacMillan, 1917), 356–359; also see Douglas Ward, "Capitalism, Early Market Research, and the Creation of the American Consumer."

24. William L. O'Neill, *The Progressive Years: America Comes of Age* (New York: Dodd, Meade & Company, 1975), 92–94; Tilman, *Thorstein Veblen and His Critics,* 99–102, 308–309; Richard T. Ely, *An Introduction to Political Economy* (New York: Kraus Reprint Company, 1969; reprint of 1901 edition), 4–42, 83–87, 102–108; and Joseph Dorfman, *The Economic Mind in American Civilization,* vol. 3 (New York: Viking Press, 1959).

25. Parlin, "Department Store Lines: Textiles," vol. A.

26. Parlin, "Why and How a Manufacturer Should Make Trade Investigations."

27. Parlin, "Department Store Lines," vol. A, 316–318.

28. Parlin, "Agricultural Implements," 281.

29. Parlin, "Department Store Lines," vol. A, 64.

30. Robert B. Ekelund Jr. and Robert F. Hébert, *A History of Economic Theory and Method* (New York: McGraw-Hill, 1983), 85–87; J. Herbert Altschull, *From Milton to McLuhan: The Ideas Behind American Journalism* (New York: Long-

man, 1990), 36–47; and Robert H. Wiebe, *The Search for Order, 1877–1920* (New York: Hill and Wang, 1967), 145–155, 164–176.

31. Parlin, "Agricultural Implements," 233.

32. Parlin, "Agricultural Implements," 114–116.

33. Beniger, *The Control Revolution*.

34. Parlin, "Department Store Lines," vol. B, 61; and Thomas C. Cochran, *The American Business System: A Historical Perspective, 1900–1955* (New York: Harper Torchbooks, 1957), 11–15.

35. "The Vital Importance of Market Knowledge," *PI*, May 20, 1915, 111.

36. Wiebe, *The Search for Order*, 151–154; Loren Baritz, *The Servants of Power: A History of the Use of Social Science in American Industry* (Middletown, CT: Wesleyan University Press, 1960), 26–29; and John Rae, "The Application of Science to Industry," in *The Organization of Knowledge in Modern America, 1860–1920*, ed. Alexandra Oleson and John Voss (Baltimore: Johns Hopkins, 1979), 249–268.

37. Ralph M. Hower, *The History of an Advertising Agency: N. W. Ayer & Son at Work, 1869–1939* (Cambridge, MA: Harvard University Press, 1939), 88–91.

38. Calkins and Holden, *Modern Advertising*, 261.

39. Calkins and Holden, *Modern Advertising*, 261–282.

40. Stephen Fox, *The Mirror Makers: A History of American Advertising and Its Creators* (New York: William Morrow, 1984), 60–61; and Parlin, "Agricultural Implements," 258–259, 281, 310–311.

41. In one case that Parlin noted, the agency had interviewed sixty-five retailers to determine their attitude toward a brand of tomato catsup. See "Agricultural Implements," 206.

42. The Thompson Blue Book on Advertising, 1904, Early Advertising Publications, Advertising Ephemera Collection—Database #A0160, Emergence of Advertising On-Line Project, John W. Hartman Center for Sales, Advertising and Marketing History, Duke University Rare Book, Manuscript, and Special Collections Library. http://library.duke.edu/digitalcollections/eaa.Q0012/pg.1/ (accessed June 2009).

43. Kreshel, "Advertising Research in the Pre-Depression Years."

44. "Chicago as a Market," advertisement, *PI*, July 6, 1911, 5; and *Book of Facts: Data on Markets, Merchandising, Advertising with Special Reference to the Chicago Territory and Chicago Newspaper Advertising* (Chicago: Tribune Company, 1928).

45. "Business Bourse Develops a Bureau of Research," *PI*, July 20, 1911, 52.

46. Jeffrey L. Cruikshank, *A Delicate Experiment: The Harvard Business School, 1908–1945* (Boston: Harvard Business School Press, 1987), 54–63; Leach, *Land of Desire*, 155–163; and *Bulletin of the Bureau of Business Research* 1 (1913): 3–15.

47. Lawrence C. Lockley, "Notes on the History of Marketing Research," *Journal of Marketing* 14 (April 1950): 733–736.

48. See, for instance, "First-Hand Facts about Farm Dealer Conditions," *PI*, February 23, 1911, 58–59; "Chicago as a Market," advertisement, *PI*, July 6, 1911, 5; "Digging for Data," *PI*, February 1, 1912, 44, 46; R. E. Fowler, "How

to Look Before You Leap," *PI,* February 8, 1912; Joseph Hamlin Phinney, "How Papers Can Dig Up Circulation Data," *PI,* April 25, 1912, 100–105; E. G. Pratt, "Data Publishers Should Furnish Agents," *PI,* January 29, 1914, 47–51; "Data Departments as Selling Aids," *PI,* April 2, 1914, 56; "Government's New Bureaus of Trade Information," *PI,* January 15, 1914, 47–48; "Your Farm Market Analyzed at a Glance," advertisement, *PI,* June 25, 1914, 8–9; William S. Jones, "Newspapers' Part in 'Co-operation,'" *PI,* June 11, 1914, 28, 31–32; and St. Elmo Massengale, "Agent Wants Central Information Bureau," *PI,* June 25, 1914, 121–123.

49. "Investigations Which Do Not Investigate," *PI,* April 30, 1914, 84–86.

50. Parlin, "Department Store Lines," vol. A, 49, 151–152, 173; Cruikshank, *A Delicate Experiment,* 59; *Twentieth Annual Report of the Secretary of Commerce* (Washington, DC: Government Printing Office), 1932, 67; and Wiebe, *The Search for Order,* 277.

51. Before that, it had been a temporary office, activated every ten years, within the Department of the Interior.

52. The number of volumes produced by the census grew from five in 1860 and 1870 to 32 in 1890. The number of census workers in Washington grew from about 250 in 1860 to 1,495 in 1880 to 3,500 in 1900, and the number of field workers grew proportionately. The 1880 census, the first to grow to "encyclopaedic proportions," required 1,500 employees to complete. By 1920, the Bureau enlisted 90,000 people just to gather data. See W. Stull Holt, *The Bureau of the Census: Its History, Activities and Organization* (Washington, DC: Brookings Institution, 1929), 24–25, 73.

53. Margo J. Anderson, *The American Census: A Social History* (New Haven, CT: Yale University Press, 1988), 83–86.

54. Joseph W. Duncan and William C. Shelton, *Revolution in United States Government Statistics, 1926–1976* (Washington, DC: U.S. Department of Commerce, 1978), 6–7; *Reports of the Department of Commerce and Labor,* 1907 (Washington, DC: Government Printing Office, 1907), 23, 234; "Trade Bulletins," typescript, 1914, 60, CP Box 37; and "Condensed Report of Advertising Conference," typescript, 1915, 39–40, CP Box 18.

55. George Bruce Cortelyou, "Some Agencies for the Extension of Our Domestic and Foreign Trade," *Annals of the American Academy of Political and Social Science* 24 (July 1904): 1–12.

56. With both the city and university research agencies, the intent was to separate politics from administration in hopes of increasing government efficiency. See Amin Alimard, "Origins, History, and Directions of the University Bureau Movement in the United States," in *The Research Function of University Bureaus and Institutes for Government-Related Research,* ed. Dwight Waldo (Berkeley: University of California, 1960), 1–10.

57. Parlin, "Why and How a Manufacturer Should Make Trade Investigations"; and Parlin, *Basic Facts of Prosperity in 1920* (Philadelphia: Curtis Publishing Company, 1920), CP Box 148, Folder 13.

CHAPTER 3. WHAT WAS COMMERCIAL RESEARCH?

1. Parlin, "Why and How a Manufacturer Should Make Trade Investigations."

2. Parlin, "Agricultural Implements," 252.

3. Parlin, "Why and How a Manufacturer Should Make Trade Investigations"; Charles Coolidge Parlin and Henry Sherwood Youker, "Encyclopedia of Cities: An Estimate of Trading Population and of Dry Goods and Ladies' Ready-To-Wear Business in All Cities of United States above 5,000 Population," 1913, 3, CP Box 25.

4. Parlin, "Department Store Lines: Textiles," vol. A, 148.

5. Charles Coolidge Parlin and Henry Sherwood Youker, "Automobiles," vol. 1B, Gasoline Pleasure Cars, 1914, chapter 1, CP Box 30.

6. Parlin, "The Philosophy of Buying," typescript, June 23, 1914, CP Box 148, Folder 1.

7. Parlin and Youker, "Automobiles," vol. 1B, 8–10.

8. Parlin and Youker, "Automobiles," vol. 1B, 22–23.

9. Parlin, *Basic Facts of Prosperity in 1920.*

10. "Recently," the agency wrote in 1916, "we have been impressed by the very great advantage there is, when taking up the advertising of any product, to really know the channels of trade which form the logical distributing machinery for the product in question." See J. Walter Thompson *News Bulletin* 22 (October 31, 1916). Also see "Data and Plan Form," c. 1919, microfilm reel 195, J. Walter Thompson Archives.

11. Parlin, "Why and How a Manufacturer Should Make Trade Investigations."

12. Noble points out that scientists of the eighteenth and early nineteenth centuries had nothing but disdain for colleagues who sought to turn science into money. See David F. Noble, *America by Design: Science, Technology, and the Rise of Corporate Capitalism* (New York: Oxford University Press, 1980), 3–4.

13. Strasser, *Satisfaction Guaranteed,* 16–28, 146–161.

14. Parlin, "Department Store Lines," vol. B, 21–26.

15. Adam Smith, *An Inquiry in the Nature and Causes of the Wealth of Nations* (1776), Book IV, chapter 8, retrieved from www.econlib.org/library/Smith/smWN18.html (accessed June 2006); Robert Ellis Thompson, *Political Economy* (Philadelphia: Porter & Coates, 1882); R. H. Inglis Palgrave, *Dictionary of Political Economy* (London: MacMillan, 1894), 394–395, 666–667. I develop this idea more fully in Ward, "Capitalism, Early Market Research, and the Creation of the American Consumer."

16. McGovern, "Sold American," 19, 60–77.

17. "Woman is a shopper," Parlin wrote. "Out of that fact has come the modern department store." See "Department Store Lines," vol. B, 7–8.

18. Parlin, "Agricultural Implements," 113–114; and Parlin, "The Philosophy of Buying."

19. Parlin, "Department Store Lines," vol. B, 7–17. Also see Parlin, *The Merchandising of Textiles* (Philadelphia: National Dry Goods Association, n.d.), CP Box 150, Folder 109.

20. Although Parlin based his theory of shopping on scores of interviews and months of compiling statistics, he later said that the core of the theory came from observing his wife. He explained that he had met her in downtown Boston one day so that they could make an important family purchase. "As we went down town, she said, 'Now I have been looking around in advance and the thing that we want to buy is at Smith's. Where shall we go first?' To that very sensible question I returned a foolish answer," Parlin said. "I said, 'Let's go to Smith's,' and that broke up the shopping tour and I did not get another invitation for many a long day." See "Testimonial Dinner," 45–47.

21. Parlin, "Department Store Lines," 7–17.

22. Parlin, "Why and How a Manufacturer Should Make Trade Investigations."

23. In 1926, for example, the *Post* had total revenues of $49,158,904. Of that, $15,683,224 came from advertising for automobiles and accessories. In 1931, advertising revenues totaled $35,492,312, of which $10,604,264 came from automobile advertising. In 1922, the *Post* accounted for the largest share—69%—of automobile ads placed among weeklies. See *Advertising in The Saturday Evening Post, 1926* (Philadelphia: Curtis Publishing Company, 1927); *Leading Advertisers—1932* (Philadelphia: Curtis Publishing Company, 1932); and "Leading Advertisers, 1911–1916," typescript, CP Box 121.

24. In 1922, automotive, foods, and toilet goods were the three top categories for advertising expenditures. The *Journal* was the top recipient of advertising for foods, soaps and cleaners, textiles, toilet goods, women's ready-to-wear clothing, and yarns, notions, and dressmaker's accessories. See "25 Largest Classes of Merchandise Advertising," Curtis *Bulletin* 25 (May 23, 1923).

25. Parlin wrote that the automobile study was conducted in part "to ascertain whether this important source of business was one which would continue." See Parlin, *The Merchandising of Automobile Parts and Accessories* (Philadelphia: Curtis Publishing Company, 1915), CP Box 148, Folder 5.

26. Parlin and Youker, "Encyclopedia of Cities," 1913 and "Encyclopedia of Cities," 1921, CP Box 77.

27. Parlin and Youker, "Encyclopedia of Cities," 1913.

28. Charles Coolidge Parlin and Henry Sherwood Youker, "Food Products and Household Supplies," vols. A, B, C, D, and E, typescript, 1914–1917, CP Boxes 38–42, inclusive; Parlin and Youker, "Farm Tractors," vols. A and B, typescript, 1916, CP Boxes 47, 48, 49; Henry Sherwood Youker with Samuel M. Kinney and Miller Munson, "Canned Soup," typescript, 1917, CP Box 50; Charles Coolidge Parlin with Henry Sherwood Youker and Norwood Weaver, "Electrical Industry," vols. A and B, typescript, 1917, CP Boxes 51, 52, 53; William Wellington Paine, "Oleomargarine," 1919, CP Box 62; Kinney, "Machine Tools," typescript, 1920, CP Box 69; Milford J. Baker, "Retail Hardware Stores,"

typescript, 1920, CP Box 73; Kinney and Baker, "Motor Trucks," typescript, 1920, CP Box 70; Parlin and Baker, "The Gas Industry," typescript, 1921, CP Box 79; Division of Commercial Research (no author listed), "Canned Beans," vols. A and B, typescript, 1919, CP Boxes 59, 60; "National Prohibition," typescript, 1920, CP Box 71; "Automobile Markets," vols. A, B, C, typescript, 1920, CP Boxes 64, 65, 66; "Automobile Tires," typescript, 1920, CP Box 66; "Department Store Lines," vols. AA, BB, typescript, 1920–1921, CP Boxes 75, 76; "Radio," vols. A, B, typescript, 1925, CP Boxes 82, 83; "Automobiles: Influence of Women," typescript, 1926, CP Boxes 85, 86.

29. Division of Commercial Research, "Merchandising Problems of Coal-Tar Dyes," 1919, CP Box 61.

30. Division of Commercial Research, "Merchandising Problems of Coal-Tar Dyes."

31. Parlin, "Agricultural Implements."

32. Parlin, "Department Store Lines," vols. A and B; and Blanche E. Hyde, "Department Store Lines: Cloths and Their Uses," vol. D, 1912, CP Boxes 23, 24.

33. Parlin and Youker, "Automobiles," vols. A, 1B, 2B, C, D, 1914, CP Boxes 28–36, inclusive.

34. Parlin and Youker, "Food Products and Household Supplies." There was also a companion volume, "The Future of Chains," 1915, CP Box 43.

35. For instance, Parlin and Youker's "Farm Tractors," 1916 (assisted by George C. Rohrs and William Shaw), consisted of two volumes, as did "Electrical Industry," 1917 (with the assistance of Norwood Weaver), and "Farm Markets," 1917 (with the assistance of William Wellington Paine), CP Boxes 47–49, 51–56. Later studies that followed a similar format included "National Prohibition," 1920; "Radio," 1925, and "Life Insurance Survey," 1934, CP Boxes 71, 82, 83, 94, 95.

36. Parlin, "The Philosophy of Buying." The company added several advertising offices in the 1920s.

37. The title page of "Agricultural Implements" and subsequent reports contains this statement: "N.B. This report is to be considered strictly confidential as to names and as to all statements concerning individual concerns."

38. "Ninth Annual Conference."

39. "Trade Diagnosis," *Obiter Dicta* 3 (July–August 1913): 10–14.

40. "New Material for Curtis Representatives," Curtis *Bulletin* 28 (September 12, 1923). In an OCLC computer search in the spring of 1994, I found abbreviated forms of Parlin's studies from the 1920s and 1930s at libraries in Virginia, Michigan, Oklahoma, New York, Indiana, Ohio, Pennsylvania, Maryland, Kansas, the District of Columbia, California, New Jersey, Georgia, South Dakota, Oregon, and Vermont. How the libraries obtained the reports is impossible to determine, but the range of states indicates that Parlin's reports and copies of his speeches were widely available.

41. Parlin, "The Philosophy of Buying"; Parlin, "Address," National Coffee Roasters Association, typescript, December 14, 1915, CP Box 148, Folder 3;

Parlin, "Address," December 28, 1915, Folder 4; Parlin, *The Merchandising of Automobile Parts and Accessories* (Philadelphia: Curtis Publishing Company, 1915), Folder 5; Parlin, *The Merchandising of Commercial Motor Vehicles* (Philadelphia: Curtis Publishing Company, 1915), Folder 7; Parlin, "Address before the Metal Branch of the National Hardware Association," typescript, June 1, 1916, Folder 8; Parlin, *The Manufacturer, the Retailer and Branded Merchandise* (Philadelphia: Curtis Publishing Company, 1916), Folder 9; Parlin, *The Merchandising of Tractors* (Philadelphia: Curtis Publishing Company, 1917), Folder 10; Parlin, *The Farm Market* (Philadelphia: Curtis Publishing Company, 1918), Folder 12; Parlin, *Basic Facts of Prosperity in 1920*; and Parlin, "Commercial Research."

42. Parlin, "Department Store Lines," vol. B, 128–129.

43. Parlin, "Department Store Lines," vols. A and B.

44. C. S. Duncan, *Commercial Research* (New York: Macmillan, 1919); and L.D.H. Weld, "The Progress of Commercial Research," *Harvard Business Review* 1 (January 1923): 175–186.

45. Parlin, National Coffee Roasters Association address.

46. Parlin, "Why and How a Manufacturer Should Make Trade Investigations."

CHAPTER 4. WINNING OVER THE SKEPTICS

1. Paul Converse also notes that Parlin had to sell the importance of information not only to advertisers but to the Curtis advertising staff. Converse writes: "He was a good salesman—he made many speeches and his ability as a public speaker stood him in good stead. In line with his high degree of ethical responsibility, his standing instructions to his assistants were: 'Go out and do the best job of research you know how to do.'" See Converse, *The Beginning of Marketing Thought*, 38.

2. Curtis made no mention of Parlin's work in its *Printers' Ink* ads until October 1913. See "At First Blush," *PI*, October 30, 1913, 25.

3. In researching this chapter, I read each issue of *Printers' Ink* from 1911 through 1915. I cite only a few of the Curtis advertisements that seem most appropriate. Many made the same point in slightly different ways. See, for example, "The largest edition of *The Ladies' Home Journal* ever printed is that for the next issue—June," *PI*, June 1, 1911, 7; "25,000 Short," *PI*, June 8, 1911, 7; "The Value of the Fittest," *PI*, May 30, 1912, 23; "Natural Selection," *PI*, May 30, 1912, 23; "Progress," *PI*, September 11, 1913, 25; and "100 Commodities Advertised In One Issue," *PI*, April 22, 1915, 22–23.

4. "Ninth Annual Conference," 79–80, 307–316, 420–422, 488.

5. "Ninth Annual Conference," 294–302, 313–315.

6. "Ninth Annual Conference," 294–302, 313–315; "Testimonial Dinner," 15–20, 42–52; and "Advertising Faith of Cyrus Curtis and How He Keeps It," *PI*, January 22, 1914, 57–68.

7. Parlin, "Department Store Lines," vol. B.

8. Charles Coolidge Parlin, "Address before the Metal Branch of the National Hardware Association," typescript, June 1, 1916, CP Box 148, Folder 8.

9. Charles Coolidge Parlin and Henry Sherwood Youker, "Automobiles," vol. 1B; Parlin, *The Merchandising of Automobile Parts and Accessories*; Parlin, *The Merchandising of Automobiles* (Philadelphia: Curtis Publishing Company, 1915), CP Box 148, Folder 6; Parlin, *The Merchandising of Commercial Motor Vehicles*; and Parlin, *The Merchandising of Tractors*.

10. "Tenth Annual Conference," 67.

11. "Curtis Service," *Obiter Dicta* 1 (September–October 1913): 21–25; "Research Papers Prepared by the Curtis School," January 1913, CP Box 27.

12. "Ninth Annual Conference," 316, 420–422.

13. "Ninth Annual Conference," 316, 420–422; *An Advertising Campaign* (Philadelphia: Curtis Publishing Company, 1915), Curtis Archives, Indianapolis, Folder 36.

14. "Curtis Service," 21–25; and *Selling Forces*, 177–191.

15. "At First Blush," *PI*, October 30, 1913, 25.

16. "Cravats to Women," *PI*, November 27, 1913, 25.

17. "Merely A Matter of Width," *PI*, November 20, 1913, 17.

18. The disdain of theory was common among advertising practitioners, who preferred to think of themselves as practical. In 1914, the F. Wallis Armstrong agency wrote in an advertisement that theories of business and advertising had been offered "ad absurdum. One might suppose we were living in a nice little cut-and-dried world where all consumers, all dealers, all commodities, and all manufacturers are simple and identical units. What a delightful business advertising would be if such were the case; establish a general rule and there you are!" See "Theory," *PI*, May 7, 1914, 41.

19. "Weight of Evidence," *PI*, January 15, 1914, 13–17.

20. See, for example, "At First Blush"; "Cravats to Women"; "On Investigation It Was Found—," *PI*, December 11, 1913, 21; "One-Cylinder Advertising," *PI*, December 18, 1913, 21; "On the Side," *PI*, December 25, 1913, 21; untitled advertisement, *PI*, January 1, 1914, 14–15; "*The Public Ledger*'s Analysis of Automobile Trade Conditions in the Philadelphia Market Proves—," *PI*, January 22, 1914, 40; and "A Local Issue," *PI*, February 12, 1914, 21.

21. Untitled advertisement, *PI*, March 26, 1914, 119.

22. "The Automobile Industry," *PI*, April 30, 1914, 34–35.

23. "The Automobile Industry"; untitled advertisement, *PI*, June 11, 1914, 21; "A Census for Salesmen," *Obiter Dicta* 6 (January 1914): 14–17; "Foodstuffs and Pacific Coast Possibilities," *Obiter Dicta* 7 (April 1914): 17–19; untitled, *Obiter Dicta* 7 (April 1914): 18; "Automobiles," *Obiter Dicta* 8 (August 1914): 3–4; "The Permanence of Automobile Advertising," *Obiter Dicta* 8 (August 1914): 10–20; and "Studying a $4,500,000,000 Industry," *Obiter Dicta* 10 (November 1915): 3–9.

24. See, for instance, Wells, "Remapping America," chapter 1; and McGovern, *Sold American*.

25. Earnest Elmo Calkins, for instance, dedicated his book *The Business of Advertising* (New York: D. Appleton, 1916) to Cyrus Curtis, the "man who has done most to put the modern conduct of advertising on the right basis." Opposite the title page is a photograph of Curtis.

26. An introduction to the book says it was prepared by Richard J. Walsh under the direction of the Advertising Department. Fred Clark's bibliography lists it as having been written by Parlin. That seems unlikely, although the book does contain a chapter on the Division of Commercial Research. As the sole member of the division at the time, Parlin would have been a likely candidate for writing about what he did. See *Selling Forces*.

27. "Fred Clark's Bibliography of the Early 1920's," *Journal of Marketing* 10 (July 1945): 54–57.

28. Hobart, *Marketing Research Practice*, 8–9; Lockley, "Notes on the History of Marketing Research."

29. Lockley, "Notes on the History of Marketing Research."

30. "Statistical Department," December 4, 1916, J. Walter Thompson Information Center records, Box 6, J. Walter Thompson Company Archives.

31. Stanley Resor to J. W. Young, July 18, 1916, J. Walter Thompson Company Archives, Newsletter Collection, Main Series, 1916–1922, Box 1; and J.W.T. Committee on Standardization, 1919, Corporate Documentation collection, Box COM-ST2.

32. "Testimonial Dinner," 8–13. Willits was toastmaster of the dinner that honored Parlin for twenty-five years of work at Curtis. Parlin said that Paul Cherington was one of the first people to invite him to lecture at a college class, indicating that he spoke at others. "Testimonial Dinner," 25.

33. Wells, "Remapping America," chapter 4; and Duncan, *Commercial Research,* 109–110.

34. In 1923, Melvin T. Copeland put forth a classification slightly different from Parlin's, but provided a long reference on how his theories related to Parlin's. See Copeland, "Relation of Consumers' Buying Habits to Marketing Methods," *Harvard Business Review* 1 (April 1923): 282–289.

35. "Testimonial Dinner," 42–43; Paul D. Converse, "The Development of the Science of Marketing—An Exploratory Survey," 14–23; and Wells, "Remapping America."

36. Parlin, "Speech before American Face Brick Association," typescript, 1923, CP Box 149, Folder 44. (The folder also contains a pamphlet of the speech.)

37. Robert Benchley, *Inside Benchley* (New York: Harper & Brothers, 1942), 298–304.

38. "Testimonial Dinner," 21–22.

39. Alderson, "Charles Coolidge Parlin, 1872–1942."

40. *Selling Forces,* chapter 11.

41. Lockley, "Notes on the History of Marketing Research."

42. "In the Interest of Sound Advertising," *Saturday Evening Post,* January 30, 1915, 34–35; and "Testimonial Dinner," 21–22, 24, 52.

43. "In the Interest of Sound Advertising," *PI,* January 28, 1915, 29; "Testimonial Dinner," 21–22, 24, 52; and "An Announcement and an Invitation," *PI,* November 4, 1915, 18–20.

CHAPTER 5. BARBARIANS, FARMERS, AND CONSUMERS

1. "An Inquiry Among Readers of the *Country Gentleman.*"

2. Charles Coolidge Parlin, *Consumer Is King,* 1920, CP Box 148, Folder 15.

3. See, for instance, Donald J. Bogue, *The Population of the United States: Historical Trends and Future Projections* (New York: Free Press, 1985), 102–106.

4. Roderick Nash, *The Nervous Generation: American Thought, 1917–1930* (Chicago: Rand McNally, 1970), chapter 5.

5. Gilman M. Ostrander, *American Civilization in the First Machine Age, 1890–1940* (New York: Harper Torchbooks, 1972), 45–47.

6. Scott J. Peters and Paul A. Morgan, "The Country Life Commission: Reconsidering a Milestone in American Agricultural History," *Agricultural History* 78 (Summer 2004): 289–316; David B. Danbom, "Rural Education Reform and the Country Life Movement," *Agricultural History* 53 (April 1979): 462–474; and William L. Bowers, *The Country Life Movement in America, 1900–1920* (Port Washington, NY: Kennikat Press, 1974), especially pages 3–6 and 128–134.

7. David B. Danbom, *Born In the Country: A History of Rural America* (Baltimore: Johns Hopkins, 1995), 161–165.

8. Carl N. Degler, *Out of Our Past* (New York: Harper Colophon, 1959), 321–325; *Cornell Countryman* is quoted on page 325.

9. Thomas J. Schlereth, "Country Stores, County Fairs, and Mail-Order Catalogues: Consumption in Rural America," in Bronner, *Consuming Visions,* 339–375; Danbom, *Born in the Country,* 132–150; Daniel J. Boorstin, *The Americans: The Democratic Experience* (New York: Random House, 1973), 89–164; Richard S. Tedlow, *New and Improved: The Story of Mass Marketing in America* (New York: Basic Books, 1990), chapter 5; and David Blanke, *Sowing the American Dream: How Consumer Culture Took Root in the Rural Midwest* (Athens: Ohio University Press, 2000), 1–11, 216–220.

10. See G. Bertram Sharpe, "The Country's Biggest Neglected Market," *PI,* March 30, 1911, 61–62, 64–67; "99,924 Illinois Farms Average Wealth $21,114," advertisement, *PI,* April 27, 1911, 57; H. Willson Ingram, "The Farm Paper Advertising Evolution," *PI,* January 26, 1911, 71–72, 74; and "More Scientific Distribution Study," *PI,* January 26, 1911, 86–87.

11. Parlin, "Agricultural Implements"; "An Inquiry Among Readers of the *Country Gentleman*"; Parlin and Youker, "Farm Tractors," vols. A and B; Charles Coolidge Parlin, Henry Sherwood Youker, and William Wellington Paine, "The Farm Market," typescript, vols. A and B, CP Boxes 54–56; Youker, "Stock Feed and Commercial Fertilizer," vols. A and B, typescript, 1917, CP Boxes 57, 58; Parlin and Youker, "Farm Tractors," vols. A and B, 1916; "An Agricultural Trading

Center," typescript, 1920, CP Box 63; and "The *Country Gentleman* Question-naire," typescript, 1920, CP Box 68. Some of the other studies apparently did not survive. They are listed in *Digests of Principal Research Department Studies*.

12. *Digests of Principal Research Department Studies,* vol. 1, 2–3, and vol. 2, 2; and Parlin, *Basic Facts of Prosperity in 1920.*

13. Parlin, "Department Store Lines: Textiles," vol. B.

14. Parlin and Youker, "Automobiles," vol. 1B, 1067–1077.

15. Parlin, *The Farm Market.*

16. Parlin and Youker, "Automobiles," vol. 1B, 1067–1077.

17. Parlin, *Consumer Is King.*

18. Parlin, *The Merchandising of Tractors*; Parlin, *The Farm Market*; Parlin, "Two Years Later—A Review of Advertising after Two Years of Travel and Reflection," typescript, 1939, CP Box 150, Folder 102.

19. Danbom, *Born in the Country,* 170–174.

20. Danbom, *Born in the Country*; and "A Valuable Ally of Advertising," J. Walter Thompson *News Letter* 43 (September 4, 1924).

21. "A Census of Farm Home Equipment," Curtis *Bulletin* 66 (November 13, 1925), CP Box 159, Folder 194.

22. Different disciplines have used varying terms for this mode of study, including sociography, human geography, and national ethnography. All evolved from social survey methods used in Europe in the 1800s. See Conrad M. Arens-berg, "The Community-Study Method," *American Journal of Sociology* 60 (September 1954): 109–124. On rural sociology, see Carl C. Taylor, "Rural Life and Rural Sociology," in Taylor et al., *Rural Life in the United States* (New York: Alfred A. Knopf, 1950), 3–12.

23. Beniger, *The Control Revolution,* 387.

24. "An Agricultural Trading Center: A Report on Some Facts of National Significance Gleaned in a Survey of Sabetha, Kansas," 1920, CP Box 63.

25. The report it did in 1922, "Sabetha: Two Years Later," is not included in the University of Pennsylvania collection. It is listed in *Digests of Principal Research Department Studies.*

26. "City A and City B: A Story of Circulation Based on an Every Home Survey of Two Cities," typescript, 1925–1926, CP Box 84; "Wayne County Survey," typescript, 1933, CP Box 92; and "Dry Waste Survey Presentation," typescript, 1936, CP Box 98. Also see *Digests of Principal Research Department Studies,* vols. 1 and 2; and Parlin, "Surveying Pantries," typescript, 1932, CP Box 149, Folder 87.

27. See, for instance, Parlin, "What Commercial Research Is Doing for Manufacturers."

28. See, for instance, Paul T. Cherington, "Some Recent Changes in the Rural and Small Town Market," J. Walter Thompson *News Bulletin* 114 (July 1925): 8–17; and "What Is Happening to the Thirteen Thousand Villages," J.W.T. *News Bulletin* 132 (September 1927): 12–17.

29. "What Do Our Rural Neighbors Buy?" J.W.T. *News Bulletin* 120 (March 1926): 1–15.

30. "What Do Our Rural Neighbors Buy?"

31. Cherington, "Some Recent Changes in the Rural and Small Town Market."

32. George Pearson, "Elementary Methods in Selecting Newspaper Media," J. Walter Thompson *News Bulletin* (June 1922): 5–8; "The Countrywoman," Curtis *Bulletin* 40 (March 5, 1924), CP Box 159, Folder 180.

33. "The Small Town Paper," J. Walter Thompson *News Bulletin* (October 24, 1916); and "Dear Jim," J.W.T. *News Bulletin* 25 (November 1, 1916).

34. Gilbert M. Tucker, *American Agricultural Periodicals: An Historical Sketch* (self-published, 1909), CP Box 170, Folder 285.

35. Bok, *A Man from Maine*, 183–187.

36. "Ninth Annual Conference," 199–202; "After Three Years," *Obiter Dicta* 8 (August 1914): 6–9.

37. Bok, *A Man from Maine*; "Cyrus H. K. Curtis Buys 'The Country Gentleman,'" *PI*, February 23, 1911, 30; "Trade Bulletins," 1914, 60; "Condensed Report of Advertising Conference," 39–40.

38. *Proofs* (Philadelphia: Curtis Publishing Company, 1916); Bok, *A Man from Maine*, 190.

39. *The Country Gentleman* (Philadelphia: Curtis Publishing Company, 1913), CP Box 170, Folder 286.

40. *A Brief History of Country Gentleman* (Philadelphia: Curtis Publishing Company, 1941), CP Box 170, Folder 295.

41. *Proofs*; "A Few Contrasts Emphasizing C.G. Quality," Curtis *Bulletin* 16 (January 18, 1923), CP Box 158, Folder 168.

42. *A Record of Leadership in American Agriculture* (Philadelphia: Curtis Publishing Company, 1929), 21–35; "The Rural Weekly," Curtis *Bulletin* 43 (April 16, 1924), CP Box 159, Folder 181.

43. "After Three Years."

44. "Population Reduced to its Lowest Terms—An Estimate," *Obiter Dicta* 9 (December 1914): 3–13.

45. Parlin, "The *Ladies' Home Journal*," typescript, c. 1926, and "The *Saturday Evening Post*," typescript, c. 1926, CP Box 149, Folder 67.

46. See, for instance, Parlin, *The Farm Market*.

47. Maxwell Droke, "What Chance Have You in the Small Town Market?" *Business Digest Service,* May 4, 1921. The article originally appeared October 20, 1920, in the *Morning Mail*.

48. *A Record of Advertising in Farm Publications* (Philadelphia: Curtis Publishing Company, 1919, 1920, 1921), CP Box 126; and "Rank of Ten Leading Publications," Curtis *Bulletin* 59 (March 25, 1925), CP Box 159, Folder 189.

49. "After Three Years"; "The *Country Gentleman* in 1926," Curtis *Bulletin* 81 (November 26, 1926), CP Box 161, Folder 204; *A Record of Leadership in*

American Agriculture 21, 35–36; "Country Gentleman," typescript, c. 1940, CP Box 170, Folder 294; "*Country Gentleman* Subscribers Own Larger-Than-Average Farms," Curtis *Bulletin* 68 (December 25, 1925), CP Box 160, Folder 195; "Some Other Letters," Curtis *Bulletin* 69 (January 8, 1926), CP Box 160, Folder 196; and "One Year's Analysis," Curtis *Bulletin* 59 (March 25, 1925), CP Box 159, Folder 189.

50. Danbom, *Born in the Country,* 161; *A Record of Leadership in American Agriculture*; and Goulden, *The Curtis Caper,* 80.

51. Goulden, *The Curtis Caper,* 80; "Farm Journal and Town Journal Acquire *Country Gentleman,*" *New York Herald Tribune,* June 13, 1955: 32, CP Box 170, Folder 303.

52. Parlin, "Commercial Research"; and *A Record of Leadership in American Agriculture.*

53. Danbom, *Born in the Country,* 194–196; and *A Record of Leadership in American Agriculture.*

54. "Current Trade Data and Conditions in the Rural Market," J. Walter Thompson *News Letter* 8 (January 3, 1924); and "What Do Our Rural Neighbors Buy?"

55. *The Parlins,* 34.

56. Ostrander, *American Civilization in the First Machine Age.*

CHAPTER 6. READERS AS CONSUMERS

Epigraph: Quoted in Goulden, *The Curtis Caper,* 26.

1. Parlin, "Department Store Lines: Textiles," vol. B, 204–205; and "Testimonial Dinner."

2. Bartels, *The Development of Marketing Thought,* 18–22, 109; and Merle Curti, "The Changing Concept of 'Human Nature' in the Literature of American Advertising," *Business History Review* 41 (Winter 1967): 335–357.

3. Pollay, "Thank the Editors for the Buyological Urge"; and Wilson, "The Rhetoric of Consumption."

4. Curtis was not the only publisher to make such claims. *Good Housekeeping,* for instance, portrayed itself as a "magazine whose advertising pages, as well as its editorial pages, keep 'clean company,'" and in doing so "wins the confidence of its readers—and, therefore, results for its advertisers." It guaranteed the products advertised within its pages and set up the Good Housekeeping Institute to test those products starting about 1909. Like Curtis's policy of "censorship," the Good Housekeeping stamp of approval was intended to make readers more comfortable with the magazine and its advertising so that readers would be more apt to buy the products advertised. See "Clean Company," *PI,* July 13, 1911, 16; and "Waldo Joins New York 'Tribune,'" *PI,* August 20, 1914, 12.

5. *Selling Forces,* 217–218, 241–244. The same sort of reasoning resonates in Curtis's house organ from 1913 to 1915 and in its advertising and promotional material from the 1880s into the 1920s. See, for example, various advertisements

in Curtis scrapbook, c. 1880–1890, CP Box 179; "The Treatment of Cuts," *Obiter Dicta* 1 (May 1913): 9–12; as well as such advertisements in *Printers' Ink* as "The Value of the Fittest," May 30, 1912, 23; "Natural Selection," July 11, 1912, 21; "160 Thousand Letters," May 7, 1914, 21; and "Where Trade Is Brisk," May 27, 1915, 17–20. Likewise, in 1905, Calkins and Holden used the *Journal* as an example of a publication that was read by a "discriminating class." See *Modern Advertising,* 71–72.

6. George Horace Lorimer, "Business Policies of the *Saturday Evening Post,*" in Curtis "Dope Book," c. 1923, CP Box 130. The unbound pages in the box are not numbered.

7. "A List of Authors," *PI,* June 4, 1914, 21.

8. "The Country Gentleman," advertisement, *Advertising & Selling* (October 1912): 12–13.

9. "The Political Influence of the *Public Ledger,*" *PI,* June 5, 1913, 45; "*The Public Ledger* Does Not Believe   " *PI,* September 18, 1913, 30.

10. "Ninth Annual Conference," 336.

11. "Tenth Annual Conference," 38–39.

12. Edward S. Jordan, "A Strictly 'Show-Me' Basis," *PI,* July 20, 1911, 24–26.

13. Parlin, "Department Store Lines," vol. B, 358.

14. See, for instance, Milton J. Blair, "Where Do The Best Customers Live? A Study of Curtis Distribution" (Curtis Chicago office, May 1, 1923), CP Box 81; and "Growth of Incomes," Curtis "Dope Book."

15. "Prosperous Philadelphia," advertisement, *PI,* December 2, 1915, 57–68; "A Christmas Pudding for Advertisers," advertisement, *PI,* December 16, 1915, 53–56; "Two New Subways in Philadelphia," advertisement, *PI,* December 23, 1915, 47; untitled advertisement, *PI,* August 19, 1915, 52–53; and "What Gives Value to Advertising?" advertisement, *PI,* November 18, 1915, 42–43.

16. Based on the inflation calculator provided by the Bureau of Labor Statistics, http://data.bls.gov/cgi-bin/cpicalc.pl, calculated August 2008.

17. "Condensed Report of Advertising Conference," 6–8.

18. *Selling Forces,* 225–241; William V. Alexander to E.G.W. Dietrich, February 29, 1904, CP Box 2; "Pattern Service," Curtis *Bulletin* 32 (November 7, 1923), CP Box 158, Folder 176; Pollay, "Thank the Editors"; and Wilson, "The Rhetoric of Consumption."

19. Scanlon, *Inarticulate Longings,* 6. Also see, for instance, Damon-Moore, *Magazines for the Millions;* Kitch, "The American Woman Series," and Waller-Zuckerman, "Marketing the Women's Journals, 1873–1900."

20. Quoted in Goulden, *The Curtis Caper,* 32.

21. Frank Luther Mott, *A History of American Magazines,* vol. 4, 688; Tebbel and Zuckerman, *The Magazine in America, 1741–1990,* 73–97; Boorstin, *The Americans,* 151; and Cohn, *Creating America,* 3.

22. Leon Whipple, "Sat Eve Post," *Journalism Quarterly* 5 (November 1928): 20–30.

23. "Condensed Report of Advertising Conference," 21–22.

24. See various clippings and advertisements in Curtis scrapbook, 324–340.

25. Curtis scrapbook, 324–340.

26. See, for instance, Parlin, "Agricultural Implements"; Parlin, "Department Store Lines," vol. B; Parlin and Youker, "Automobiles," vol. 1B; and Parlin and Youker, "Food Products and Household Supplies," vols. B and C.

27. In *Selling Forces* in 1913, Curtis said that 3,000 merchants were asked by an impartial investigator (presumably Parlin): "What periodicals are mentioned most by your customers when referring to advertised goods?" Of those respondents, 679 said the *Journal*, 675 said the *Post*, and many said both. See *Selling Forces*, 241.

28. "Tenth Annual Conference," 36; "Department Store Lines: Textiles," vol. B, 131–136; and "Attitudes Toward *The Ladies Home Journal* and *The Saturday Evening Post* as Advertising Mediums," typescript, 1916, CP Box 45.

29. Parlin, "Department Store Lines," vol. B, 134–136.

30. Bartels, *The Development of Marketing Thought*, 18–22.

31. Parlin, "Department Store Lines," vol. B, 204–205; and "Testimonial Dinner," 54–55.

32. It is difficult, if not impossible, to determine when the first readership study was done. In most cases, the documents for individual publications were confidential and would not have been widely distributed outside the companies that had done the research. Both Leo Bogart and David Nord estimate that newspapers began doing audience studies in the 1930s. The Curtis surveys were done in the 1910s. As I have shown in earlier chapters, the type of research that Curtis conducted was rare in the 1910s, and that would make readership studies rare as well. I have also done extensive searching and have found no other such studies. So it seems safe to say that Curtis's readership studies were "among the first." I go into more depth on readership studies in Douglas B. Ward, "Readers, Research, and Objectivity," in *Fair and Balanced: A History of Journalistic Objectivity*, ed. Steven R. Knowlton and Karen L. Freeman (Northport, AL: Vision Press, 2005), 167–179. Also see Bogart, *Press and Public: Who Reads What, When, Where, and Why in American Newspapers*, 2nd ed. (Hillsdale, NJ: Lawrence Erlbaum, 1989), 76; Nord, "The Children of Isaiah Thomas: Notes on the Historiography of Journalism and of the Book in America," *Occasional Papers in the History of the Book in American Culture* 1 (Worcester, MA: American Antiquarian Society, 1987), 19; Nord, "Working-Class Readers: Family, Community, and Reading in Late Nineteenth-Century America," *Communication Research* 13 (April 1986): 156–181; Lockley, "Notes on the History of Marketing Research"; Duncan, *Commercial Research*; Bartels, *The Development of Marketing Thought*; and Walter Dill Scott, *The Psychology of Advertising* (Boston: Small, Maynard and Company, 1908).

33. Although no readership study of the *Journal* was done until the 1920s, the Curtis Advertising Department was directed in 1915 to analyze the magazine's editorial correspondence, presumably to gain more specific information about readers. See "Condensed Report of Advertising Conference," 13.

34. See Ward, "Readers, Research, and Objectivity."

35. "An Inquiry Among Readers of the *Country Gentleman,*" vol. A.

36. "The *Country Gentleman* Questionnaire," typescript, 1920, CP Box 68.

37. See "Announcement in the *Country Gentleman,*" Curtis "Dope Book." The announcement is in the form of a letter dated April 29, 1921. The contest offered $50 for the best letter, $25 for second place, $10 for the next five, and $5 for the next ten. The company received 4,463 replies, which it tabulated by sex, number written by typewriter, occupation, and features preferred.

38. *Digests of Principal Research Department Studies,* vols. 1 and 2.

39. The *Public Ledger* survey was done solely by interview. Company representatives conducted more than nine hundred interviews in Philadelphia and the Philadelphia area, as well as in Pennsylvania, Maryland, and Washington, DC, during 1919 and 1920.

40. "Daily Newspaper Investigations," *PI,* July 6, 1904, 1–7. A reprint of the article can be found in John M. Hein, ed., "Notes and References Relating to the History of Philadelphia Newspapers" (Philadelphia: Free Library, 1937). Also see "The *Public Ledger* Report," vol. B, 1920; Bok, *A Man from Maine,* 197–212; and Oswald Garrison Villard, *The Disappearing Daily* (New York: Books for Libraries Press, 1969; reprint of 1946 edition), 218–228.

41. For more on this argument, see Ward, "Readers, Research, and Objectivity."

42. "The *Public Ledger* Report," vol. B, 308–359. The *Ledger* study consists of two volumes. Volume A is a typescript volume of all interviews. Volume B contains the analysis and recommendations. The Curtis papers contain only Volume A. I found Volume B in 1994 in the managing editor's office of *The Philadelphia Inquirer,* which absorbed the *Public Ledger* in the 1930s.

43. See, for instance, Hein, "Notes and References Relating to the History of Philadelphia Newspapers"; "*Ledger* Ends as It Began, in Era of World Turmoil," *Philadelphia Inquirer,* January 6, 1942, *Inquirer* clip file; "Curtis's Newspaper Dynasty Grew from Humble Beginning," January 6, 1942, *Philadelphia Inquirer* clip file; Villard, *The Disappearing Daily,* 218–228; Kenneth Stewart and John Tebbel, *Makers of Modern Journalism* (New York: Prentice-Hall, 1952), 199–216; and "North American Is Sold to Curtis," *The Fourth Estate,* May 16, 1925, 3. Also see several "Dear Father" letters, presumably from Curtis's daughter, Mary Louise Curtis Bok, to Curtis in the 1920s, Cyrus Curtis papers, Historical Society of Pennsylvania, Philadelphia.

44. F. R. Feland, "A Curious Place Is Ad-Land," *PI,* January 28, 1915: 88–89.

45. "1909 Advertising in Retrospect," *PI,* January 19, 1910: 16–21.

46. See, for instance, Carolyn Stewart Dyer, "Census Manuscripts and Circulation Data for Mid-19th Century Newspapers," *Journalism History* 7 (Summer 1980): 47–48, 67.

47. Nathaniel C. Fowler Jr., *Fowler's Publicity* (New York: Publicity Publishing Company, 1897), 358–362; and Calkins and Holden, *Modern Advertising,* 71–77.

48. Donald Hurwitz, "The Culture of Business and the Business of Culture: Social Research, Scientific Management and the Collection of Media Audience Data," in *Marketing in the Long Run*, ed. Hollander and Nevett, 43–53.

49. Quentin J. Schultze, "The Trade Press of Advertising: Its Content and Contribution to the Profession," in *Information Sources in Advertising History*, ed. Richard W. Pollay (Westport, CT: Greenwood, 1979), 49–62. Also see Hurwitz, "The Culture of Business and the Business of Culture."

50. Lockley, "Notes on the History of Marketing Research"; Duncan, *Commercial Research*, 106–109; Bartels, *The Development of Marketing Thought*; and Scott, *The Psychology of Advertising*.

51. George Batten, "An Advertising Agent's Talk to Salesmen," *PI*, February 23, 1911, 23–24.

52. "Tenth Annual Conference," 13–36; and *Selling Forces*, 210–213.

53. See, for example, "Retail Dry Goods and Ready-to-Wear"; "Department Store Centers"; "Market for Electrical Merchandise"; "Rental Analysis in the City of Chicago"; and "Market Opportunity," all in the Curtis "Dope Book."

54. "Women's Interest in the *Saturday Evening Post*," Curtis *Bulletin* 88 (April 22, 1927); "Industrial Executives and Technical Men Prefer the *Post*," Curtis *Bulletin* 98 (1928); "Dear Mr. Parlin," Curtis *Bulletin* 71 (February 12, 1926); and "Will an Advertisement Pull Better in a Large Issue or a Small One?" Curtis *Bulletin* 91 (July 22, 1927).

55. *Digests of Principal Research Department Studies*, vol. 2, 11.

56. "The Number of Readers, in Proportion to Circulation," Curtis *Bulletin* 60 (April 8, 1925).

57. Curtis said that 4.9 percent of readers subscribed to both the *Post* and *Country Gentleman* and that 5.9 percent subscribed to both the *Journal* and *Country Gentleman*. See "Duplication of Circulation Among *Post* and *Country Gentleman* Subscribers," and "Duplication of Circulation Among *Journal* and *Country Gentleman* Subscribers," Curtis "Dope Book." Also see "City A and City B: A Story of Circulation Based on an Every Home Survey of Two Cities," typescript, 1925–1926, CP Box 84.

58. See, for example, "Retail Dry Goods and Ready-to-Wear"; "Department Store Centers," "Market for Electrical Merchandise," "Rental Analysis in the City of Chicago"; and "Market Opportunity" in the Curtis "Dope Book."

59. "The Reading Habits of *Saturday Evening Post* Readers," Curtis *Bulletin* 68 (December 25, 1925); "Reader Responsiveness," Curtis *Bulletin* 94 (October 28, 1927); "The Demand for the *Post*," Curtis *Bulletin* 106 (December 1928); and *Digests of Principal Research Department Studies*, vol. 2, 31, 72, 124–125.

60. *The Saturday Evening Post* (Philadelphia: Curtis Publishing Company, c. 1930), CP Box 140.

61. "Looking Ahead," typescript, c. 1931, CP Box 140.

62. "Advance in Price," advertisement in Curtis scrapbook, c. 1880–1890.

63. "Reduction in Price of the *Ladies' Home Journal*," Curtis *Bulletin* 31 (October 24, 1923); "The *Ladies' Home Journal*," Curtis *Bulletin* 39 (February 20,

1924); "Market For *Ladies' Home Journal,*" 1933, J. Walter Thompson Company Archives, microfilm reel 38; and "Pictorial Review Circulation," Curtis *Bulletin* 71 (February 12, 1926). *Journal* circulation did drop below that of *Woman's Home Companion* and *McCall's* for a time in the 1930s, but the *Journal* regained its dominance in the late 1930s and maintained its spot as the top selling women's magazine in the United States through the 1950s. See Mary Ellen Zuckerman, *A History of Popular Women's Magazines in the United States, 1792–1995* (Westport, CT: Greenwood Press, 1998), 105–107.

64. "Tenth Annual Conference," 13–36.

65. Parlin, "Department Store Lines," vol. B, 35–38; and "What Gives Value to Advertising?"

66. "The Value of the Fittest," advertisement, *PI,* May 30, 1912, 23; "Natural Selection," advertisement, *PI,* July 11, 1912, 21.

67. See, for instance, various issues of *Curtis Folks* from 1921 to 1927, CP Boxes 154–157. In the issue after Curtis Day each year, the in-house publication devoted several pages to the festivities at the country club and the park, including a separate page of photos of black employees and their families. On circulation, see "Quality Installment Circulation," Curtis *Bulletin* 16 (January 18,1923), CP Box 158, Folder 168.

68. Blacks recognized this economic prejudice and attempted to act on it around the turn of the century. August Meier notes that some black leaders thought that if blacks could achieve high economic status and high moral character, whites would recognize their worth and allow them their rights and participation in the political process. During Reconstruction, elite leaders, who had some financial stability, stressed political and civil rights and the importance of education. Economic improvement was a lower priority. The masses, who had little economically, sought land ownership, education, and politics, in that order—the reverse order of what the elite sought. See August Meier, *Negro Thought in America, 1880–1915* (Ann Arbor: University of Michigan Press, 1969), 8–15, 25–35.

69. "Condensed Report of Advertising Conference."

70. See, for instance, Parlin and Youker, "Encyclopedia of Cities," 1913, and Parlin, "The Philosophy of Buying." On economic differences in the South, see *Sales Quotas* (Philadelphia: Curtis Publishing Company, 1928), CP Box 129.

71. Nord, "Working-Class Readers: Family, Community, and Reading in Late Nineteenth-Century America"; Douglas B. Ward, "The Geography of the *Ladies' Home Journal*: An Analysis of a Magazine's Audience, 1911–1955," *Journalism History* 34 (Spring 2008): 2–14; and Ward, "Mapping the Audience of an Icon: A Geographic Analysis of the Circulation of the *Saturday Evening Post,* 1915–1935," a paper presented to the American Journalism Historians national convention, 2005.

72. Parlin, "Department Store Lines," vol. B, 25; Parlin and Youker, "Food Products and Household Supplies," vol. B; and Parlin and Youker, "Encyclopedia of Cities."

73. Parlin, untitled address to Western Company, typescript, February 16, 1923, CP Box 149, Folder 42; "Population Reduced to Its Lowest Terms—

An Estimate," *Obiter Dicta* 9 (December 1914): 3–13; Parlin, "Department Store Lines," vol. B, 44–56; Parlin, *The Merchandising of Textiles* (Philadelphia: National Dry Goods Association, n.d.), CP Box 150, Folder 109; and "Sales Quotas and City Markets," Curtis *Bulletin* 32 (November 7, 1923).

74. Stanley Coben, *Rebellion Against Victorianism: The Impetus for Cultural Change in 1920s America* (New York: Oxford University Press, 1991), 38.

75. *The Parlins,* 19, 208.

76. "Quality Installment Circulation."

77. *Curtis Circulation Combined* (Philadelphia: Curtis Publishing Company, 1921).

78. "Population Reduced to its Lowest Terms."

79. "Population Reduced to its Lowest Terms."

80. Parlin, untitled address to Western Company; and Parlin, "National Advertising and How It Fits in with Local Advertising for the Jobber and Dealer," typescript, June 4, 1924, CP Box 149, Folder 49.

81. The company portrayed women as a forgotten element in the sales of automobiles, saying that "at least 50 percent of the impression leading to the sale of a car must be created on the woman." Women, Curtis said, were chiefly responsible for overseeing style, comfort, convenience, and economy in every family. "Any decision that hangs upon these must be her decision." See "The Automobile and the Woman," *PI,* July 15, 1915, 33–36; also see *Selling Forces,* part II, chapter 2.

82. Parlin, "Department Store Lines," vol. B, 7–19.

83. "Men's Wear and the Woman's Influence," *PI,* August 19, 1915, 33–36; also see "The First Long Pants Suit," *PI,* August 26, 1915, 33–36.

84. "The Automobile and the Woman"; "The Public Ledger Report," vol. B, 326–329.

85. Parlin, "The Philosophy of Buying."

CHAPTER 7. CHASING THE CONSUMER, PROTECTING THE COMPANY

1. Charles Coolidge Parlin, "Advertising and Selling," CP Box 149.

2. *Leading Advertisers—1921* (Philadelphia: Curtis Publishing Company, 1922); Chandler, *The Visible Hand,* 456–457; and "The Dismal Rout of Magazines," *Business Research Digest,* May 18, 1921, 242. The article originally appeared in *Advertising Age.*

3. "Busiest Season in History of Research Department," J. Walter Thompson *News Letter* 59, December 26, 1924.

4. *Twentieth Annual Report of the Secretary of Commerce,* 1932, 52.

5. Parlin, "What Commercial Research Is Doing for Manufacturers," typescript, September 14, 1931, CP Box 149, Folder 82.

6. Mac Martin, "Getting Responses from Dealer Questionnaires," *PI,* August 3, 1916.

7. McGovern, "Sold American," 363–374.

8. Parlin, "Motor Accessory Speech," c. 1921, CP Box 148, Folder 17; Parlin, "Address to Salesmen's Association of the Paper Industry," April 12, 1921, Folder 19; Parlin, "The Present Selling Problem," typescript, May 10, 1921, Folder 20; and Parlin, "Address to the National Pipe and Supplies Association," May 11, 1921, Folder 21.

9. Parlin, "Address before the Ice Cream Manufacturers Association," 1924, CP Box 149, Folder 50.

10. Parlin, "Address to Salesmen's Association of the Paper Industry"; and Parlin, "Address to the National Pipe and Supplies Association."

11. Parlin, "Magazines Are Especially Effective in the Present Crisis," typescript, 1932, CP Box 149, Folder 88.

12. "A Debate on Whether Advertising Pays," Curtis *Bulletin* 81 (November 26, 1926).

13. "Dear Mr. Parlin." 14. "An Answer to an Inquirer's Question," Curtis *Bulletin* 107 (January 1929).

15. *Curtis Circulation 1922* (Philadelphia: Curtis Publishing Company, 1922), Curtis Archives, Indianapolis.

16. *Circulation, 1920* (Philadelphia: Curtis Publishing Company, 1921). Also see *Curtis Circulation—1923*; *Curtis Circulation—1924*; *Profitable Selling—1928–1929*; and *Sales Opportunities—1927–28*.

17. For instance, Pennsylvania had 539,172 tax returns, a combined Curtis circulation of 394,181, and an advertising cost of $1,519 34. Nebraska had 87,344 income tax returns, circulation of 57,299 and a cost of $219.55.

18. *Curtis Circulation Combined* (Philadelphia: Curtis Publishing Company, 1921), Curtis Archives, Indianapolis; and *Curtis Circulation 1922*.

19. "Sales Quotas and City Markets," Curtis *Bulletin* 32 (November 7, 1923).

20. Parlin, "Music Master" address, c. 1921, CP Box 148, Folder 30; Parlin, untitled address to Dry Goods Association, January 1926, CP Box 149, Folder 53; Parlin, untitled address to Common Brick Association, 1925, CP Box 149, Folder 56; Parlin, untitled address to American Management Association, April 23, 1925, CP Box 149, Folder 54; and "Some Manufacturers Who Use the Curtis Quota Plan," Curtis *Bulletin* 61 (April 22, 1925), CP Box 160, Folder 190.

21. *Curtis Circulation 1922*.

22. "Automotive Statistics in Sales Quota Books," Curtis *Bulletin* 32 (November 7, 1923).

23. "Quota Application," Curtis *Bulletin* 62 (June 3, 1925); "How the Corona Typewriter Company Uses *Saturday Evening Post* Circulation in Establishing Sales Quotas," Curtis *Bulletin* 66 (November 13, 1925); "Another Leading Manufacturer Uses Curtis Circulation as 100% Basis for His Own Sales Quota," Curtis *Bulletin* 67 (December 5, 1925); and "Another Leading Advertiser Adopts Curtis Combined Circulation as a Basis for Sales Quotas in 1925," Curtis *Bulletin* 56 (February 11, 1925).

24. "Some Manufacturers Who Use the Curtis Quota Plan"; "Companies Using Sales Quotas," Curtis *Bulletin* 91 (July 22, 1927); "How the Corona Typewriter Company Uses *Saturday Evening Post* Circulation in Establishing Sales Quotas"; Parlin, "Music Master" address; Parlin, untitled address to Common Brick Association, 1925; Parlin, untitled address to American Management Association, 1925. On later sales guides, see for instance, "Where People Buy" in *Digests of Principal Research Department Studies,* vol. 3, 39; and *Market Areas in the United States,* 4th ed. (Philadelphia: Curtis Publishing Company, 1961).

25. *Woman's World Guide to Profitable Distribution* (Chicago: Woman's World, 1916).

26. E. G. Pratt, "Data Publishers Should Furnish Agents," *PI,* January 29, 1914, 47–51; *Population and Its Distribution* (New York, 1912); *Population and Its Distribution,* 3rd ed. (1921); *Prize Competition* (New York, 1922), J.W.T., Publications, Box 8; Stephen Fox, *The Mirror Makers,* 84–85. Also see "Suggestions for the Use of Circulation Statement," Curtis *Bulletin* 9 (October 11, 1922); "A Few Contrasts Emphasizing C. G. Quality," Curtis *Bulletin* 16 (January 1923); "Automotive Statistics in Sales Quota Books," Curtis *Bulletin* 32 (November 7, 1923); "Sales Quotas and City Markets," Curtis *Bulletin* 32; "What Is Market Opportunity?" Curtis *Bulletin* 45 (May 14, 1924); and "Telephone Subscribers Not a Safe Guide to Market Opportunities," Curtis *Bulletin* 54 (January 14, 1925). Thompson published the winning essays in William A. Berridge, Emma A. Winslow, and Richard A. Flinn, *Purchasing Power of the Consumer: A Statistical Index* (Chicago: A. W. Shaw, 1925).

27. See, for instance, *A Study of All American Markets* (Chicago: The 100,000 Group of American Cities, 1927). The organization was a promotional tool for daily newspapers in about eighty cities.

28. Parlin, address to the Western Company.

29. Emery and Smith, *The Press and America,* 402, 600–666.

30. Michael Emery and Edwin Emery, *The Press and America,* 6th ed. (Englewood Cliffs, NJ: Prentice Hall, 1988), 375.

31. "Sales Quotas and City Markets."

32. Quoted in "How Procter and Gamble Salesmen Are Using 'Sales Opportunities,'" Curtis *Bulletin* 74 (April 30, 1926).

33. "A Letter from the President to the Senior Salesmen," Curtis *Bulletin* 90 (June 17, 1927). The J. Walter Thompson advertising agency made a similar case against small-town newspapers in the late 1910s. See J.W.T. *News Bulletin* 25 (November 21, 1916).

34. See, for example, "More Newspaper Advertising This Spring," Curtis *Bulletin* 19 (February 28, 1923); and "Sales Increase Resulting from Newspaper Advertising of the March Issue of the *Country Gentleman,*" Curtis *Bulletin* 90 (June 17, 1927). Also see various entries in Curtis's Board of Directors Minutes for the 1920s.

35. "Advertising Revenue for 1923," Curtis *Bulletin* 35 (December 26, 1923); "Leading Advertisers Table," Curtis *Bulletin* 101 (1928); "Advertising Rev-

enue of the *Saturday Evening Post*," and Curtis *Bulletin* 100 (1928). The company said combined ad revenue for the *Post* from 1897 to 1914 was $44,965,407.

36. "A Page of Advertising," Curtis *Bulletin* 37 (January 23, 1924); and "Curtis Circulation over Seven and a Quarter Millions," Curtis *Bulletin* 110 (April 1929).

37. Emery and Emery, *The Press and America*, 375.

38. His salary was still below the $25,000 made by the Chicago advertising manager and the $18,000 made by the New York manager. For salary and employee information, see Curtis Board of Directors Minutes for the 1910s and 1920s, Curtis Archives, Indianapolis. On Commercial Research in the 1930s, see Parlin, "What Commercial Research Is Doing for Manufacturers."

39. Parlin, "Commercial Research." Also see Curtis Board of Directors Minutes for the 1920s.

40. The first issue, which was addressed to "Representatives of the Curtis Publishing Company," said its aim was to collect from various departments information that would be of use to the advertising and circulation departments. See Curtis *Bulletin* 1 (June 8, 1922).

41. "Dope Book."

42. "Tales Told by the Time Clock," *Curtis Folks* (January 1925), 7; Walter D. Fuller, "Where the Pay Roll Comes From," *Curtis Folks* (May 1925), 3–5; "New *Country Gentleman* Rates," Curtis *Bulletin* 9 (October 11, 1922); and Cohn, *Creating America*, 149–150.

43. I am following an argument made by Terrence E. Deal and Allen A Kennedy in *Corporate Cultures*: "Every business—in fact every organization—has a culture. Whether weak or strong, culture has a powerful influence throughout an organization. . . . Because of this impact, we think that culture also has a major effect on the success of the business." See Deal and Allen, *Corporate Cultures: The Rites and Rituals of Corporate Life* (Reading, MA: Addison-Wesley, 1982), 4.

44. *Curtis Folks* 1 (November 1921), 2.

45. The numbers are for research reports that either survive in the Curtis collection at the University of Pennsylvania or are mentioned in Curtis literature. Based on Parlin's accounts of Commercial Research, the division apparently did many smaller studies—probably for individual businesses—that have not survived or were not listed among the division's major work. See Maggie Kruesi, "Register, Curtis Publishing Company Records," the finding guide for the Curtis collection at the University of Pennsylvania. Also see *Digests of Principal Research Department Studies,* vols. 1 and 2.

46. Parlin, "Commercial Research."

47. Parlin, "Commercial Research," 4–5.

48. Parlin, "Commercial Research." Also see Curtis Board of Directors Minutes for the 1920s.

49. Division of Commercial Research, *Radio,* vol. B, 1925.

50. Emery and Emery, *The Press and America*, 375.

CHAPTER 8. THE LEGACY OF
COMMERCIAL RESEARCH

Epigraph: "Testimonial Dinner," 53.

1. Parlin, "What Does the Customer Want?" An overview of research conducted by the Division of Commercial Research can be found in the finding guide to the Curtis Papers, as well as in vols. 1 and 2 of the company's *Digests of Principal Research Department Studies*; Parlin, "Selling Mutual Insurance," typescript, October 13, 1936, CP Box 150, Folder 93; Donald M. Hobart, "Introduction," *Digests of Principal Research Department Studies,* vol. 1, 6–7; and Parlin, "What Commercial Research Is Doing for Manufacturers."

2. Parlin, "Two Years Later—A Review of Advertising after Two Years of Travel and Reflection," typescript, 1939, CP Box 150, Folder 102.

3. Samuel B. Eckert, *Fundamentals of Sound Marketing* (Philadelphia: American Marketing Association, 1950).

4. The concept of consumer sovereignty is far more complex than this, of course. I provide only a shorthand definition to raise the issue in relation to Parlin. For more detail on the concept, see, for instance, Harold G. Vatter, "Another Look at the Theory of 'Consumer Choice,'" *Challenge* 5 (February 1965): 35–39; and W. Duncan Reekie, "Consumers' Sovereignty Revisited," *Managerial and Decision Economics* 9 (Winter 1988): 17–25.

5. Peggy Kreshel makes the same argument about the research of J. Walter Thompson. See Kreshel, "Advertising Research in the Pre-Depression Years."

6. "Tenth Annual Conference," 68–70; Parlin, "Agricultural Implements," 114–116, 362; Parlin, *The Merchandising of Textiles*; and Parlin, "Why and How a Manufacturer Should Make Trade Investigations."

7. Parlin, untitled manuscript, 1931. The manuscript was published as a chapter in *Careers in Advertising,* ed. Alden James (New York: Macmillan, 1932), CP Box 148, Folder 86.

8. Bartels, *The Development of Marketing Thought,* 108–109.

9. For more on these types of changes, see Strasser, *Satisfaction Guaranteed*; and Olivier Zunz, *Making America Corporate, 1870–1920* (Chicago: University of Chicago Press, 1990).

10. David Nord suggests that journalism history in general needs to pay more attention to the structure of media institutions and to the power they wielded. See Nord, "A Plea for *Journalism History,*" *Journalism History* 15 (Spring 1988): 8–15.

11. This is part of a move toward what James Beniger calls "bureaucratic rationality," administration based on logical and statistical rules rather than on intuition. See Beniger, *The Control Revolution: Technological and Economic Origins of the Information Society* (Cambridge, MA: Harvard University Press, 1986), 21.

12. Quentin Schultze has called this view, which was widespread among those associated with advertising in the early twentieth century, "the ideology of economic efficiency and social control." See Schultze, "The Rise of a Professional Ideology in the Early Advertising Business, 1900–1917," in *Proceedings of the*

Annual Conference of the American Academy of Advertising, ed. Keith Hunt (Provo, UT: Institute of Business Management, Brigham Young University, 1981).

13. McGovern explores this connection between buying and "casting votes" in *Sold American.* Gary Cross argues that the consumer culture that emerged in the twentieth century "concretely expressed the cardinal political ideals of the century—liberty and democracy—and with relatively little self-destructive behavior or personal humiliation." See Cross, *An All-Consuming Century: Why Commercialism Won in Modern America* (New York: Columbia University Press, 2002), 2. And Leiss, Kline, and Jhally argue that "it seems almost inconceivable that we could enjoy the benefits of industrial democracy without the activities of the commercial media." See *Social Communication in Advertising,* 70

14. Parlin, *Basic Facts of Prosperity in 1920*; and Parlin, untitled address, October 11, 1926, CP Box 149, Folder 62.

15. See *Selling Forces,* 210–218.

16. Leiss, Kline, and Jhally, *Social Communication in Advertising,* 56–61.

17. On the hurdles blacks faced, see J. Chambers, "Equal in Every Way: African Americans, Consumption and Materialism from Reconstruction to the Civil Rights Movement," *Advertising & Society Review* (2006), vol. 7, no. 1, http://muse.jhu.edu/journals/asr/v007/7.1chambers.html (accessed August 2007); on black elites and consumption, see B. J. Branchik and J. Foster-Davis, "Black Gold: A History of the African-American Elite Market Segment," in *Marketing History at the Center: Proceedings of the 13th Biennial Conference on Historical Analysis and Research in Marketing,* ed. Branchik (Durham, NC, 2007). I go into more depth on the creation of the American consumer in Ward, "Capitalism, Early Market Research, and the Creation of the American Consumer."

18. As Sam Wineburg observes, the use of broad terms like "racism" poses problems for historians, tending to paint an issue much too simplistically. Though I have used the term "racist," I have tried to show the nuances involved at Curtis. See Wineburg, *Historical Thinking and Other Unnatural Acts,* 17. On "Rat-Trap Elmer," see Frank Stiefel, "The Lion and the Mouse," *Curtis Folks* VI (August 1927), 2–3, CP Box 157, Folder 159; on Walter Jones, see "The Best in His Line," *Curtis Folks* I (March 1922), CP Box 154, Folder 148.

19. Parlin, "Evolution of Industry Leads to Legislation," typescript, c. 1936, CP Box 150, Folder 94.

20. "An Agricultural Trading Center." Although Parlin's name is not listed as author of the report, he indicated in later speeches that he conducted many of the Sabetha interviews himself. The writing style of the report is also similar to other works that do bear his name. See Parlin, "Two Years Later" and Parlin, "Motor Accessory Speech," c. 1921, CP Box 148, Folder 17.

21. Parlin, "Evolution of Industry Leads to Legislation."

22. Stapleford, "Market Visions," 424–425.

23. Parlin to J. J. Gibbons, reprinted in "A Debate on Whether Advertising Pays," *Curtis Bulletin* 81 (November 26, 1926), CP Box 161, Folder 204; and untitled article, *Obiter Dicta* 8 (August 1914): 4.

24. "Testimonial Dinner," 10.

25. "Testimonial Dinner," 22.

26. Hobart, *Marketing Research Practice,* 17–21; Hobart, "Curtis Research," typescript, 1945, Curtis Archives, Indianapolis.

27. Parlin, "Selling a Parade," *The Red Barrel,* August 15, 1929, 14–16, CP Box 149, Folder 79; and Parlin, "What Commercial Research Is Doing for Manufacturers."

28. Richard Saul Wurman, *Information Anxiety* (New York: Doubleday, 1989), 37–39.

29. Parlin, "What Commercial Research Is Doing for Manufacturers."

EPILOGUE

1. Parlin, "Fifteen Years Later," typescript, June 16, 1938, CP Box 150, Folder 101; Parlin, "Two Years Later"; "C. C. Parlin Gives Fine Talk before Club," the *Adcrafter,* May 14, 1940, 14, Folder 103; Parlin, untitled address to Association of Financial Advertisers, typescript, October 30, 1940, Folder 104; and Parlin, "Address on Advertising," typescript, April 11, 1941, Folder 106.

2. Parlin, "Address on Advertising."

3. Alderson, "Charles Coolidge Parlin, 1872–1942"; Assael, *The Collected Works of C. C. Parlin;* Drucker, "Marketing and Economic Development"; Hollander, "Some Notes on the Difficulty of Identifying the Marketing Thought Contributions of the 'Early Institutionalists'"; and Hobart, *Marketing Research Practice.*

4. Parlin, "Why and How a Manufacturer Should Make Trade Investigations."

Index

Advertising: as religion, 145; credibility
of, 17–18, 35, 146–147, 155–156;
criticism of, 144–145; defense of,
144–148, 174–176; growth in early
twentieth century, 19–20, 147;
importance to Commercial Research,
51–52; importance to publications,
28–29, 121, 124, 187–188n13;
national vs. local, 79, 110, 156–158;
questions about, 17–18, 50; readers
of, 121, 129; research about, 53–55,
126–128; restrictions on (see Censorship); role of, 27, 70–71, 74–75;
spending on various media, 156; theories of, 53–55, 110–111, 145–148;
truth in (see Truth in advertising); use
of to promote Curtis magazines, 21–
22, 37, 106. See also Advertising
Agencies; Automobiles, advertising
of; Clothing, advertising of; Curtis
Publishing Company, defense of
advertising; Education; Efficiency,
in advertising; Household supplies,
importance of advertising; Marketing,
ties to advertising

Advertising agencies, 10–11, 54, 103–
104; change in approach, 30; commissions for, 34; Curtis Publishing's
pressuring of, 81, 85–86; customer
service at, 30–31, 33–34; pressuring
of publishers, 118–119; professional-
ization of, 31–32; role of, 33. See also
Advertising; Thompson, J. Walter,
agency
Advertising Code, 18, 31–32
Advertising Department (Curtis), 4;
annual conferences, 25, 27–29, 37–
39; collection of statistics, 37–39;
expansion of, 23; influence of, 18–19,
32–34; offices, 16, 23, 38–39; role of,
16–18, 25, 27–29, 33–34; specialization of, 38; statistical division, 38
"Advertising Land," 125–126
African Americans, 132–137, 176–178
Agricultural implements: industry problems, 112; study of, 43–44, 46–49,
51–52, 65, 67, 72; as a utilitarian
good, 66
Agriculture Department, U.S., 106
Antiformalist thinking, 48

Audiences, 10; defining, 136–137; studies of, 118–119, 122–125, 126–127. *See also* Readership
Audit Bureau of Circulations, 126
Automobiles: advertising of, 33, 52, 67–68; changes in consumer buying habits, 61–62; desire for, 60–61; influence of, 96–97, 101, 104, 140, 165; influences on purchase of, 79, 140; as a measure of wealth, 149–152; research on, 85; speedometers, 32–33
Average. *See* Typical

Baker, Milford, 69
Bargain hunting, 66
Batten, George, 127
Benchley, Robert, 87–88
Blacks. *See* African Americans
Bok, Edward, 20, 28–29, 117, 119
Boyd, William, 78, 90; photograph, 26
Bradley Knitting Company, 151
Brands, 15
Bureaucracy, increase among businesses, 25–26
Bureaucratic thinking, 7, 51
Bureau of Business Research, 55
Business: change in structure of, 4–6, 25–26, 173, 180–182; desire for information, 6–8, 52–53, 63, 89, 116–118, 165; ideals, 58; image of, 30; pursuit of customers, 142–143, 153–154; theory of, 62, 79–80
Business Bourse, 55
Buying. *See* Consumption
Buying class, 119
Buying power, 132–133

Capitalism, 173; legitimizing, 169. *See also* Business
Case studies, 102
Catalogues, 95
Censorship: cost of to Curtis, 35; creation of formal policy, 34–35; Curtis philosophy of, 28–29, 31–32; increased strictness, 35

Census, Bureau of, 39; data, 49, 83; data gathering, 55; growth of, 56, 198n52
Census of distribution, 68, 142–143
Change: comprehending, 181–182; in early twentieth century America, 41, 164; explaining, 48–49; uncertainties about, 82–84, 183–184
Cherington, Paul T., 87, 103–104
Chicago, 138
Chicago Tribune, 54–55, 105
Circulation: audits of, 126; "dimensions" of, 102; doubts about claims, 117–118; "duplication" of, 118–119, 127–129; as a means of judging sales potential, 149–158; methods of increasing, 36–37
Citizen: study of, 130; tied to consumption, 65, 119. *See also* Readers
Class, 12, 131–132, 176; defining, 119, 132; divisiveness of, 134–136; of readers, 130; white elites, 137
Clothing, 66, 69; advertising of, 67; color in, 70–71. *See also* Textiles; Department Stores
"Coal-Tar Dyes," 70–71
Commercial Research, Division of: distribution of reports, 72; doubts about, 40–42, 47, 76–77, 89–90; early days of, 42–47, 49–52; establishing credibility of, 58–59, 80–81; form of reports, 71–73; influence of, 85–90, 168–171, 176–177, 180–181; location of, 41, 90; methods of, 46–52, 102–103; office staff, 72; philosophy behind, 35–36, 58–69, 174; promotion of, 81–85; rationale for creating, 2–3, 16–19, 24, 38–39, 72–75; role of, 81–85, 122–123, 161–165, 169–170; shift in focus in 1920s, 143–146; ties to advertising, 51–52, 70–71; types of studies, 70–71, 96, 163–164, 168–169; use of graphs and charts, 48–49, 164
Community studies, 99–100
Comparison shopping. *See* Shopping

Concentration of business, 66
Constitution, 135–136
"Consumer is king," 115–117
Consumer products, 33–34
Consumers: classes of, 64, 119, 129–
130, 132–133; finding, 148–158;
habits of, 61, 95, 123; image of, 93,
119–120, 169–170; as key to merchandising, 64; men as, 61; power of,
65; psychology of, 65, 97–98, 115–
117, 146–147; types reached by Curtis magazines, 23–24, 117, 119; use
of term, 65; women as, 65–66; "yeoman," 113–114. See also Consumer
society; Consumption
Consumer society, 10–11, 48, 95; justi-
fication for, 71, 175–177, 179–180
Consumer sovereignty, 170
Consumption, 131; barriers to, 62–63;
as a measure of worth, 134–136,
176–177; methods of spurring, 149–
154; need for information about, 41,
57; as progress, 146–147, regional
nature of, 74–75; theories of, 60–61,
65–66, 97–98, 100–104, 112–113,
116–117, 138–140, 146–148
Convenience goods, 65–66
Cooperative Extension Service, 98–99
Corona Typewriter Company, 151
Country Gentleman, 9, 22, 43–44, 102–
111; advertising revenue, 158–160,
166; competitive position of, 111–
112; philosophy of, 106; readers of,
101–102, 109–110, 117, 122–123;
role in equipment census, 99. See also
Circulation; Curtis Publishing Company; Magazines; Readers
"Country Gentlewoman," 108
Country Life Movement, 94–95
Courtelyou, George, 56–57
Curtis, Cyrus H. K., 2, 20, 22, 44, 124,
163; business philosophy, 28–29, 115,
121; on importance of information,
36; on promotion of Commercial
Research, 78; start of his company,
105

Curtis Circulation, 149–155
Curtis Publishing Company, 50;
Advertising Department (see separate
entry); advertising revenue, 9, 142,
158–161; as an authority on sales,
150–154; Boston office, 16; business
strategy, 156–157, 162–165, 181;
circulation of its magazines, 127–
128, 158–161; corporate culture,
44, 163; defense of advertising,
155–156; growth of, 9, 20, 22–25;
importance of, 3–4, 8–12, 27–35,
158, 173–175; new building in Philadelphia, 23–24, 125; promotion of,
145–146, 149, 151–154, 158; training of employees, 80–81; treatment
of black employees, 132–134, 178–
179. See also Circulation; Country
Gentleman; Ladies' Home Journal;
Saturday Evening Post
Culture: definition of, 12, 217/n43;
ideals in, 60, 93–95. See also Rural
America
Currie, Barton W., 135
Customer service: as a business philosophy, 27–30; changes in, 29–31; at
Curtis, 18–19, 27–29, 32–35, 81.
See also Customers; Paternalism
Customers, 64–65, 98, 174; attracting,
141–142, 145, 155, 157–158; in con-
tract to consumers, 15

Demand, creation of, 63
Demographics, use of, 126–128, 132
Department stores, 52; structure of, 65–
66; study of, 47, 49, 67–70, 77, 96.
See also Textiles
Desire, as a component of consumption,
61, 147
Distribution, 57
District agents, 36–37; map of, 37
Dry goods, 69
Durand, E. Dana, 39

Eastman, R. O., 127, 131–132
Economic man, 64

Economics: study of, 45–46, 64; theory, 51, 146–147

Economy, U.S., post–World War I, 141–143

Education, as a concept in advertising and consumption, 51, 65, 99, 145, 148, 175

Efficiency: of advertising, 34, 53, 118–119; in business, 51, 142; in magazine circulation, 137; scientific, 36, 51

Ely, Richard T., 45–48

Emergency goods, 65–66

Encyclopedia of Cities, 60, 67–70

Exclusion, 132–140, 176–177

Expert opinion, 46, 51, 53, 55

Farmer: as a business owner, 106, 108; as a consumer, 94–95, 97, 103–104; as a romantic ideal, 93–94, 113; stereotypes of, 91–92, 104, 113

Farm Journal, 111–112

Farming, as a business, 94

Facts. See *Information*

Federal government: regulation by, 179–180; role in research, 39, 55–57, 116, 142–143

Feland, F. R., 125–126

Food products, 52, 67–68. *See also* Household supplies

Formalist thinking, 48

Fowler, Nathaniel, C., 126

Frederick, J. George, 55

Fundamental tendencies (fundamental economic laws), 60, 75

General Federation of Women's Clubs, 99

Geography, importance of to manufacturers, 62, 64. *See also* Location

Germany, importance as a dye maker, 70

Gimbel Brothers, 50

Good Housekeeping, 208n4

Government. *See* Federal government

Great Depression, 179–182

Hazen, Edward W., 40–41, 43–44, 77; as advertising director, 26–28; photograph, 26

Household products, 52, 66, 68; importance of advertising, 67. *See also* Food products

100,000 Group of American Cities, 155

Immigrants, 132–134, 138–139, 176, 178

Industrialization, 52–53, 93–94

Information, 13; as a business tool, 6, 8, 53, 63, 71, 77, 82–84, 118, 173–174, 181–182; definition of, 188n15; gathering of, 36, 47–52; importance of, 6, 8, 26, 184; lagging behind industrial process, 26; need for context in, 38–40; statistical, 83; ties to consumer society, 71, 116–117; value of, 42, 49, 59. *See also* Knowledge; Research

Interviewing, importance to early market research, 46–47, 49–50, 60, 63, 72–73, 100, 122, 130, 166. *See also* Research methods

Jeffery Company, Thomas B., 118

Jews, 136

Jobbers, 17, 46, 57–58, 62, 65, 116, 122, 155, 170. *See also* Middleman, bypassing

Journalism, as a commodity, 124–125

Kellogg's, 127

King, Caroline B., 108

Kinney, Samuel, 69

Knowledge: belief in power of, 41, 58, 154, 172, 184; dynamic nature of, 80, 181; promoting the value of, 81, 83

Ladies' Home Journal, 28–29, 34, 105, 115; advertisement for, 152; advertising in, 67; advertising revenues, 21–23, 68–69, 158–161; business strategy, 156–157; circulation, 20–21, 36; erosion of its dominance, 144, 158–

160; as a guide for retailers, 122, 151; importance of, 3, 8–9, 20, 180; perceptions of, 12, 50; readers, 28–29, 101–102, 109–110, 117, 119–120, 122, 127–128, 130–132, 134, 139–140, 156; screening of advertising, 34–35. *See also* Bok, Edward; Censorship; Circulation; Curtis, Cyrus H. K.; Curtis Publishing Company; Readers; Readership studies; Women

Lamb, Chauncey T., 32

Lasker, Albert, 54

Latshaw, Stanley, 16–18, 25, 27–28, 33, 51; photograph, 26; role in creating Commercial Research, 2, 39, 41–42, 44, 168

Literacy, 20, 132, 134–136

Location, as a factor in retailing, 64, 66, 154

Lord & Thomas, 54

Lorimer, George Horace, 24, 117, 120

Magazines, 9, 11–12, 20, 35, 103, 116, 142, 144; advertising in, 102, 156, 158–160; advertising revenue, 23, 68–69, 160–161; criticism of, 118; readers of, 126–132, 150. *See also* Circulation; *Country Gentleman*; *Ladies' Home Journal*; Readers; *Saturday Evening Post*

Mahin, John, 126–127

Management, 17; philosophy at Curtis Publishing, 44; scientific, 53, 172; uncertainty among, 25–26, 82–83

Manufacturers, 19, 26, 51–53; categories of, 66; consumers' effect on, 116; expansion to national markets, 15, 95, 141–142, 150–151, 153–154; reaching out to, 121–122, 132, 137, 145, 147, 174; use of research by, 172, 181, 184. *See also* Agricultural implements; Automobiles; Bureaucracy; Business; Clothing; Consumer Products; Management; Mass Market

Maps: of sales areas, 153; use of in Commercial Research, 49, 71–72, 74, 88, 132, 143, 149. *See also* Commercial Research, Division of

Marketing: approaches to, 65–66, 97–98, 137; dynamic, 181; micro-, 7; pull vs. push, 78–79; ties to advertising, 74–75, 108; use of magazine circulation for, 37. *See also* Advertising; Commercial Research, Division of; Consumers; Customer Service; Information; Market Research; Mass market; Niche markets

Marketplace of ideas, 51

Market research: cost of, 55–56; early, 54–55; experimentation in, 88, 168, 177; growth of, 7, 54–55, 85–87, 142–143; importance of, 7–8, 63, 89, 172–173, 180–182; limits of, 165–167, 182; need for, 62, 140; rationale behind, 6–7, 13, 71, 177; skepticism about, 2–3, 6–7. *See also* Commercial Research; Information; Research

Markets, 145, defining, 122, 131, 137; desire to control, 6; desire for information about, 25–26, 54–55, 118, 126; expanding, 148, 150–151; farm, 94–98, 102, 104–105, 109–114; index of, 136–137, 149–156; national, 15, 59, 81–84, 93, 95, 141–142; regional variations in, 74–75, 135–136; theories of, 59–63, 74–75, 79–80. *See also* Farmer; Mass Market; Niche markets; Rural America

Marquis, J. Clyde, 105–106

Mass market, 9–10, 14–15, 19, 53, 115; defining, 119, 156, 176; dynamics of, 62–63; theory of, 59–65, 79–80, 97–98. *See also* Advertising, national vs. local; Consumers; Consumer society; Customers; Marketing; National markets; Niche markets

Mass media, 9–10, 12, 20, 156; competition among, 144; reach of, 104–105

Men: as automobile buyers, 61; clothing for, 33; as readers of the *Saturday Evening Post,* 117, 128–129; as shoppers, 65, 139–140. *See also* Consumers; Readers; Women

Merchandisers, 18–19, 191n40. *See also* Retailers; Sales

Middle class. *See* Class

Middleman, 17, 62; bypassing, 121. *See also* Jobbers

Modernity, 4, 51, 172–173, 176

Mulattoes, 136

Musical instruments, 69, 166

Nationality. *See* Immigrants

National markets, 15, 67, 79, 82–84, 102, 105, 115–116, 141, 165, 173; breaking into regions, 155–156; fuzzy nature of, 74–75, 155; inclusion of rural areas, 92–95; questions about, 59–60. *See also* Consumers; Consumer society; Customers; Marketing; Mass market; Niche markets

National Publishers Association, 179

Nebraska, 91–92

Negroes. *See* African Americans

Newspapers: for advertising, 22, 67, 104–106, 121, 144; business aspects of, 124–125; competition with magazines, 149, 156–158; share of advertising, 156. *See also* Mass media; *Public Ledger;* Readers

Niche markets, 12, 66, 118, 137, 173

Nichols-Finn Advertising Company, 31

N. W. Ayer & Sons, 53–54

Nystrom, Paul W., 86–87

Obiter Dicta, 22, 81

Office supplies, 69

100,000 Group of American Cities, 155

Packard auto company, 117

Parlin, Charles Coolidge: background, 40, 42, 45, 113; creed, 116–118; doubts about research department, 40–45; influence of, 1–2, 86–90, 162; photograph, 5, 26; reputation of, 79–81; role at Curtis, 6–7, 121–122, 144–147, 163–164, 170–171, 183; significance of, 1–3, 171–172; speeches, 77–78, 164–165; spread of his ideas, 3, 73–74, 179, 183–184

Paternalism, 18–19, 27–29, 84, 174, 181

Payne, William Wellington, photograph, 26

Peerless auto company, 117

Philadelphia, 123–124; map of Curtis readership in, 153

Pictorial Review, 131, 159–160

Pierce-Arrow, 117

Population: as a measure for circulation, 36–37; use in market indices, 149–150, 154. *See also* Class; Demographics

Pragmatism, 84

Price: cutting, 62; as a factor in buying, 66, 146, 166. *See also* Consumers; Sales

Printers' Ink, 31, 55, 81, 95

Procter & Gamble, 157

Producer culture, 147

Producers. *See* Manufacturers

Productivity, 53, 163

Progress, 17, 34, 48, 65, 71, 116, 146, 175, 179; in rural America, 92–93, 108

Progressive Era, 56, 94, 99

Progressivism, 8, 17–18, 51, 83, 175

Promotion. *See* Marketing; Advertising

Psychology: of buying, 65–66; use in advertising and marketing, 53–55, 116, 140, 146, 177

Public Ledger (Philadelphia), 22, 81, 122, 140; editorial policy, 124–125; readers of, 117, 123–124

Public relations, 144, 165

Publicity. *See* Advertising; Marketing

Qualitative analysis. *See* Research methods, qualitative

Race, 68, 118–119, 131–138, 176–178. See also African Americans
Radio: advertising, 144, 156, 159, 166–167; study of, 165–167
Rambler Motor Cars, 118
Readers, 50, 91–92, 97, 109–111, 158; of advertisements, 121; attracting, 116–117, 124–125; compared to subscribers, 128; ethnic and racial characteristics, 131–139; income levels of, 119; perceptions of, 125–126; "quality" of, 29, 108, 117–124, 129–131, 134, 176 179; questions about, 118–119; research about, 118–119, 121–123, 126–128, 131–132; in rural areas, 101–103; as a tool for measuring consumption, 148–156. See also Audiences; Circulation; Country Gentleman; Ladies' Home Journal; Public Ledger; Saturday Evening Post; Women
Readership studies, 122–131, 176, 182, 210n32; example of, 130
Research, 7, 10, 13, 88, 143, 180 181; bias in, 59; bureaus, 56–57; by government agencies, 56 57; limits of, 112–113, 165–167, 169, 172; need for, 62; promotion of, 108–109; purpose of, 140; scientific, 108–109. See also Commercial Research; Information; Market Research; Readership studies
Researchers, characteristics of, 135
Research methods, 12–13, 36–37, 63, 106, 134–135; qualitative, 60, 63, 144, 169; scientific, 6, 48, 172, 176. See also Commercial Research, methods of; Interviewing; Social science
Retailing, 17–18, 52–53, 59; advertising to reach, 148–149; changes in methods, 61; lack of statistics about, 57; theory of, 61–64, 75, 87, 97–98, 148–156; volume of, 70. See also Census of distribution; Consumers; Consumption; Customer service; Customers; Department Stores; Encyclopedia of Cities; Household products; Sales
Rural America: changes in, 96–97; consumption in, 96–103, 112–113; as a market, 91–95, 103–104, 108–110; merchants, 110–111; problems in reaching, 95, 104–105; promise of, 94–95; research of, 96, 103–105, 112 114. See also Sabetha, Kansas
Rural sociology, 99–100

Sabetha, Kansas, 99–103. See also Rural America
Sales, 19, 62, 177; competition to find predictor, 154–155; judging potential of, 36–37, 65, 103, 126, 148–150, 155; measuring, 59, 67, 70–71, 169, 173; quotas, 154; theory of, 59, 157–158, 175; use of Curtis circulation to increase, 148–154. See also Census of distribution; Consumers; Consumption; Customer service; Customers; Encyclopedia of Cities
Salesmanship, 32–33, 53, 62
Saturation survey, 100–101
Saturday Evening Post, 3–4, 8–9, 12, 20, 157, 28; advertising in, 32–33, 51–52, 67–69, 128; advertising revenues, 21–23, 147, 158–161, 166–167; circulation, 20–21, 36, 151, 156; competition with other media, 156–161; as a guide for retailers, 122, 151; influence of advertising, 32–33; perceptions of, 50; readers, 101–102, 109–110, 117, 120, 122, 127–131. See also Circulation; Curtis, Cyrus H. K.; Curtis Publishing Company; Lorimer, George Horace; Magazines; Readers; Readership studies
Science, 10, 41, 51, 53; applied to business, 63, 172; belief in, 83–84. See also Social science
Scientific management. See Management, scientific

Scientific method. *See* Research methods, scientific

Scott, Walter Dill, 54

Segregation, 132–138

Service. *See* Customer service

Shoe industry, 38–39, 55

Shopping, 68; comparison, 65–66; districts, 97; theory of, 65–66, 87, 138–139, 200n20; value in, 66. *See also* Consumers; Consumption; Department stores; Retailing; Men, as shoppers; Women, as consumers

Shopping goods, 65–66, 87, 170. *See also* Retailing

Short, Floyd T., 77–78

Smith, Melville H., 38–39

Soap and cleansers, 68

Social science, 45–47, 54–55, 63, 116; use of to discriminate, 134–137, 176. *See also* Science

Source material, 12–13

Southern states, 135, 149

Specialists. *See* Expert opinion

Standard of living, 147–148

Starch, Daniel, 130

Statistics. *See* Information

Stereotypes, 178. *See also* African Americans; Class; Exclusion; Immigrants

Stewart & Clark, 32–33

Studebaker Corporation, 60

Style goods, 66

Successful Farming, 111

Supply and demand, 79

Surveys, 88, 91–92, 96, 100, 102–103, 108, 118, 122–132. *See also* Readership studies; Research; Research methods

Swift & Company, 86

Textiles, 52; advertising of, 67; study of, 3, 47, 49, 57, 67, 72, 77, 115. *See also* Department stores; Retailing

Theory: of buying and communication, 97; skepticism of, 84; use of in market research, 65–66, 138

Thompson, Harry A., 105

Thompson, J. Walter, agency, 54, 86–87, 99, 106, 142; promotion of sales quotas, 154–155; studies of rural America, 99, 103–104. *See also* Advertising agencies

Tobacco products, 69

Toilet goods, 68

Trends, 49, 177; monitoring, 16, 38, 48–49, 146, 182

Tribune and Farmer, 20, 105, 121

Truth in advertising, 31–32, 35

Two-step flow of communication, 97–98

"Typical" towns, 99–105

Urban areas, influence on rural consumption, 103–104

U.S. Rubber Company, 86

Utility goods, 60–61, 66

Wanamaker's department store, 49–50

Warner Instrument Company, 32–34

Watertown, New York, 128

Weld, L.D.H., 86

Wholesalers, 52–53, 69. *See also* Jobbers

Willys, John, 78

Wisconsin, 39, 42, 45

Wisconsin, University of, 45–46

Woman's World, 154

Women: as consumers, 65–66, 119–120, 139–140, 176, 214n81; clubs for, 99, 108; as readers, 108, 117, 131, 139–140. *See also* Consumers; *Ladies' Home Journal*; Men; Readers

Yeoman farmer. *See* Farmer

Youker, Henry Sherwood, 60, 68, 135; photograph of, 26

Douglas B. Ward is Assistant Professor in the William Allen White School of Journalism and Mass Communications at the University of Kansas. He was formerly an editor on the business desk at the *New York Times*.